Ernst Troeltsch
and the Future of
Theology

Ernst Troeltsch and the Future of Theology

EDITED BY

JOHN POWELL CLAYTON

LECTURER IN RELIGIOUS AND ATHEISTIC THOUGHT
DEPARTMENT OF RELIGIOUS STUDIES, UNIVERSITY OF LANCASTER

CAMBRIDGE UNIVERSITY PRESS

CAMBRIDGE

LONDON · NEW YORK · MELBOURNE

Published by the Syndics of the Cambridge University Press
The Pitt Building, Trumpington Street, Cambridge CB2 1RP
Bentley House, 200 Euston Road, London NW1 2DB
32 East 57th Street, New York, NY 10022, USA
296 Beaconsfield Parade, Middle Park, Melbourne 3206, Australia

First published 1976

Printed in Great Britain
at the
University Printing House, Cambridge
(Euan Phillips, University Printer)

Library of Congress Cataloguing in Publication Data
Main entry under title:
Ernst Troeltsch and the future of theology.

Essays based on a colloquium sponsored by the Dept
of Religious Studies, University of Lancaster.
'Bibliography, compiled by Jacob Klapwijk': p.
Includes index.
1. Troeltsch, Ernst, 1865–1923 – Congresses.
I. Clayton, John Powell. II. Lancaster, Eng. University
Dept. of Religious Studies.

BX4827.T7E76   230'.092'4   75–44576
ISBN 0 521 21074 7

Contents

Contributors

JOHN POWELL CLAYTON lectures on modern religious and atheistic thought in the department of religious studies at the University of Lancaster. With S. W. Sykes, he coedited *Christ, Faith and History: Cambridge Studies in Christology* (C.U.P.: Cambridge, 1972).

HANS-GEORG DRESCHER is professor of protestant theology and director of the Seminar für Religionspädagogik at the Pädagogische Hochschule Ruhr. At Marburg Drescher wrote his doctoral dissertation on Troeltsch, which later appeared as *Glaube und Vernunft bei Ernst Troeltsch* (1957).

A. O. DYSON was until recently principal of Ripon Hall, Oxford. He is now a canon of Windsor. Dyson wrote his doctoral dissertation at Oxford on the problem of history in Troeltsch's philosophy and theology. He has also published two books: *Who is Jesus Christ?* (S.C.M.: London, 1969) and *The Immortality of the Past* (S.C.M.: London, 1974). The latter volume originated as the Hensley Henson Lectures at Oxford.

B. A. GERRISH is professor of historical theology at the divinity school of the University of Chicago. He has written *Grace and Reason* (O.U.P.: London, 1962), and has edited *The Faith of Christendom* (World: Cleveland, 1963) and *Reformers in Profile* (Fortress: Philadelphia, 1967). Gerrish has been engaged in research on the thought of Ernst Troeltsch with a fellowship from the Guggenheim Foundation. He is coeditor of the *Journal of Religion*.

JACOB KLAPWIJK is lecturer in modern philosophy at the Free University of Amsterdam. He is author of a major study of Troeltsch's philosophy of culture and religion entitled *Tussen Historisme en Relativisme* (Royal Van Gorcum: Assen, 1970). He also coedited *The Idea of a*

Christian Philosophy (University of Toronto Press: Toronto, 1973). Klapwijk is currently editing a new edition of Troeltsch's *Glaubenslehre* and a fifth volume of the *Gesammelte Schriften*, both to be published by Scientia Verlag.

ROBERT MORGAN has taught christian theology at Lancaster since the department of religious studies opened in 1967. He has edited *The Nature of New Testament Theology* (S.C.M.: London, 1973) and has coedited with Michael Pye a Lancaster symposium entitled *The Cardinal Meaning: Essays in Comparative Hermeneutics* (Mouton: The Hague, 1973).

MICHAEL PYE teaches comparative religion at the University of Leeds. From 1968 to 1973 he taught history of religions at Lancaster. He has published a book introducing *Comparative Religion* (David & Charles: London, and Harper & Row: New York, 1972) and has coedited with Robert Morgan, *The Cardinal Meaning*. Pye and Morgan are currently translating and editing a collection of essays mainly from Troeltsch's *Gesammelte Schriften* to be published by Duckworth as *Ernst Troeltsch: Writings on Theology and Religion*. Pye is an editor of the journal *Religion: Journal of Religion and Religions*.

S. W. SYKES is the Van Mildert Professor of Divinity at the University of Durham. Until 1974 he was fellow and dean of St John's College, Cambridge, and university lecturer in divinity. He has written two books, *Friedrich Schleiermacher* (Lutterworth: London, & John Knox: Richmond, 1971) and *Christian Theology Today* (Mowbrays: London, 1971, and John Knox: Richmond, 1974). Sykes also coedited *Christ, Faith and History*.

Preface

For some years now there has been in Germany and North America especially, and more recently in Britain as well, a renewed interest in nineteenth-century religious thought. Nor is this interest merely antiquarian. For many of the mainly methodological issues which are central in contemporary religious studies were either raised first or refocussed significantly during that century. In addition, a growing number of theologians are coming round to the view that the constructive task of christian theology will be advanced only after a thorough reassessment of certain developments in nineteenth-century religious thought, including some which are closely associated with the name of Ernst Troeltsch (1865–1923).

Partly in recognition of this growing area of concern, the department of religious studies recently sponsored a colloquium at the University of Lancaster on Troeltsch's intellectual legacy. The present volume of essays is based on that colloquium, which was attended by scholars from Canada, Germany, Holland, Ireland and the United States, as well as Great Britain.

The contributors to the present collection focus on some main issues raised in Troeltsch's thought which remain central in contemporary theological discussion and regarding which, it is believed, something yet remains to be gained from a critical reassessment of his writings. The contributors have consequently sought to engage Troeltsch as a discussion partner. But, ultimately, it is the issues themselves which are held to be important. Troeltsch is of interest today only to the extent that he continues to speak to the issues with which we are concerned or, perhaps, *ought* to be concerned. The authors have therefore dealt both critically with Troeltsch and con-

structively with the issues. It is hoped that the collection will
make a contribution not only to an increased understanding
of Troeltsch, but also to the on-going debates in contemporary
christian theology about such problems as the relationship of
Christianity to 'other' religions, faith and history, the nature
and tasks of theology.

No effort has been made to cover the whole range of
Troeltsch's thought, nor even all those areas where he might
be regarded as having made an original and lasting contribution. Troeltsch's importance for the study of church history,
the sociology of religion and the philosophy of history and
culture is generally acknowledged and well covered in the
secondary literature. It was felt, however, that his contribution
to theology in particular has not received sufficient attention.

Reasons for this neglect are not difficult to find. Nor can all
of them be attributed to what Richard R. Niebuhr once aptly
described as 'the Barthian captivity of the history of modern
Christian thought'. For there are occasions in his writings
when Troeltsch himself exhibits manifest lack of concern as
to whether his thought should be described as 'christian' or
not. And in his lectures intended for delivery in England,
published posthumously as *Christian Thought: Its History and
Application*, his grounds for commending Christianity as a
faith to live by are at best pragmatic. The view is widely held,
and not only amongst those who would discredit him, that
Troeltsch may have begun as a christian theologian but that,
in the end, he turned rather to a more general philosophy of
culture [cf. *Gl.*, p. vi]. Despite such considerations, there is
today evidence of a renewed interest in Troeltsch's more
specifically theological writings and of an increasingly uneasy
conscience that the extent of his contribution to christian
thought might remain one of the 'unsettled questions for
theology today'. It is to be hoped that this symposium will add
in some measure to the discussion of that question.

The collection consists of three parts, the first of which
concerns Troeltsch's standing as a christian theologian. In his
introductory essay on Troeltsch's intellectual development,
Hans-Georg Drescher emphasises that, contrary to the widely-
held view mentioned above, Troeltsch remained throughout
his life principally (though not narrowly) a theologian. This

judgment is reinforced by Robert Morgan's subsequent observation that when Troeltsch remarked that he had outgrown the theological faculty [*GS* IV, 12], this need not be taken to imply that he had also outgrown theology [p. 76]. The so-called 'dialectical' theologians have taught us to believe otherwise. Indeed, the emergence and subsequent ascendancy of this sort of theology has unmistakably been a major factor in Troeltsch's not having been taken seriously in the twentieth century as a christian theologian. Consequently, it is right that a volume which lays stress on his specifically theological contribution should at the outset contain an assessment of the justice of Troeltsch's fate at the hands of Barth, Bultmann and Gogarten especially.

The quotation from Troeltsch with which Mr Morgan concludes his essay provides a bridge to Part II, in which the question is raised as to 'what we take theology and its task to be' [*GS* II, 227]. Here basic issues of theological method are raised and examined, though from different perspectives, by A. O. Dyson and B. A. Gerrish. Dr Dyson approaches the problem of theology's task at a formal level, 'looking at the structure and relationship of Troeltsch's closely argued historical, philosophical and theological standpoints with a view to exploring their implications for the task of systematic theology' [p. 83]. Professor Gerrish, on the other hand, approaches the same methodological question at a material level through a careful and detailed analysis of Troeltsch's own 'systematic theology', namely his posthumously published and frequently neglected *Glaubenslehre*, a volume which is fortunately soon to be reissued. These two papers complement each other and interconnect at a number of specific points.

Professor Gerrish's question whether it is possible for christian theology to be 'historical' as regards *content* or *substance* as well as regards *form* raises the unavoidable issue as to what makes Christianity christian and as to whether christian truth-claims can be regarded as in any sense 'absolute'. Troeltsch's approach to this issue – or, rather, this cluster of issues – is weighed in Part III by S. W. Sykes, who measures the strengths and weaknesses of the essay, 'Was heißt "Wesen des Christentums"?', and by Michael Pye, whose paper though last is not merely an appendage in the sense that

'other' religions are sometimes treated as appendages in
christian theologies (and even university faculties!). For, as is
being acknowledged increasingly in recent religious thought
in Britain and elsewhere, it is precisely at this point that an
important task lies for the theology of the future: namely,
doing christian theology from within the context of the universe of faiths. And here, too, Troeltsch points a way forward,
even if – as Mr Pye argues – his approach requires substantial
modification.

In addition to those who prepared papers for the colloquium at Lancaster, others assisted in different ways. A
number of scholars served as interlocutors: W. F. Bense (Wis-
consin), D. W. Hardy (Birmingham), Van Harvey (Pennsyl-
vania), Jacob Klapwijk (Amsterdam), R. W. A. McKinney
(Nottingham), G. M. Newlands (Cambridge), D. E. Nineham
(Oxford), Thomas Ogletree (Vanderbilt), D. A. Pailin (Man-
chester), James Richmond (Lancaster), Ninian Smart (Lancaster), and M. F. Wiles (Oxford). Professor Drescher was
chairman of the two lively discussion sessions which were
conducted in German. Special mention should be made of the
assistance and encouragement given by James Luther Adams,
whose enthusiasm and advice throughout the planning stages
and in the compiling of the Bibliography were much appreciated and whose insightful comments about specific details of
interpretation added immeasurably to the quality of discussion
during the colloquium itself.

Bailrigg   J.P.C.
Lancaster
1976

Abbreviations

Where possible references to some of Troeltsch's main works have been incorporated into the text and enclosed within square brackets. The following abbreviations have been used throughout the volume.

AC *The Absoluteness of Christianity and the History of Religions*, trans. David Reid. Richmond, 1971; London, 1972.

CT *Christian Thought: Its History and Application.* London, 1923.

Gl. *Glaubenslehre nach Heidelberger Vorlesungen aus den Jahren 1911 und 1912*, ed. Gertrud von le Fort. Munich and Leipzig, 1925.

GS *Gesammelte Schriften.* 4 vols. Tübingen, 1912–25.

PP *Protestantism and Progress: A Historical Study of the Relation of Protestantism to the Modern World*, trans. W. Montgomery. London and New York, 1912.

STCC *The Social Teaching of the Christian Churches*, trans. Olive Wyon. 2 vols. London and New York, 1931.

Part I

1. Ernst Troeltsch's intellectual development

HANS-GEORG DRESCHER
TRANSLATED BY MICHAEL PYE

The beginning of Ernst Troeltsch's intellectual career is marked by his encounter with the person and the theology of Albrecht Ritschl. Troeltsch spoke of Ritschl as a 'personality of great stature and originality' [*GS* IV, 5][1] and recalled that it was through him that he was really first won over for theology.[2] In the history of theology Ritschl signified 'the end of the old theology of mediation and the beginning of a new one'.[3] Ritschl made a break with the old theology of mediation and the pietistic presuppositions which it still maintained. He worked historically, while orientating himself in matters of faith towards a positively conceived revelation and its renewal in Reformation terms. It is of course problematical as to whether and how far this orientation was itself a barrier to radically historical understanding.

It was precisely this set of problems that the young Troeltsch found himself coming up against, and the first few years of his own intellectual work were mainly characterised by his wrestlings with Ritschl's theology. Ernst Troeltsch, who was born in 1865 and was the son of a doctor, went first to study theology at Erlangen where the faculty of that time was reckoned to be particularly important. But as Troeltsch remarked in retrospect: 'We had a cool respect for the professors and thought of them as antiquities from the time of the German Confederation, relics of the battle between neo-pietism and Enlightenment. Our interests were different, lying partly in the political and social problems of the time and partly in the

---

[1] *Gesammelte Schriften* IV, 5. References to the *GS* are given in abbreviated form hereafter.
[2] 'Die "kleine Göttinger Fakultät" von 1890', in *Die christliche Welt* 34 (1920), 282.
[3] E. Hirsch, *Geschichte der neuern evangelischen Theologie*, 5 (Gütersloh, 1954), 558ff.

world-view of the natural sciences then current.'[4] So before long Troeltsch left Erlangen and went to Göttingen, above all to study under Ritschl. Others teaching in Göttingen at the time included the theologians Paul de Lagarde and Bernhard Duhm who worked in the perspective of the history of religions and had a lasting influence on Troeltsch. The philosophical authority in this period of his development was Hermann Lotze, who was indeed also an important philosophical guarantor for Ritschl. The decisive set of problems underlying Troeltsch's formation of his own intellectual position lay in the competitive influence of Ritschl on the one side and that of the history of religions specialists on the other side. Ritschl was certainly able to satisfy his critical mind better than the Erlangen Lutherans, but Troeltsch pursued things further, and the direction of his questions was essentially determined by the stimulus of ideas arising from the history of religions. Ritschl impressed Troeltsch through his intellectual clarity, his attention to the historical development of dogma in the elaboration of a systematic theology, and his lively philosophical interest, and in these matters he exercised a lasting influence upon him.

There were above all two points which sparked off Troeltsch's *criticism of Ritschl*. First Troeltsch questioned Ritschl's historical perspective. Did Ritschl understand sufficiently radically the alien character of the middle ages and the changes taking place in the modern world? Secondly Troeltsch became increasingly critical of Ritschlian dogmatics. The central questions here were these: is the isolated reference to revelation and its claim on mankind theologically justified?; what are the presuppositions of such a 'theology of claim' and to what consequences do they lead?

Troeltsch's thesis on 'Reason and revelation in Johann Gerhard and Melanchthon' corresponds entirely to Albrecht Ritschl's way of working and thinking in being an exercise in the history of dogma against the background of questions in systematic theology.[5] It is no longer possible today, he argued, to determine the relationship between faith and reason either

[4] 'Die "kleine Göttinger Fakultät" von 1890', p. 282.
[5] *Vernunft und Offenbarung bei Johann Gerhard und Melanchthon* (Göttingen, 1891). This work originated as Troeltsch's doctoral dissertation and was subsequently expanded into his habilitation dissertation.

along Reformation lines (Melanchthon) or along orthodox lines (Johann Gerhard). The continuity is broken.

A distinct and stable relationship between reason and revelation, such as the old theologians enjoyed and worked out with great strength and clarity, is something which the new theologians do not have. The former had a settlement of this relationship which altogether satisfied them, with its dualism and its thesis of *lex* and *evangelium*. For all its narrowness and insufficiency its clarity, firmness and trenchancy still fill us with a certain admiration today [*Ibid.* p. 213].

In showing the importance of the concept of natural law Troeltsch's examination came to conclusions similar to those of Wilhelm Dilthey. In contrast to Ritschl he determined that 'the continuity of the Lutheran church itself with the past is greater, and that of modern theology with the older theology is less, than one usually assumes' [*Ibid.* p. 212].

Ritschl himself emphasised in his criticism of Melanchthon that the latter, in the Augsburg Confession and his defence of it, followed 'the leading ideas of Luther'. Nevertheless he had maintained the medieval scheme in this theological textbook, the *Loci communes*, and thereby lost sight of the initial Reformation impetus of Luther who had broken clear beyond the confines of medieval theology.[6] Troeltsch interpreted the matter differently. Above all he took a more positive view of Melanchthon. Melanchthon's contribution lay in the recognition that christian faith needs 'a preparation and a point of connection in natural man'.[7]

Walter Bodenstein's account of Troeltsch's intellectual development [*Neige des Historismus* (Gütersloh, 1959)] ascribes a programmatic importance to Troeltsch's work on Johann Gerhard and Melanchthon, and in this vein he gives the first part of his book the heading 'The initial work of 1891 as an attempt to win independence from Ritschlian theology'. The importance of this first work of Troeltsch is clearly overplayed here. It was less dramatic than that. In the main it is Ritschl's historical appraisal which is corrected. Luther's strong connection with the middle ages comes out very clearly, as also the idea that in the train of a new church a new dogmatic system had to be formed as well, one which could appeal to Luther's

---

[6] *Drei akademische Reden* (Bonn, 1887), pp. 17ff.
[7] In the review of R. Seeberg's *Lehrbuch der Dogmengeschichte*, 2nd half, *Göttingische Gelehrte, Anzeigen* (1901), p. 28.

religious experience and his connection with certain aspects of the development of doctrine up until then (Augustine, mysticism and humanistic theology). In this largely historically orientated investigation Bodenstein tends to perceive the systematic insights which Troeltsch conceived later, though admittedly he already let it be seen here that he believed the rejection of natural theology and metaphysics to be untenable [*ibid.* p. 14]. Troeltsch's conclusion in the first instance was that the Ritschlian theology, framed in terms of an isolated claim to revelation on the part of Christianity, could not be justified by reference to the dogmatic tradition of protestantism. If Troeltsch's argument had already gone as far as Bodenstein seems to think, his further theological development would be difficult to understand.

This can be seen not least in that in subsequent writings, above all in the long essay on 'The christian world-view and its counter-currents' ('Die christliche Weltanschauung und ihre Gegenströmungen'),[8] he is still operating on the basis of a Ritschlian theology. It is particularly clear from his talk of the 'claim' of Christianity, and the recourse implied therein to a purely factually given revelation with no need of further rational justification. The unbroken link with Ritschl is also clearly visible when Troeltsch distinguishes religion from world-views formed by the combination of various theories and thus takes over Ritschl's distinction between theoretical and practical value judgments [*GS* II, 240]. The connection is also there in terms of philosophical perspective, for Troeltsch, like Ritschl himself, was strongly influenced by the philosophy of Lotze and defined the relationship between mind and nature in the same way as Lotze, namely in terms of the priority of mind [*GS* II, 242, 246f.].

At the same time however a *new influence* now makes itself felt. Troeltsch recognised more and more the importance of the work of the history of religions and perceives the effect which it has on theology. To think in the categories of the history of religions is bound to put a question mark against christian theology's claim to exclusiveness, because analogies to christian spirituality are to be seen on all sides. Faced with this set of

---

[8] *Zeitschrift für Theologie und Kirche* (1893/4), III and IV (hereafter *ZThK*), reprinted in *GS* II, 227–327.

problems Troeltsch attempted, by contrast with Ritschl, to delineate 'the spirit of Christianity' which would be 'comprehensible and alive even without its first historical formation' [*GS* II, 239]. For the historically disciplined view must see the anthropomorphic character of biblical and ecclesiastical supernaturalism which 'is merely one particular case of the understanding of the world and of nature common to antiquity' [*GS* II, 247]. These are indeed new notes which no longer harmonise with the basic conception of Ritschlian theology. They demonstrate the power of historical thinking and the problems which it raises for theology. In the long run Troeltsch found the idea of ranging Christianity within the history of religions inescapable. With this idea came the question about the absoluteness of Christianity. Methodologically considered, the whole problem arose as a result of the uncompromising recognition of the historical method. In the essay, 'The christian world-view and its counter-currents', Troeltsch was essentially still trying to solve these questions by means of the theology of Ritschl. This writing is therefore eloquent testimony to the transition from a Ritschlian viewpoint to a theology conditioned by the history of religions. Ritschl's 'theology of claim', which saw Christianity as filled with the claim 'to be the perfect religion beyond the other types and stages',[9] was the basis of his conclusion that only Christianity could count as religion in the full sense of the word. Over against Christianity there was only that deficient mode of religion, the non-christian nature religion, whose inadequacy lay in its lack of intellectual and moral refinement. Thus Ritschl substantially failed to take account of the objective significance of the history of religions because he was dealing on a conceptual rather than a historical level and reserved the concept 'religion' in its true fulness for Christianity. So when Troeltsch emphasised that Christianity was 'the purely intellectual and moral world religion' [*GS* II, 321] he was still thinking in agreement with Ritschl. He took this purely intellectual and moral character of Christianity to be its special quality as a religion.

Troeltsch's own history of religions approach at first ran

---

[9] *Unterricht in der christlichen Religion*, reprint of the first edition (Gütersloh, 1966), v, 13.

parallel to these ideas but gradually went beyond the Ritschlian starting point until it brought about a change in his theological thinking. Christianity cannot be isolated from the general history of religions. The meaning of Christianity is only to be perceived in the context of the development of religious life in general. Therefore the idea of a 'ready-made' redemption which only requires to be accepted by man cannot be made the starting point of theological reflections. Troeltsch attempted to convey this new perspective in his essay, 'The autonomy of religion' ('Die Selbständigkeit der Religion), in *Zeitschrift für Theologie und Kirche* (1895/6) v and vi. In response to a critical comment by Julius Kaftan he justified and developed his position once again in an essay entitled 'History and metaphysics'.[10]

Troeltsch's reply was based on the conception that religion is an independent area of spiritual or mental life. Over against modern immanentist views and the rapidly proceeding historicisation of thought in general it is necessary to justify and develop religion's own right to exist. The content of religious statements cannot simply be logically deduced, and they also cannot be traced back to fundamental moral attitudes. It is above all Schleiermacher's position which we see in the background mediating a decisive influence.

But it is only by bringing the idea of development into the picture that the liveliness and fulness of religious life truly appears. We have then an enquiry into religion, freed both from rationalising constructionism and from any reduction to moral concepts. It was Hegel's merit to have taken up the idea of development and linked it together with an appreciation of the driving ideas of history. Troeltsch's criticism of Hegel was that the latter understood the development of religion as a purely human intellectual movement. Nevertheless it is clear that Schleiermacher and Hegel were necessary to make possible the position in the philosophy of religion now unfolded by Troeltsch. He saw the philosophy of religion not as a philosophical treatment of religious objects but as coming to terms with living religion itself. This had the consequence that the philosophy of religion must concern itself with the psychology of religion and the history of religions. As an

[10] *ZThK* VIII (1898), 1–69.

autonomous area of life religion proffers a sphere of its own for psychological investigations, and in so far as the contents of this area are articulated within historical movements one is brought to look at things from the perspective of the history of religions.

The psychology of religion sees religion and its moorings in the human consciousness as a complicated specific case of a fundamental human function. The task of the history of religions is to seek out 'laws and connections in the historical varieties of religion, and the basis of a criterion for the evaluation of these varieties' ['Selbständigkeit der Religion', *ZThK* v, 370]. The intention is to seek a solution to the question of the criterion for evaluating the development, not from outside, as for example by a dogmatic decision, but from inside, that is, from within the development of the history of religions itself. One must strive to recognise the driving ideas of the development of the history of religions and on that basis solve the question of a criterion for judging the historical multiplicity of forms. Troeltsch saw both the psychology of religion and the history of religion as having a bearing on the question of truth in religion. The psychology of religion seeks the locus of religion in the consciousness and thus also the origin and meaning of religion. Thus it 'alone can make clear what can indeed be worked out about the question of truth in religion' [*ibid.*]. As to the history of religions, this seeks out laws and connections in the multiplicity of history and works in this way for a criterion to appraise the historical varieties.

What may be concluded about the contribution of each of these to the question of truth, and how the relationship between the psychological and the historical criteria of evaluation is to be seen, seem to remain not quite clear. Troeltsch tried to get over this by linking the two ideas: he brought the psychological and the history of religions aspects of the truth question together by pointing out that the psychology of religion ought to pursue not an abstract, individualistic method, but a historical or socio-psychological one. He felt that the main questions lay in the historical field and required to be solved through a philosophy of history aligned with a metaphysics of mind. But if the philosophy of religion is a philosophical treatment of the historical development of religion as it exists in living fact, then the philosophy of religion can be defined as the philosophy of the history of religion. In that sense the philosophy of religion is linked both with the psychology of religion and with the history of religion. According to Troeltsch the psychology and the history of religion can also be understood as subordinate disciplines of the science of religion. Troeltsch did not always commit himself to one terminology on this matter. He was more concerned about the problems and the implications of the content than about a consistent terminology. Thus he speaks sometimes of the two great leading problems of the science of religion as being that of the psychology of religion and that of the history of religion [ZThK VI, 71 f.]. Yet it is clear that he could also speak of them as sub-disciplines. Furthermore the science of religion can also be referred to as the philosophy of religion, though with this difference, that the use of the latter term pushes more strongly to the foreground the problem of the criterion for evaluating the multiplicity of religious developments. In this sense, the philosophy of religion tends to become a philosophy of history for religion, giving a metaphysical interpretation to the concept of development and assuming a motivation within history towards the unfolding of ultimate meaning.

Eckartd Lessing attributes encyclopaedist intentions to Troeltsch during this stage in his development, and speaks of him as presenting an 'outline of a system of the sciences'.[11] referring particularly in this connection to the essay, 'History and metaphysics' ('Geschichte und Metaphysik'). Troeltsch himself showed here that as his position developed on the basis of religion, and the problems in the philosophy of religion and the philosophy of history arising out of it, there was a need for a comprehensive scientific treatment and justification for it. He did this in response to Kaftan's attempt to reproach him here for inconsistencies and inadequate scientific reflection.[12]

---

[11] E. Lessing, *Die Geschichtsphilosophie Ernst Troeltschs* (Hamburg, 1965), p. 17.

[12] E.g. thus: 'Either empirical analysis and then at the right place a transition to a standpoint in the ideal, that is, to personal conviction, to faith, – or a doctrine of religion in the sense of a metaphysics; there is no in-between. And that is why it comes to be as declared above: Troeltsch attempts an impossible standpoint and falls between two stools. He has not carried his scientific reflection through as far as the problem demands.' J. Kaftan, 'Die Selbständigkeit des Christentums', *ZThK* VI, 391.

Troeltsch was concerned to meet a reproach of this kind by demonstrating the extent to which he was conscious of the demands of science. Nevertheless his whole response consisted of hints about interconnections, indications of where the problems lie and suggestions about where the solutions are to be sought, rather than aiming at the real outline of a system. Troeltsch expressed himself on these matters very aphoristically and contented himself with declaring a basic position in the form of a rejection of supernaturalism, with advocacy of a historical, that is, of a history of religions approach in theology, and with the resultant set of questions and tasks. With that occasional perspicacity of an opponent Kaftan did in fact strike a weak point in Troeltsch's presentation, namely its lack of terminological strictness and its aphoristic brevity instead of more persistent and more theoretically scientific reflection.

In spite of this Lessing remains true to his idea that Troeltsch was a systematic thinker, even though he himself was to take note of difficulties which arise in the course of his account.[13] He holds to his scheme with a determined consistency, which however becomes dubious when it refuses to yield even to Troeltsch himself.

In his consideration of the development of the history of religions Troeltsch emphasised that one should presuppose faith in the reason running through the historical development, understanding this developmental process not merely as the effects of human activity but seeing it as the consequence of divine impulses. In this sense, then, Troeltsch could speak of the divine humanity of the history of religions. The objective basis of history is thereby presumed and declared to be a divine basis. Taking account of the driving ideas of history Troeltsch took it to be beyond dispute that Christianity can finally be recognised as the highest form of religion. 'The inner dialectic of the religious idea' [*ZThK* vi, 200] points in the direction of Christianity. As a perfectly spiritualised and moralised religion Christianity is the deepest and richest product of the religious idea itself.

One can of course ask whether Troeltsch distanced himself sufficiently with this kind of justification from the Ritschlian

[13] Cf. Lessing, *Die Geschichtphilosophie Ernst Troeltschs*, p. 17 and pp. 51f.; or when Lessing has to say with respect to psychology that Troeltsch 'has merely developed a few principles of this psychology', *ibid.* p. 52.

theology with its definition of the perfect religion. His concept of religion itself remained strongly influenced by Ritschl, and on the question of a criterion for appraising the historical development of religion one can read: 'The criterion grows up in and with the history itself as the higher phenomenon carries in itself the certainty of its greater power and depth' [*ZThK* VI, 78]. This kind of reference to the certainty of greater power and depth might be taken as a modified form of a claim to revelation. And yet, it must be said that the overall plane of argument has shifted. Troeltsch did not argue from the standpoint of a special position for Christianity but immersed himself in history with a view to solving the problem of a criterion from within history. He sought to achieve it with the help of a philosophy of history centred on a metaphysically intended concept of development. The interpretation of the concept of development is anchored in the 'conviction that the reason which holds sway in the human mind also holds sway in the world in general, and here too includes within itself an instinct towards the unfolding and articulation of its final meaning and its deepest content' [*ZThK* VI, 79]. Troeltsch wished therefore not to give himself over precipitately, in the form of a decision of faith, to the impression made by the personality of Jesus, but rather he wished to entrust himself to 'the factual procession of ideas' [*ibid.* p. 78]. The idea of a 'decision' ['History and metaphysics', *ZThK* VIII, 6of.] must, for him, accept the considerations in the philosophy of religion which he set out, together with their foundation in the basic datum of religion. Or at least this must be so if it is to be a question of scientific presentations of the matter, which seek to take into account the main body of contemporary scientific thought [*ibid.* p. 67].

Troeltsch's philosophy of religion was rejected by Julius Kaftan from the point of view of the Ritschlian school.

At least one thing must be most strictly excluded, and that is the idea that theology might somehow be based on the philosophy of religion. The matter must be allowed to rest as theology in opposition to philosophy of religion. The basis is and always will be revelation alone, that is, Jesus Christ, holy scripture. This is what is demanded by faith as we confess it and the christian community which it is theology's task to serve. And it is this too that corresponds to common sense ['Die Selbständigkeit des Christentums', *ZThK* VII, 382].

For Kaftan it is in the end an either/or, either faith in a principle or faith in a person, that is, faith in the person of Christ as redeemer [cf. *ibid.* p. 394]. That Troeltsch might succeed in finding a standpoint beyond these alternatives is in Kaftan's view most doubtful. Troeltsch's answer in the essay, 'History and metaphysics' ('Geschichte und Metaphysik'), traces the differences between Kaftan and himself back to the fundamental opposition between supernaturalist and historical thought. 'Only one who merely careers through the history of religions from the point of view of apologetics, like a hunter on the look-out for game, namely evidences of the inferiority of religions other than Christianity, only such a one could return home from these expeditions with his supernaturalism unimpaired' [*ZThK* VIII, 9].

This essay is of particular importance for the understanding of Troeltsch's intellectual development because Troeltsch himself clarifies what was going on in his mind in connection with this attack from the Ritschlian school. He put it as follows:

My first philosophical authorities were Kant, Albert Lange and Lotze, through whom I have found myself gradually pushed forward to the idea of a critical metaphysics. My theological teacher was Ritschl; but gradually I have come to see that there are two things in the Ritschlian system which I cannot accept. The first is its supernaturalism, which appeared to me to be not maintainable in the face of history of religions research either within the field of Christianity or outside it. The second is the much too simple resolution of the problems of natural philosophy and metaphysics through the theory that nature is merely phenomenal, a solution which proved inadequate as I studied philosophical literature further. It was in the end B. Duhm who most decisively pointed out the way to be pursued, although of course I do not go along with all his idiosyncrasies. But once my attention was drawn to the concept of development it was necessary to learn from Hegel and the Hegelians. Finally I noticed that in all this I was very close to Schleiermacher [*ZThK* VIII, 52, n. 1].

The first period of Troeltsch's development ended approximately with the year 1902. His work on *The Absoluteness of Christianity* marked the transition to the second period of his thought. A detailed treatment of this first period was desirable above all for two reasons. First it was a time when the scientific foundation of Troeltsch's work was laid, which was to influence what came later and of which the basic intention was maintained throughout. Thus in 1920 Troeltsch could write in retrospect of his studying and lecturing in Göttingen: 'For my part I was already devoting my time to philosophy very much at that time, searching out a conception of the development of mind in which I could range the christian world. That search was also one of the germs of all my later work, for indeed such germs must arise during youth.'[14] Secondly, Troeltsch's final investigations into the philosophy of history display a clear connection, even extending to matters of content, with his early work.[15]

Thus the first phase of Troeltsch's activity covers roughly one decade. Seen biographically it covers his lectureship at Göttingen, a short spell at Bonn as an associate professor (1892–4), and the first part of his activity as occupant of the chair for systematic theology at Heidelberg (1894–1902).

The matter is seen differently by Walter Bodenstein in *Neige des Historismus*. He views the first section of Troeltsch's development as running from 1894 to 1909. 'That is the time...during which Troeltsch was professor in Heidelberg, and when he was only a theologian. In the year 1910 when Troeltsch also took on teaching responsibilities in philosophy a new phase began, in the course of which he grew out beyond the narrow framework of the theological faculty [*ibid.* p. 17]. But Ernst Troeltsch is hardly correctly judged when he is thought for a time to have been 'just a theologian'. On the contrary the relationship between philosophy and theology is a basic constituent of his theological work. Theological statements must be based as indicated on a foundation in the philosophy of religion, as was seen above; and the question of a criterion for evaluating the development of the history of religions can only be answered from the point of view of a philosophy of history. Troeltsch's works show that as a theologian he was also a philosopher. The acceptance of a university position in philosophy is a quite secondary indication as compared with the inner connection of Troeltsch's work with philosophy. It is therefore not correct to say that the official facilitation of lectures in philosophy marks the beginning of a new phase for Troeltsch.

There is a much clearer turning point in his work as early as

[14] 'Die "kleine Göttinger Fakultät" von 1890', p. 282.
[15] Cf. H. G. Drescher, 'Das Problem der Geschichte bei Ernst Troeltsch', *ZThK* N.F. 57 (1960), 224ff.

the year 1902, and this can be objectively placed in Troeltsch's
new attention to the south-west German Kantian school.
Troeltsch himself characterised his interest in these new
philosophical authorities as follows: 'The differences in the
later works lie...crudely stated, in a shift of philosophical
standpoint from Dilthey and Lotze to Windelband and Rickert' [*GS* II, 227, n. 11]. The mention of Dilthey and Lotze, and
not of Hegel or Schleiermacher, can be explained above all by
their contrapuntal position to Windelband and Rickert, for by
this direct comparison the difference of positions can be clearly
expressed. These polarised positions are clarified for example
in Troeltsch's review of Rickert's book *Kulturwissenschaft und
Naturwissenschaft* from the year 1899. Troeltsch lets it be known
here that he can 'not share the immanentist, anti-metaphysical
starting point of this whole argument'.[16] Above all Troeltsch
cannot 'take the usual classification into natural sciences and
human sciences (i.e. that of Dilthey) to be so mistaken' [*loc. cit.*].
For Troeltsch the difference in method here continues to be
determined by the difference in the objects treated. According
to Rickert, by contrast, the forms of scientific work are
dependent 'on the formal characteristics of the aims pursued
by the knowing subject'.[17]

Troeltsch followed Windelband and Rickert because he
thought he would find help in their philosophy towards
solving the problem of the transition from psychological
description to the procedure of evaluation. We recall that the
debate with Kaftan centred around this problem. The transition to the question of truth or evaluation was now felt to be a
problem which could no longer be solved along the lines of
Dilthey's thought, and also not with Eucken's clear metaphysical admixture. Troeltsch now attempted to solve this problem
above all by linking up with Heinrich Rickert, whose position
was defined by a philosophy of validity or of value which was
anti-metaphysical in type. For Rickert the problem was to find
'timelessly valid values'. The multiplicity and fulness of history
is then to be correlated with these.[18]

---

[16] *Theologische Literaturzeitung* 24 (1899), 377.
[17] Cf. H. Rickert, 'Geschichtsphilosophie' in *Die Philosophie im 20. Jahrhundert*
(Heidelberg, 1907), p. 332.
[18] 'Only when the attainment of supra-historical values is possible can the
philosophy of history be carried on as a special science of the principles of
the historical universe, and the meaning of the history of the universe be

Troeltsch's well-known book *The Absoluteness of Christianity and the History of Religions* (Tübingen, 1902) is a document which marks his transition from a more Hegelian position to the neo-Kantianism of Windelband and Rickert. In the same sense as Rickert and Windelband he put forward here the idea of that which is individual, as a historical category, and from that basis he criticised the orientation towards general concepts. At the same time Troeltsch thereby departed from his earlier position which believed it possible to extract the criterion for the evaluation of the historical development of religion from within the historical process itself. Thinking out from within the historical movement was now modified by the emphasis on requiring values to be defensible. 'It is just for this reason that history knows no values and norms which coincide with factual generalities but knows these always only as generally *valid* ideas, or ideas claiming validity, which always appear in individual form and proclaim their general validity only in the struggle against mere factuality' [*ibid. German original*, p. 24]. Looking back on his position at the time of the essay, 'History and metaphysics', Troeltsch commented: 'The strongly Hegelian standpoint which I took there is one which I now find it necessary, under Rickert's influence, to criticise' [*ibid.* p. 11, n. 4].

In tackling the question of the absoluteness of Christianity Troeltsch rules out two possible courses. He finds unacceptable both the modern, supra-naturalist theory with its interventionalist view of miracle and the evolutionist form of apologetics with its belief in the historical realisation of the idea. The consequence of this is that 'the setting up of Christianity as the absolute religion [is] not possible in terms of the historical way of thinking and with historical means' [*ibid.* p. 20]. Christianity is a historical phenomenon through and through. Every investigation of its history has to be carried out with the usual methods of historical research. But if being 'historical' means at the same time being 'relative' then the problem of arriving at norms over against the historical and relative is found at the centre of the enquiry. The idea of relativity does not exclude

interpreted', Rickert, *ibid.* p. 394; or 'The foundations of the philosophy of history are therefore coterminous with the foundations of any philosophy conceived as a science of values' (*ibid.*).

human decision, but includes it. What is at stake is a final decision which is arrived at through appraising and surveying the whole. The concept of decision takes on a heightened meaning for Troeltsch's position. In the first period of his thought the objective features of the ideas were so strongly emphasised that by contrast the subjective aspect of the decision was overshadowed.

Even though this emphasis on the individual and on the normative follow Rickert's thought in the manner indicated, there is nevertheless a characteristic distancing from the neo-Kantianism of Windelband and Rickert in the question of metaphysics. Troeltsch modifies Rickert's position when he formulates: 'The (historical) idea demands a metaphysical resolution' [p. 58]. The normative and the generally valid cannot be defined as valid goals; they must be referred back to 'a supra-sensual reality which strains forward in concert with the spiritual kernel of the world' [p. 58]. Thus Troeltsch does not share Rickert's anti-metaphysical attitude but stands instead by a fundamentally metaphysical position.

It remains to indicate Troeltsch's answer to the question as to the absoluteness of Christianity. Methodologically he proceeds as follows. He enters fully into the historical and thus the relative, and thereby seeks to recognise at the same time the generally valid as that which objectively emerges. But there is only a certain amount of support in what is objectively there.

The rest is based on the personal decision of the individual. This decision is scientifically secured to the extent that one can claim the historical way of thinking not to exclude 'the recognition of Christianity as the highest truth valid for us' [*ibid.* p. 65]. Troeltsch is seeking no either/or, therefore, but instead his concept of decision arises out of a both/and. One must do justice to the historically relative. At the same time one must take account of the pressure of the believer towards religious certainty. Again and again Troeltsch tried new formulations to justify the combination of relativity and certainty. Finally 'absoluteness' is described as a mark of naive thinking [p. 89]. Naively conceived and asserted absoluteness in the religious sense can be accepted so long as it remains naive and does not betake itself into a system of artificial theory and proofs of sole truth. Out of such artificial absoluteness arises the idea of a supernatural absoluteness. Thus artificial absoluteness is to be found, for Troeltsch, midway between the natural naive absoluteness and thought in comparisons and relationships. It is mistaken to replace naive absoluteness with artificial absoluteness. The final passage of the book concludes that it is all right for religious feeling to forget history again and to live with a sense of naive absoluteness in the presence of God.

One must ask, however, whether there is not a break to be observed here. How does the naiveté of religious feeling relate to reflective thought about this same naive position? Can the pious believer with his feeling of naive certainty free himself from the claims of critical thought? And if he cannot do so, what then becomes of his naiveté?

Wilhelm Herrmann in his review of Troeltsch's book accepted precisely this idea of naive absoluteness. Troeltsch spoke for him in the idea 'that religion is only living when it possesses what he calls naive absoluteness'.[19] If one pursues the line *via* Wilhelm Herrmann to Rudolf Bultmann it can be shown that on the one hand Bultmann accepts the result of Troeltsch's enquiry[20] while on the other hand he maintains, down to the form of words, the line of Wilhelm Herrmann.[21] Bultmann accepts Herrmann's argument when he says of the claim to absoluteness of the christian faith: 'This claim can only be raised, but also must be raised, by each believer, and then not as a result of comparison with other forms of faith but in response to the Word which itself addresses him personally' [*Kerygma und Mythos* III, 59]. There persists here the problem about the relationship between the purely historical view and the interpretation of the past along the lines of existential address responded to by the one who is addressed. For

---

[19] *Schriften zur Grundlegung der Theologie*, Part I (München, 1966), p. 199.

[20] 'For [the claim to absoluteness of christian faith] is not [properly understood] when it is taken as the assertion of the absoluteness of the christian religion. Such a claim has no meaning. The christian religion is a phenomenon of world history, just like other religions.' Rudolf Bultmann, 'Zur Frage der Entmythologisierung', *Kerygma und Mythos*, III (Hamburg, 1954), 58.

[21] Wilhelm Herrmann: 'But if the absolute religion cannot be discerned in the history which is known to science, it may perhaps be otherwise with history as it is experienced in the present by the individual.' *Schriften zur Grundlegung der Theologie*, part I, p. 197.

Bultmann this becomes a question about the dualism of *Historie* and *Geschichte*. Whereas Bultmann divides the objectivising question about the historical meaning of religion from the existential avowal of faith through history (*geschichtlich*), Troeltsch attempted to bring the historical comparison between the religions into the decision. The decision is understood as one based upon a considered point of view, one which brings itself about only on a broad basis of comparison as the final axiomatic deed of the individual.

Following on from these reflections it is appropriate to turn to Troeltsch's more specifically theological discussions. These are found mainly in his articles in the encyclopedia *Religion in Geschichte und Gegenwart*. In his own brief autobiography Troeltsch said that he put forward his 'positive views' here. These partially coincide with a record of his lectures assembled by Gertrud von Le Fort which was later published as his *Glaubenslehre* [i.e. 'Dogmatics', Heidelberg, 1924]. In Troeltsch's thought, these positive views have a definite significance, and this can be perceived when his differentiation between the scientific and confessional ways of thinking is seen against the background of his distinction between philosophy of religion and theology. The philosophy of religion has to do with the general phenomenon of religion and its work precedes any form of theological statement or teaching. Scientific theology in the strict sense can only be historical theology. Dogmatics understood as systematic doctrine (*Glaubenslehre*) has subjective, confessional traits and really belongs to practical theology.[22] Thus Troeltsch's statements all have their own particular place in the articulation of his thought and thereby for him their own varied area of validity.

An interesting example of these more strictly theological statements is Troeltsch's article on eschatology [*RGG*, 1st ed., II, 622–32]. Religion itself is interpreted here as being the perception, or more precisely, the sensation, of the last things,

---

[22] Troeltsch is admittedly far from offering a strictly consistent use of the term 'theology'. He can say of theology as a whole that it is unscientific [*GS* II, 362], and then again he can say of the images of faith, 'that in their free and imaginative flexibility they are brought together and regulated in terms of their general conceptual substance by means of scientific doctrine' [article on 'Dogma' in *Religion in Geschichte und Gegenwart* (hereafter *RGG*), 1st ed., II, 106].

and this in the sense of having to do with the absolute and the unconditional as opposed to any possible form of relativisation of reality in the form of science. Morality, science and art come into it in so far as they have to do with the idea of religion itself and with the absolute which becomes apparent through it. As a perception of the absolute, eschatology has worked itself out in two diverse doctrinal forms. One form comprehends the absolute as the definition of reality in the form of totality and constancy, against the background of that which is merely partial and changeable in our understanding of the world. The other form thinks in personal and ethical terms of a free act of self-giving to the absolute. Both of these forms are available to man for his decision. In spite of the emphasis on the personal character of the decision Troeltsch does not omit guidance on how to take it. The considerations which lead to the practical decision should pursue the question, in which of these two forms 'the absolute takes up the finite into itself most comprehensively and penetratingly' [*ibid.* column 627]. This interpretation of eschatology shows starting points which lead on to Bultmann and Tillich. The connection with Bultmann lies in the common feature that both consider eschatology as a kind of existential interpretation of being human, as the orientation of man towards a final reality. For Bultmann the *eschaton* becomes the overall determining criterion for the present life of man [*Glaube und Verstehen*, II, 75f.]. At the same time Troeltsch did not wish to give up the purely chronological perspective in the interpretation of the eschatological. Three things link Troeltsch with Tillich: talk of the unconditional, inclusion of the idea of the kingdom of God into eschatology, and finally the inseparability of religion and culture [cf. P. Tillich, *Gesammelte Werke*, I, 329].

Troeltsch can be differentiated from both in that, characteristically, he speculates freely at the end of the article on the doctrine of the restoration of all men and on the possibility of a modern form of the eschatological myth to replace the traditional one of the church. These speculations at the end of his essay are in accord with Troeltsch's conception of theology as the total expression of the freely ranging religious imagination, and are therefore quite personally intended. On the basis of this example we can therefore conclude as follows. The content and form of theological communication are both variables for Troeltsch; they must be examined with respect to their intention and differentiated accordingly.

After going into this detail on the transition from the first to the second creative phase in Troeltsch's thought, it is now necessary to discuss the formula which belongs to the second period: *the religious a priori*. Troeltsch's name is linked with this phrase again and again. His shift towards Kantianism in connection with the persistent emphasis on the autonomy of religion prepared the way for an enquiry in the philosophy of religion which led to the religious *a priori*. This formulation is first found in an article on philosophy of religion in the volume in honour of Kuno Fischer, *Die Philosophie im Beginn des 20. Jahrhunderts* (1904). This piece, together with another entitled 'Das Historische in Kants Religionsphilosophie' ('The historical in Kant's philosophy of religion', 1904), was followed by the lecture 'Psychologie und Erkenntnistheorie in der Religionswissenschaft' ('Psychology and epistemology in the science of religion', 1905). On publication this lecture was sub-titled 'An enquiry into Kant's account of religion for the science of religion today'.

The empirical psychology of religion of William James with its emphasis on the multiplicity of religious experience based upon an elementary form led Troeltsch to the question of the truth or reality content of the religious phenomena. This question could not be answered at the empirical level but was, he said, 'the question of what is valid' [p. 18]. He believed that it could be shown precisely in the case of James how the psychological question had to lead to the epistemological one. While the living concreteness of the phenomena is known from within experience, a secure knowledge of reality follows from science. Thus the problem is defined as that of the relation between irrational factuality and rational validity. The task of the religious *a priori* is to determine the truth content of religion. It provides the final scientifically possible basis for such a determination of the truth content and is to that extent a means for the critical testing and purification of factually existing religion.

In the context of the further discussion we then find an interesting modification of Kant's philosophy. The phenomenal 'I' and the 'I' known to mind should not be seen as side by side, according to Troeltsch, but they must lie in and over each other. For if the interwovenness of the phenomenal world and the world of ideas can be assumed, then with respect to the philosophy of religion the empirical can be rationally shaped, for the interconnection of the two asserts 'the interruption of causal necessity and the intervention of autonomous reason [*ibid.* p. 40]. In this way the claim of the irrational beside and within the rational can be recognised, while irrational events can come to pass without causal necessity. With this conception of irrationality the right of religion's understanding of itself is maintained when it claims to be based on a transcendent initiative. The religious *a priori* is supposed 'to determine the element of necessity in the empirical phenomenon, without any reduction in its perception, and on the basis of this element to correct confusions and one-sidednesses in the human psychological condition without doing away with the element itself' [*ibid.* p. 45].

The 'actualisation of the religious *a priori*' means therefore the bringing about of real religion through a combination of the rational element and the psychological activity of the individual. The critical regulator of living religion is the science of religion, and it is so on the basis of the recognition that it only regulates and criticises religion in terms of its own *a priori*. For our discussion here it is indeed important to add that there is a metaphysics lying behind all these considerations. Troeltsch speaks of a 'hidden unity of cosmic reason, in which the general, the necessary and the rational enjoy an incomprehensible unity with the factual, the individual and the given' [*ibid.* p. 49].

The fundamental question raised by this conception of the religious *a priori* can only be briefly characterised here. The religious *a priori* is intended to be two things: a principle of validity in formal rationality, and an irrational, material principle of history. The difficulties in combining these with each other cannot be resolved.

There are two more matters which belong in this second section of Troeltsch's work, namely his preoccupation with the 'History of protestantism' (*Geschichte des Protestantismus*, 1902), and his *Social Teachings of the Christian Churches and Sects (Die Soziallehren der christlichen Kirchen und Gruppen,* 1912). The history of protestantism, from the Reformation up to modern times, appeared as a contribution to the volume *Kultur der Gegenwart.* The quality and scope of this work justify us in speaking of it as a significant monograph in the modern history of theology. In fact historical works figure in every period of Troeltsch's writing and demonstrate his persistent interest in history. But between 1902 and 1910 however this historical interest was particularly prominent. Together with these historical works belongs the major work on *The Social Teachings of the Christian Churches and Sects,* albeit with a specific set of problems. The double character of Troeltsch's work is to be seen in the combination of his historical interest with a systematic approach to the materials. In the foreword to the first volume of his collected writings he declared for himself the role which the historical enquiries played in the overall pattern of his work. 'Thus there naturally arose for me the double task of getting clear the ecclesiastical dogmatic tradi- tion of protestantism in its own historical terms and the true fundamental tendencies of the present spiritual and practical situation. Hence arose the two-sided form of my investiga- tions' [*GS* I, vii]. In the context of these reflections Troeltsch mentions that his attention to the modern state of the question led him to put the accent more and more on ethics [*ibid.* p. viii]. His work on the social teachings is evidence of this. Max Weber's influence on Troeltsch certainly supported the pro- cess of this shift of emphasis in his work and stimulated him in the articulation of the questions about social ethics. At any rate this second phase of Troeltsch's development, along with the philosophical influence of Windelband and Rickert, was deci- sively determined by his sociological studies and their results in the enquiries into social ethics. The role played by Max Weber in this new direction in his work is repeatedly emphasised by Troeltsch. In his autobiographical sketch 'My books' ('Meine Bücher') he comments: 'All the previous solutions gave rise to new problems. At the same time I came under the spell of the powerful personality of Max Weber, for whom the marvels now dawning upon me had long been a matter of course. And from that point on I was powerfully seized by the marxist theory of infrastructure and superstructure' [*GS* IV, II].[23] In the *Social Teachings* there is a clear agreement with Weber's works *The Protestant Ethic and the Spirit of Capitalism* (1904–5) and *The Protestant Sects and the Spirit of Capitalism* (originally 1906, altered 1920), as regards both subject matter and methodology, and extending as far as terminology such as 'inner-worldly asceticism' and 'sect-type'.

Troeltsch limited his task in the *Social Teachings* to questions framed in terms of the history of dogma [1, 2] and he saw his work as complementary to Harnack's *History of Dogma* [IV, 11]. There is no contradiction here when one sees that Troeltsch, unlike Harnack, makes room in his account for the sociological self-construction of Christianity and for its social relations. Troeltsch knew that his methodological starting point should really lead him further, namely not only to an account of the history of social theories but to an examination of the historical reality itself. He comments that his powers were not adequate for this. Altogether his account covers the ancient church, the middle ages and protestantism up to the eighteenth century. A concluding chapter summarises the results, and in this Troeltsch indicates the intention and the meaning of the language of ideal types (church, sect, mysticism) and explains once again the methodological principle, which to him also appears as the result, of his enquiry. This is 'the dependence of the whole world of christian ideas and dogma on fundamental sociological factors and the social conception of the time' [*GS* I, 967f.].

It is evidence that this result gave a lead to the method of the enquiry, and this is not inconsistent in the sense that Troeltsch worked heuristically with this method while the result of the historical enquiry in turn proved to justify the procedure. The application of the socio-historical or marxist method to Christianity is limited by Troeltsch however in that he rejects a doctrinaire application of it. The method may be said to be applied in a doctrinaire way when it is not able to accept in what

[23] And in his obituary for Max Weber Troeltsch wrote: 'For my own part I will simply observe that I experienced the endlessly stimulating power of the man from day to day for many years, and I am conscious of being indebted to him for a large part of knowledge and ability.' *Deutscher Geist und Westeuropa* (Tübingen, 1925), p. 249.

is specifically religious 'an independent expression of the religious life' [*GS* 1, 975]. In historical perspective, and with a view to future tasks, Troeltsch emphasises that a reconciliation should be sought for the three types, church, mysticism and sect, in a higher unity, an idea which in history was already anticipated and presupposed in so far as these three fundamental social forms were already marked by increasing interpenetration. In this way Troeltsch calls for a flexibility in the christian ethos to be understood as a continually renewed adaptation to the situation and thus to changing circumstances.

A discussion of these same problems arising out of Troeltsch's *Social Teachings* and also of his relationship to Max Weber is found Hans Bosse's book, *Marx–Weber–Troeltsch* [München, 1970].

This combination may seem strange at first sight, but it is understandable in terms of Bosse's perspective on the critique of religion and the sociology of religion which is linked with it. Bosse is in fact able to show how relevant research into the history of theology can be when it is not pursued in an antiquarian way. Because of this relevance we must discuss this work here critically. The central critical starting point for Bosse is the question whether the bourgeois sociology of religion has not so systematised the marxian critical model in its attempt to turn his critique of religion into a scientific procedure that the real criticism of religion thereby failed to be taken over. The loss of critical potency and the lack of social relevance to be found in socio-political analyses and models would then presumably be evidence in the case of Weber and of Troeltsch, because they could have brought about this substantial loss when converting the critique of religion into a form of science.

The question itself leads to problems. Considering the chronological spread between Marx, Weber and Troeltsch, with the substantial difference in what each one was attempting, should such an enquiry not explicitly consider the methodological problem as to whether such a direct comparison is possible at all? Can Weber and Troeltsch be measured against Marx by assuming the importance of the criticism of religion and of the *praxis* of social change as a presupposition for this evaluative comparison? Weber and Troeltsch were scientists and not activists who understood themselves in marxist terms. The reception of theoretical elements into another theory is only one problem, and there is also the question of criteria to be critically discussed so that one of the theories – in this case the marxian – does not unwittingly provide the standards of judgement. Thus the critique of religion (Marx) and the sociology of religion (Weber and Troeltsch) are only comparable, provided that thorough attention is given to their diverse presuppositions and interests. Is it surprising that Bosse can then discover a loss of substance, a falling away of the critical impulse into scientific theorising without relevance to practice? If one follows Troeltsch himself, and his interests, the fact remains that he used the marxian starting point in extending and completing research in the pure history of ideas. Whether one regrets it or not, he never did engage in systematic debate with Marx's critique of religion. There are some hints in this direction from the time of the composition of 'The autonomy of religion' ('Selbständigkeit der Religion') when Troeltsch attended, in terms of the psychology of religion, to Feuerbach's explanation of religion as illusion.

If Troeltsch is to be measured like this by the yardstick of Marx it is not surprising that what comes out at the end is – Marx. Troeltsch is being used here more as a peg on which to hang interesting problems of today rather than being considered for his own sake in terms of his own intentions. This does not mean that it is wrong to actualise and reformulate Troeltschian statements and themes. But this must be done explicitly and not presume to be understood biographically and historically. Bosse asks, for example, whether Troeltsch's view of the codetermination of socio-economic causal factors within the history of culture holds good for his own theoretical studies and work in the history of religions. The biographical answer to this is that Troeltsch's theoretical works were mainly conceived before his recognition of the importance of these codetermining factors. Bosse's question can only be understood as retrospective to works in which Troeltsch's perception was not so far advanced, and when the marxian teaching of infrastructure and superstructure did not yet have the relevance as a methodological principle for his writings implied for it. That is not to deny that there is a substantial question here which could be posed in a new systematic treatment. But Bosse should have made clear the nature of the question and then conceived and evaluated the result correspondingly.

When these presuppositions of interpretation are taken into account it is also clear that Troeltsch's talk of the autonomy of religion cannot be directly confronted with Marx. The assertion that religion is autonomous has in Troeltsch a different opponent, not the marxian critique of religion. He is rather, like Schleiermacher, emphasising the autonomy of religion by contrast with metaphysics and morals. And unlike the stress on the autonomy of Christianity in the Ritschlian school it involves an extension of thought into the history of religions. The basic problem with Bosse's book is that on the one hand he is working in terms of the history of theology and on the other he is intending to reformulate for the present. But the distinction between the two is not sufficiently clear.

The last main section of Troeltsch's work covers approximately the time from 1914 to the end of his life in the year 1923. In 1915 he went to Berlin to take up a chair in philosophy. The teaching responsibilities connected with this involved the philosophy of religion, society and history, as well as the history of the christian religion. The works which he published at this time relate above all to the philosophy of history and appeared while he was still alive as the third volume of his collected writings (*Der Historismus und seine Probleme*). Since some of the contents of this volume first appeared separately and were then provided with additions and linking passages there are not a few overlaps and repetitions. The first 'book' of the whole account, now before us, has as its theme 'the logical problem of the philosophy of history'. The second book was to deal with the substance of history in a philosophical manner in the form of a cultural synthesis, but it remained unwritten. Troeltsch died on 1st February 1923. The lectures prepared for delivery in England, *Christian Thought, Its History and Application*, are no substitute for what remained to be done, and their German title, *Der Historismus und seine Überwindung*, is misleading in that it suggests that historicism is overcome.

Troeltsch began his book *Der Historismus und seine Probleme* by referring to the crisis in historical thought. This lay for him in its philosophical foundations. His reflections in this context were written out of the direct experience of the time, that is from the time of the first world war and the revolution in Germany. This historical situation needs to be taken into account. Looking both at the historical conditioning of the time and the radical resolve to be free from it he said: 'We have to carry our burden onwards. We can shift it about and set it on the other shoulder. But since all our life's possessions and tools are in it we cannot simply throw it away' [*GS* III, 4]. Troeltsch was concerned to strike the right balance, to retain the right selection of the old which history has conveyed to us while advancing with the required openness towards the new. It was necessary to support the capability of creating anew in sovereign freedom, without abruptly breaking off the orientation towards the values of the (European) past.

The solution of the crisis, a crisis in the philosophy of history, could only be achieved by a fundamental philosophical treatment of the nature of history and the question of its intellectual and spiritual aims.

This task was pursued in the subsequent chapters. They deal with the problem of appraising historical events, that is to say with the question of criteria and with the historical concept of development, and to that extent with the question of a universal history. Troeltsch's characteristic linking of historical review with a systematic perspective informs the whole undertaking. The third chapter of the book is by far the longest and deals with the concept of development. In the treatment of this theme it is evident how strongly Troeltsch's approach links up with the concerns of his early years, when it was also the concept of development which had had central importance for him. The articulation of a philosophy of the factual content of history was to be linked on to this discussion, because the further development, and that means the formation of the future, is decisive for it. The philosophy of the content of history is to be aligned with history itself in order to seek from it the possible solutions for the shaping of the future. At this point the philosophy of history leads over into ethics, so that the former exists as a discipline between the science of history on the one hand and ethics on the other.

Troeltsch sets before us two different types of work in the philosophy of history in his account of the positions of the cultural philosophers Nietzsche and Dilthey and the more formal neo-Kantian thinkers Rickert and Windelband. Troeltsch himself sees the solution in a synthesis. The contemplation of the historical fullness of life must be maintained, without the control of this concrete fullness of historical life through regulative categories being lost. The search for this synthesis leads according to Troeltsch into the field of epistemology. A Leibnizian doctrine of monads is needed here for the solution of the problem of maintaining historical vision in the face of the logical grasp of the historical. A monadology teaches us to understand the individual 'I' through its identity with the consciousness of the 'All' and thus allows it to participate in the overall content of reality. 'Not Spinoza's identity of thought and being, or of nature and spirit, but the substantial and individual identity of the finite minds with the infinite mind, and precisely thereby the intuitive participation in its concrete content and active unity of life, this is the key to the solution of our problem' [*GS* III, 677]. The problem of the grasp of historical, and that means again and again individual, reality is solved when reality is spoken of in the sense of a 'visualisable reality which at the same time like all reality is soaked through with idea, law and meaning' [*ibid*]. Troeltsch's epistemological foundation for the synthesis of perception and form is thus inspired by a metaphysics of monadological provenance. It is therefore evident that a metaphysical orientation, and indeed a characteristic mystical trait, persists through all Troeltsch's works from the earlier to the latest. The mystical concept of religion from the early period appears broadened out at the end to a mystical philosophy of cosmic fullness and extent.

The concluding chapter of *Der Historismus und seine Probleme* already contains the first suggestions for an elaboration of the philosophy of the content of history. Troeltsch himself did not stick to the division of the work into the form and the content of the philosophy of history. Are the doubts perhaps justified which have been expressed (Scheler) about Troeltsch's ability for systematic philosophical work? Troeltsch himself closes the book with the diffident words: 'That shall be treated in the next volume as far as it lies within the power of an individual to do so' [GS III, 772]. The doubts are probably not justified, in that Troeltsch would probably have remained true to his principle of 'surmounting history through history' [ibid.], even in the systematic elaboration of the philosophy of history, and carried it out very much as a study in the history of ideas. To that extent Hans Baron, the editor of the fourth volume of the collected writings, is right when he feels able to see in the essays in the history of ideas which it contains a 'certain substitute for the missing second part of the work on historicism' [GS IV, viii]. Troeltsch may seem to have distanced himself rather clearly, in the execution of his work in the philosophy of history, from the theological beginning of his development. But did he really? I believe that such a judgement is only partially true, for there is a historically orientated theological and philosophical thought which persists through all the stages of Troeltsch's development.

Finally something needs to be said about the so-called failure of Ernst Troeltsch, a judgment which has been handed down since the twenties about the outcome of Troeltsch's work. Yet this talk of Troeltsch's failure seems to me increasingly suspect. It is too scanty a label to stick over the life-work of this great theologian and historian and it hands him over to a quick and pejorative criticism. His achievements thereby go unrecognised. His generous abililty to hold theological thinking widely open, without losing an eye for radical questions and doubts, could be described as exemplary precisely in contrast to the following generation. And it cannot surely be denied that the end of the dialectical theology is bound up with a breaking free from the narrowness of revelational theology into philosophy, theory of science, the sociological dimension and the socio-ethical.[24] How does it stand with this so-called failure of Troeltsch, spoken of by the following theological generation and handed down so happily to this day as the generally accepted view? Such talk must be called into question in so far as it was used as a justification for the right of the following generation of theologians to begin afresh. Perhaps a more just and more objective appraisal of the conclusion of Troeltsch's work might begin with his own comment on the inclusion of earlier works in the collected writings. Troeltsch declared here

[24] Cf. in this connection the work of Pannenberg, Sauter, Marsch and others.

that he had always indicated old points of view which had been left in the text [*GS* II, vii]. To take up contemporary questions and allow them to influence his thinking was normal for Troeltsch, while the conservation of old viewpoints was not normal for him. There is a profound reason for this, namely that for him theology is always something to be articulated in connection with the time in question. Theology always has to be the timely expression of the religious questions. But if theology was not something isolated, not a science which could make objective statements without regard to the time and the society in which it was carried on, then one should ask about the conditions in which Troeltsch found himself in the time of the first world war and thereafter. In that depressing time, when the downfall of the west forecast by Spengler seemed no longer to be a distant possibility, Troeltsch himself did not lose hope. Even when the Zeitgeist ran contrary and theological and other critics like Gertrud von Le Fort (who turned catholic) could not or would not see it, Troeltsch spoke repeatedly of boldness and courage, of spontaneity and creative power. From the same time can be found his plans for a philosophy of religion [*GS* III, viii]. There were therefore indeed starting points in Troeltsch for a way through the understandable sense of resignation, starting points which however were prevented from flourishing because of his sudden death.

When all the values of culture and church appeared to be in ruins a different path led to a strengthened reliance on biblical revelation and on the Reformation. The concentration on a 'pure' theology based on the bible which was provoked by the first world war shattered the broad scientific horizon of influence and experience in academic theology. Unlike the theology of Barth, Bultmann and Gogarten, Troeltsch had had an influence which went beyond theology as a single university discipline, out to philosophy, the history of ideas and sociology. It is only today that these impulses are being taken up again and that links with other sciences are being forged.[25]

Troeltsch's ability to relate his work to other disciplines is

---

[25] Cf., e.g., *Die Theologie in der interdisziplinären Forschung*, eds. J. B. Metz and T. Rendtorff (Düsseldorf, 1971).

once again becoming most relevant, and it is his permanent
contribution to have demonstrated that theology is an open
discipline which lives by cooperation with other sorts of
intellectual endeavour. The problem of the open and historical character of the basic criteria of theology, a responsibility
which must be accepted in all theological work, found in his
writings an exemplary expression which will continue to have
significance for the future of theology.

2. Ernst Troeltsch and the dialectical theology

ROBERT MORGAN

The theme of this volume is Ernst Troeltsch and the future of theology. It is a characteristic Troeltschian idea that we delve into the past in order to find resources out of which to shape the future. Some fifty-odd years after his death Troeltsch himself belongs to the tradition which has formed our thinking and which can be returned to as a possible source of illumination and instruction. Genuine openness to the tradition requires that we re-read him in the expectation of learning something. If we only come to bury him we are half a century late for the funeral. Within German protestant theology at least, he was all too thoroughly and prematurely buried in the 1920s, by 'the latest theological movement',[1] known as the theology of crisis, neo-orthodoxy, neo-reformation theology, theology of the Word of God, or dialectical theology.

In view of the enormous influence of the dialectical theologians' generally negative verdict on Troeltsch it is appropriate that we reopen the question at the point where the debate was broken off.[2] Whenever a violent reaction occurs in the history of thought, polemic takes the place of balanced judgment, and in this case it is fair to ask whether it was based upon a solid knowledge of Troeltsch's actual writings. The first part of this essay considers the dialectical theologians in their historical relation to Troeltsch in an attempt to clear away the *debris*, the dust of which has clouded the proper appreciation

---

[1] R. Bultmann, 'Liberal Theology and the Latest Theological Movement' (1924). ET in *Faith and Understanding* (SCM Press: London, 1969).

[2] A. O. Dyson, 'History in the Philosophy and Theology of Ernst Troeltsch' (Diss. Oxford, 1968), p. iv: 'It has become well nigh impossible to see Troeltsch except through the eyes of Neo-Orthodoxy', and p. 10: 'The treatment accorded to Troeltsch from Neo-Orthodoxy is perhaps the best explanation for the neglect, disrepute and ambiguity which surrounds his name today.'

of Troeltsch's work for over a generation. This will open the way for a more thematic comparison of Troeltsch with the most important of his successors, and some consideration of the legitimate concerns of both sides.

I

The 'dialectical theology' was a movement within German-speaking protestant theology in the 1920s whose organ was the periodical *Zwischen den Zeiten*.[3] It repudiated the development of protestant liberalism from the Enlightenment and German idealism, and sought to combat this through a recovery of the Reformers', especially Luther's, understanding of the pauline gospel. Their understanding of Paul and Luther was sharpened by an appreciation of Kierkegaard whose works had recently become available in German.

The clearly defined time-span, the shared journal, an enthusiasm for Luther and admiration for Kierkegaard, but above all the common front against a clearly designated opposition – the dominant intellectual theology of the day – was enough to unite some able and energetic young theologians into a movement. It was not sufficient to weld them into a 'school' or establish the shared platform upon the more substantial foundation of positive theological agreement. The variety which existed between the leaders of the movement complicates the question of its relation to Troeltsch, and requires a brief account of each of the main figures, in their relation both to each other and to Troeltsch.

The movement was essentially constituted by the alliance of Barth and Gogarten – in retrospect an extremely improbable combination. In his 'leave-taking'[4] Barth could speak of their alliance having been based upon a 'misunderstanding', and his view of Gogarten's political thought has hindered a proper appreciation of Gogarten as a theologian.[5]

[3] *ZZ* was published by Kaiser, Munich, and edited by G. Merz, with Barth, Gogarten and Thurneysen forming the editorial board, 1923–33.
[4] 'Abschied von Zwischen den Zeiten', *ZZ* XI (1933), reprinted in *Anfänge der dialektischen Theologie*, 2, ed. J. Moltmann (Munich, 1963), 313–21; see esp. p. 318. Hereafter cited as *Anfänge*.
[5] For a recent vindication of Gogarten, see B. Stappert, 'Glaube in der Welt. Zum Problem der Säkularität in der amerikanischen Theologie und bei

The two men were very different. The son of a conservative professor of theology in Bern, Barth was marked out as a church theologian from the cradle. His enthusiasm for Harnack, Gunkel and Kaftan in Berlin, followed by a closer relationship to Herrmann in Marburg, could not eradicate strong calvinist ecclesiastical roots.[6] Herrmann himself, who will be found to haunt any discussion of the dialectical theology, also had, for all his freedom and independence, the strong churchly and conservative side to his character which one might have expected from a pupil of Tholuck deeply influenced by Ritschl. Bultmann's statement that 'the latest movement originated not from within orthodoxy but out of liberal theology'[7] is only a part of the truth about its background. Barth's christian doctrinal roots run deeper, and one should not be surprised that he produced his first and only complete sketch of a dogmatics while still a young man in his mid thirties.[8]

Gogarten, by contrast, came from a thoroughly secular background and was for some years a non-churchman. He studied art history, philosophy and German for a semester at Munich before switching to theology at Jena, Berlin, and finally Heidelberg where he wrote his licenciate on Fichte for Troeltsch. His break with liberalism and idealism was no less dramatic than Barth's, but his theological thinking was always guided by the question of the relationship between revelation and culture.[9] He was sufficiently influenced by Barth to repudiate some of his earlier writings[10] and it seems that Barth

Friedrich Gogarten' (Diss. Tübingen, 1972). See also Peter Lange, *Konkrete Theologie? Karl Barth und Friedrich Gogarten 'Zwischen den Zeiten' (1922–33)* (Zurich, 1972).

[6] His early essay, 'Moderne Theologie und Reichsgottesarbeit', *ZThK* xix (1909), 317–21 shows how far he had as a student adopted Herrmann's stance. But this article also shows the practical concerns of one who had chosen the parochial ministry rather than a university career.

[7] *Faith and Understanding*, p. 28.

[8] I.e. his Göttingen lectures of 1923–4, to be published in the *Gesamtausgabe*. See W. Trillhaas, 'Karl Barth in Göttingen' in *Fides et Communicatio. Festschrift für Martin Doerne* (Göttingen, 1970), pp. 362–75.

[9] In the introduction to *Gericht oder Skepsis* (Jena, 1937), p. 7, he explains how from the outset he and Barth went different ways. Barth raised specifically theological questions, being guided in both questions and answers by the history of christian thought and dogmatics, whereas he himself was always guided by debate with the modern world. See also *Anfänge*, vol. 2, p. 331.

[10] E.g. *Religion Weiter* (Jena, 1917), repudiated in *Illusionen* (Jena, 1926), p. 15.

was stimulated by a visit from Gogarten to rewrite his *Romans* commentary,[11] but it was not long before they both discovered that they were going different ways. Barth had reservations as early as 1922[12] and these crystallised in 1926.[13] By 1930 the break was virtually complete, though the journal continued until 1933.

At the time the 'dialectical theology' meant above all Barth and Gogarten. The perspective provided after 50 years inevitably concentrates attention upon Barth and Bultmann. It is they who have dominated the intervening period and who in view of their monumental achievements remain the chief debating partners for anyone who today returns to the study of Troeltsch.[14]

Again it is important to recognise that they too had less in common than they themselves thought at the time – or less than Bultmann thought; Barth was probably more aware of the gulf that divided them, though anxious to have the weighty support of Bultmann's academic respectability in his front against Hirsch.[15] Bultmann's approval of the second edition of

[11] See *Revolutionary Theology in the Making*, Barth–Thurneysen correspondence, 1914–25, tr. & ed. J. D. Smart (Epworth: London, 1964), p. 53. In this letter of 1920 Barth tells of a 'highly enjoyable' visit from Gogarten – 'Here is a dreadnought on our side and against our opponents' – and then 'a strange and decisive bit of news: when Gogarten, with whom I had so many good conversations by day and night, was gone, suddenly the *Letter to the Romans* began to shed its skin.' Also interesting is Barth's comment that 'together with anthroposophy' Gogarten had settled 'Troeltsch and the modern theology'. Cited by G. Merz, 'Die Begegnung Karl Barths mit der deutschen Theologie', *Kerygma und Dogma* 2 (1956), 163. See *Gesamtausgabe*, v.3, 435.

[12] See *Revolutionary Theology in the Making*, p. 110 (7 Oct. 1922): 'The christological problem is dealt with and solved by him with the help of a speculative I-Thou philosophy...Heaven only knows where that will yet lead. Also in this respect I am really anxious about the future.' See also *Anfänge*, vol. 2, pp. 313ff.

[13] When he read Gogarten, *Ich glaube an den drei-einigen Gott. Eine Untersuchung über Glaube und Geschichte* (Jena, 1926).

[14] The theologian who more than anyone has taken up Troeltsch's tasks is Wolfhart Pannenberg (see now his *Wissenschaftstheorie und Theologie*, Suhrkam: Frankfurt, 1973). Pannenberg owed his rapid fame to the vigour of his debate with the kerygmatic theologies of the Word of God.

[15] In the reprint of the first edition of his *Romans* (1963) Barth remarked that 'on the grounds of the second edition of *The Letter to the Romans* [Bultmann and himself] came for a time quite close to one another'. Cited by B. Jaspert, editor of the *Karl Barth – Rudolf Bultmann Briefwechsel 1922–1966* (*Gesamtausgabe* v.1.; Zurich, 1971), p. 4; hereafter cited as *Briefwechsel*. This

his *Romans*[16] came as a pleasant surprise[17] and the cordial relations maintained over forty-odd years of disagreement is a tribute to the character of both men.[18] But one detects a certain reserve in Barth's letters as he staves off Bultmann's repeated requests for a *tête-à-tête*. He had no wish to be catechised by the Marburg philosophers and had perhaps already seen in the argument about *Sachkritik* the seeds of the subsequent split between his own version of the theology of the Word of God, and Bultmann's – a split which has dominated German protestant thought during this century.[19]

These two greatest pupils of Herrmann have enough in common to make a contrast with Troeltsch meaningful, but what Bultmann has in common with Troeltsch will prove more significant. Barth, Thurneysen and Brunner, and to some extent Gogarten, understood their early work primarily as a *reaction* against the preceding development; the critical note is dominant for a short period before yielding to more constructive systematic work. Bultmann's relationship to his predecessors is quite different, thanks to the cumulative progress of New Testament scholarship. In his 'Autobiographical Reflections' (1956) he relates how he 'attempted to enter into discussion with this [dialectical] theology' but insists that this

volume also contains an interesting letter to Barth from one O. Urbach, who had quickly discerned the difference between the two: pp. 215–20. Barth was later very critical of Bultmann's *Jesus* (1926). This probably marked a turning point in their relationship and was followed in due course by the break-up of the common front on the issue of natural theology (see *Briefwechsel*, pp. 100ff.). Earlier on, in February 1925, Barth could acknowledge Bultmann's reproach about his inadequately clarified conceptuality, and although 'he seems to me too anthropological – Kierkegaardian – Lutheran (+Gogartenian) ('To speak of God means to speak of man'), [and] deals with the Bible after Luther's example with a shocking eclecticism, [and] also has not yet got free of the historical egg-shells' – nevertheless, 'all of these are points of difference about which it will be worthwhile to talk further' (*Revolutionary Theology in the Making*, p. 206). See also below, n. 27.

[16] Bultmann's important review article in *Die Christliche Welt* (1922), is reprinted in *Anfänge*, vol. 1, pp. 119–42; ET ed. J. M. Robinson, *The Beginnings of Dialectical Theology* (John Knox Press: Richmond, 1969).

[17] Barth's response occurs in the preface to the third edition (1922), ET *The Epistle to the Romans* (Oxford, 1933), pp. 15–20. Bultmann replied privately. See *Briefwechsel*, pp. 8–13.

[18] The *Briefwechsel* is characterised by a magnificent frankness about their theological and personal disagreements.

[19] For a discussion of this issue, see my *Nature of NT Theology* (SCM Press: London, 1973), pp. 42–52.

'has never led me to a simple condemnation of "liberal" theology; on the contrary, I have endeavoured throughout my entire work to carry further the tradition of historical-critical research as it was practised by the liberal theology and to make our more recent theological knowledge fruitful for it'.[20]

That 'tradition of historical critical research', within which Troeltsch, as 'the dogmatician of the history of religions school', also belonged, was itself theologically motivated. The liberal protestant theologians (and they *were* theologians!) wished to fulfil the theological tasks of criticism and reconstruction in and through their historical work. Like them, Bultmann also is a theological critic of the christian tradition who exploits the negative aspect of modern critical history as an appropriate means of doing theological criticism in the modern world,[21] but *unlike* them he doubted the capacity of a historical reconstruction to bear the positive theological weight of presenting the christian message. He saw certain weaknesses in his teachers' positions and expected help from the new movement in overcoming these. Even Herrmann, who 'saw the mistakes made by the usual liberalism'[22] must be corrected by means of the kerygmatic theology of Barth's *Romans*. In appealing to the 'inner life of Jesus' Herrmann had 'forgotten that the ground of faith is solely the Word of proclamation (Rom. 10.17)'.[23] But Bultmann nevertheless remained theologically closer to Herrmann than Barth did,[24] and found it a small step from Herrmann to Heidegger.[25] It was in character with his rather one-sided interpretation of the new movement that he judged that 'Barth and Gogarten state the conclusions

---

[20] *Existence and Faith* (Collins, Fontana: London and Glasgow, 1964), p. 340.

[21] I have argued this in *The Cardinal Meaning. Essays in Comparative Hermeneutics*, ed. M. Pye and R. Morgan (Mouton: The Hague, 1973), pp. 92–101.

[22] *Faith and Understanding*, p. 132. This essay of 1927 contains Bultmann's fullest discussion of Herrmann.

[23] *Ibid.* p. 137. Bultmann does not explain why all theology must follow this pauline model.

[24] See below, n. 26. The proximity is stressed by O. Schnubbe, *Der Existenzbegriff in der Theologie Rudolf Bultmanns* (Vandenhoeck: Göttingen, 1959), and Roger A. Johnson, *The Origins of Demythologizing* (Brill: Leiden, 1974). See also Barth in the *Briefwechsel*, pp. 53, 102, 305, and in *Revolutionary Theology in the Making*, p. 204.

[25] 'Because I had learned from Herrmann I was prepared for Heidegger': *Briefwechsel*, p. 188.

which are actually inherent in liberal theology'[26] and that he
himself related what he learned from it to Dilthey's existential
view of history and Heidegger's analysis of human existence. It
is intelligible that whereas Barth was already in 1924 writing his
first dogmatics, Bultmann, like Gogarten, was equally early
radicalising their theology of the Word into a theology of
existence.[27]

Like Gogarten, Bultmann also was persuaded by Barth's
attack upon the liberals' apologetic, based upon the notion of
'religion':

It seemed to me that in this new theological movement it was rightly
recognized, as over against the 'liberal' theology out of which I had
come, that Christian faith is not a phenomenon of the history of
religion, that it does not rest on a 'religious *a priori*' (Troeltsch), and
that therefore theology does not have to look upon it as a phenomenon of religious or cultural history. It seemed to me that, as over
against such a view, the new theology had correctly seen that Christian
faith is the answer to the word of the transcendent God that
encounters man, and that theology has to deal with this word and the
man who has been encountered by it.[28]

Bultmann thus joined his contemporaries in their repudiation of the idealists' account of the relations between God and
the world. But he nevertheless shared a common perspective
with Troeltsch. For all their differences both in theology and
philosophy these two philosophical theologians were above all
else *historians* formed in their thinking by the nineteenth-
century German tradition of historiography. This constitutes

---

[26] *Faith and Understanding*, p. 45 (1924). The quotation continued: 'For who has
emphasized more forcibly than W. Herrmann that there is no specifically
Christian ethic? And who has shown more convincingly than Troeltsch
[*Social Teachings*] the problematic character of the relation of the Christian
to the world?' Troeltsch's insights are here made to serve a Herrmannian
purpose which is diametrically opposed to Troeltsch's own intentions. See
also p. 33, where Herrmann's anticipation of the views of Barth and
Gogarten is noted – that 'there is no direct knowledge of God. God is not a
given entity.'

[27] J. D. Smart, *The Divided Mind of Modern Theology* (Westminster: Philadelphia, 1967), provides an excellent account of their relationship.

[28] *Existence and Faith*, p. 340. Cf. also *Faith and Understanding*, pp. 118f., where
Troeltsch and J. Wendland are sharply criticised for the 'fatal mistake that
here "religion" and Christianity are presented definitively as functions of
the human mind, as cultural phenomena. Faith will reject any such
apologetic'.

the greatest difference between Barth and Bultmann and is rightly identified as such by the latter during the first year of their published correspondence. He draws attention to their different 'educational experience' and says that Barth lacks the 'inner relationship to historical studies' which he so clearly has to idealist philosophy.[29] Both Bultmann and Troeltsch, on the other hand, were very closely associated with the 'history of religions school' – Troeltsch as its so-called dogmatician and Bultmann as its leading representative of the second generation.[30] In their work the problem of history remains central and fundamental.

Barth, also, in his own way, was seeking to resolve the problems posed by modern historical study for christian faith and theology. This is not the place to evaluate his highly original constructive contributions which fall outside the period of 'dialectical theology'.[31] His dogmatic counter-achievement to the idealist metaphysics of history rightly excites admiration as an attempt to rescue dogmatics from the strangle-hold of historical studies. But the question whether his new account of the relationship (which is still insufficiently clarified), does justice to the legitimate claims of historical science, continues to draw a negative response from exegetical and historical theologians.

Barth's comment in his *Protestant Theology in the Nineteenth Century*[32] that, 'Proper theology begins just at the point where the difficulties disclosed by Strauss (i.e. the questions posed by historical criticism of the Christian tradition)...are seen and then laughed at' is perhaps less a comment on his famous sense of humour and more one on the 'limits to the vision' of one

---

[29] *Briefwechsel*, p. 9 (31 December 1922).

[30] Bultmann joined von Soden as editor of *Theologische Rundschau* when the new series began in 1929. He succeeded Bousset as coeditor with Gunkel *Forschungen zur Religion und Literatur des Alten und Neuen Testaments* in 1920, since Gunkel believed he would 'pass on our traditions to a younger generation': W. Klatt, *Herrmann Gunkel* (Göttingen, 1969), p. 6. He was also a major contributor to *RGG*[2]. These were the main organs and monuments of the history of religions school.

[31] It is illuminatingly analysed by R. H. Roberts, 'Eternity and Time in the Theology of Karl Barth' (Diss. Edinburgh, 1975).

[32] ET SCM Press: London, 1972, p. 568. Although this book was not published until 1947 the chapter on Strauss had already appeared in 1939 and had been worked on in the 1920s.

who was 'not a professional historian', referred to in the foreword to the same book [p. 11]. His personal account of his own relationship to historical studies is no less compromising than the quotation from Strauss' correspondence which he cites.[33] In a letter to Thurneysen in 1916 he admits

how frightfully indifferent I have become about the purely historical questions. Of course that is nothing new for me. Already under the influence of Herrmann I always thought of historical criticism as merely a means of attaining freedom in relation to the tradition, not, however, as a constituting factor in a new liberal tradition, as apparently Wernle and his like want to have it.[34]

'Wernle and his like' meant above all the history of religions school, and amongst them preeminently Ernst Troeltsch; men who wanted to give history a constitutive place in their reconstructions of christian theology.

The implication of Herrmann in this judgment is particularly relevant to our theme because it goes some way towards explaining why Bultmann, though an outstanding historian of early Christianity, would allow theological significance to history only in the attenuated form of human historicity, and also why neither Barth nor Bultmann was disposed to take Troeltsch's philosophy of history seriously as systematic theology.

It is important to recall that Herrmann and Troeltsch were *the* two great antipodes in systematic theology and ethics at the time when all the dialectical theologians were impressionable students. In 1908, the year in which Barth began to 'absorb Herrmann through all [his] pores'[35] H. Diehl referred to the *opposition* between Herrmann and Troeltsch as central to the then current discussion: 'Especially from Herrmann's side it was on occasion made quite unmistakeable what a great gulf he saw between his own work and the methods and scientific aims of Troeltsch.'[36] The well-attested personal aspect to their mutual hostility could also have contributed to some of Herrmann's pupils proving unable to contemplate Troeltsch

---

[33] 'I am not a historian; with me everything has proceeded from dogmatic (or rather anti-dogmatic) concerns.' *Ibid.* p. 543.

[34] *Revolutionary Theology in the Making*, p. 36 (1st January 1916).

[35] From Barth's autobiographical sketch of 1927: *Briefwechsel*, p. 305.

[36] *ZThK* XVIII (1908), 473.

as a live theological option.[37] When the two masters died within a year Karl Bornhausen wrote that

Anyone beginning the study of protestant theology in Germany at the start of the twentieth century would, in the course of his study inevitably be led to two theological positions that it seemed both necessary and impossible to unite. Wilhelm Herrmann and Ernst Troeltsch often and without success exchanged statement and reply in their life-time. They even almost took umbrage at any of their pupils trying to synthesise their views.'[38]

Two contentions of this essay are, first, that Barth, like Herrmann, had no patience with 'the methods and scientific aims of Troeltsch', and that his theology is consequently vulnerable to counter-questions from the theologian who saw most clearly the implications of modern critical historiography for christian faith; and, secondly, that the philosopher-historian-theologian Bultmann was better equipped than anyone to fulfil Bornhausen's dream and 'synthesise their views', but that in fact he never sufficiently freed himself from Herrmann's ahistorical theology. The main reason why the task which Bornhausen rightly saw to be urgent remains still outstanding is that the two giants of the next generation were unfortunately such decided pupils of Herrmann that they never grew into the mantle of Troeltsch.

But before returning to Barth and Bultmann it is necessary to describe briefly the relationship to Troeltsch of the other 'pillars'[39] of the dialectical theology.

When the time came for him to leave Berlin, Gogarten was faced with the choice between Marburg and Heidelberg. True to his secular background and romanticist leanings he chose the latter and became the only theologian of the movement to

---

[37] Barth mentions the *rassentiment* in *Theology and Church* (SCM Press: London, 1962), p. 261, in an essay on Herrmann from 1925, referring to the *Gesammelte Schriften* II, 768, where 'Troeltsch, answering spite with spite, called Herrmann "one of the liveliest of our edifying writers."' Barth's reference to 'the Marburg students who shrugged off [Herrmann's] "advanced confirmation instruction"...at a time when the star of Troeltsch with his world-wide programmes and perspectives was nearing its zenith!' (*ibid.* p. 258), shows that Troeltsch was not alone in his verdict on Herrmann and also that professorial sarcasm outlived them both.

[38] *ZThK* N.F.4 (1923/4), 196.

[39] Bultmann's play on Gal. 2.9 (*Briefwechsel*, pp. 107, 113, 123) has a touch of pauline irony and reflects his distance from the Swiss dogmaticians and pastors.

have been a genuine pupil of Troeltsch. Thurneysen also had studied briefly at Heidelberg as well as Marburg and never concealed his admiration for Troeltsch. In retrospect Barth could speak of 'the most impressive figures of [Thurneysen's] youth and student days' as the younger Blumhardt at Bad Boll, and the 'in his own way [*sic!*] equally great man of understanding among the theologians: Ernst Troeltsch'.[40] But during their formative period 'your friend Troeltsch' was the subject of ironical comment from the self-confessed less historically minded Barth,[41] and though like all the dialectical theologians Thurneysen accepted Troeltsch's analysis of the contemporary intellectual and religious situation[42] he never settled the account he owed his honoured teacher.[43] There is therefore little to be said about his relationship to Troeltsch except what might be gleaned indirectly from an extensive analysis of his writings.[44]

The situation is quite different with Gogarten, whose 'whole theological work can be understood as an ever deeper thinking through of the antithesis between modern autonomy and christian authority, and so shows how the debate with Troeltsch was the starting-point of his thought'.[45] In a *curriculum vitae* he wrote in 1923 when applying for a lecture-ship in Jena, Gogarten wrote as follows:

It is perhaps clear enough from my choice of universities that my theological development has from the outset been decisively influenced by 'liberal' theology. For me the decisive thing about this theology was its unconditional openness for the problems of the

[40] In his introduction, written in 1935, to a projected new edition of Thurneysen's essays, *Das Wort Gottes und die Kirche* (1927). This was finally published in the 1971 Kaiser (Munich) reprint of that collection, pp. 227–30. See p. 229.

[41] *Karl Barth – Eduard Thurneysen Briefwechsel* I, *1913–1921 Gesamtausgabe* v. 3 (Zürich, 1973), 40. Barth writes, 'you have more of a historical view.'

[42] See for example, *Anfänge*, vol. 2, p. 259, where Thurneysen appeals to Troeltsch's account of the historical critical method.

[43] *Karl Barth – Eduard Thurneysen Briefwechsel* I, 144.

[44] Thurneysen's extremely sensitive treatment of the canon question in 'Schrift und Offenbarung' (1924), reprinted in *Anfänge*, vol. 2, pp. 247–76, owes much to his historical schooling.

[45] W. Bodenstein, *Neige des Historismus: Ernst Troeltschs Entwicklungsgang* (Gerd Mohn: Gütersloh, 1959), p. 16, n. H. Fischer, *Christlicher Glaube und Geschichte: Voraussetzungen und Folgen der Theologie Friedrich Gogartens* (Gerd Mohn: Gütersloh, 1967), devotes the substantial first part (pp. 13–64) to Troeltsch.

modern spirit and the attempt without any artificiality to assert
Christianity in the face of the profound crisis caused by the
emergence of this modern thought since the beginning of the
sixteenth century, in honest debate with the difficulties resulting from
this crisis.[46]

But if Gogarten was always moved by Troeltsch's questions
he did not remain satisfied with his answers. In 1917 he bought
the Erlangen edition of Luther's works with a publisher's fee
and moved to a country parish in Thuringen to study it.

But then I was more and more compelled by an intensive study of
Luther and by various signs that the modern spirit had run into a
profound crisis, to subject my position to a thorough-going revision.
The first attempt to indicate my newly gained position was the lecture
given at the Wartburg in the Autumn of 1920 to the Friends of the
Christian World[47] entitled 'The Crisis of our Culture'[48] and the other
lectures and essays contained in my collection. *The Religious Decision*
(1921).[49] I regard these pieces as simply a first attempt. They by no
means say all that still has to be said and made clear on this topic.[50]

Troeltsch rightly recognised in the 1920 lecture an implied
criticism of his own position[51] and responded briefly in the
Christliche Welt with 'An Apple from the Tree of Kierkegaard'
(1921).[52] Gogarten replied with 'Against Romantic Theology'
(1922)[53] in which he acknowledges his debt to his teacher
'precisely at the point at which I turn against his ideas'.[54] Yet he
continues to be a learner, as he had been throughout the
'constant debate with Troeltsch' which had accompanied him
since his student days.[55] Troeltsch is said to have lost the object
of theology by subjecting the divine event to the general laws of
history. He therefore posed for theology the problem of

[46] Cited by B. Stappert, 'Glaube in der Welt', p. 243.
[47] Concerning this group, see J. Rathje, *Die Welt des Freien Protestantismus*
(Klotz, 1952).
[48] 'Die Krisis unserer Kultur', *Anfänge*, vol. 2, pp. 101–22; ET *Beginnings*, pp.
283–300.
[49] *Die religiöse Entscheidung* (Jena, 1921).
[50] Cited by B. Stappert, 'Glaube in der Welt', p. 243.
[51] The second part is entitled, 'The psychological philosophical and religious
way of looking at the matter' and the alternatives posed were religion as the
soul or the crisis of culture.
[52] 'Ein Apfel vom Baume Kierkegaards' *Anfänge*, vol. 2, pp. 140–53; ET
Beginnings, pp. 317–27.
[53] 'Wider die romantische Theologie', *Anfänge*, vol. 2, pp. 140–53; ET
Beginnings, pp. 317–27.   [54] *Ibid.* p. 141; ET p. 318.
[55] *Ibid.* p. 149; ET p. 323.

revelation while he himself refused to answer it positively by remaining within the sphere of historical knowledge.[56]

Troeltsch's death on 1st February 1923 prevented a prolongation of the debate, but Gogarten sharpened his attack in an important essay, 'Historismus' (1924)[57] and in *Ich glaube an den dreieinigen Gott* (1926) where he takes Troeltsch's *Der Historismus und seine Probleme*[58] as an important statement of an idealist view of history. The earlier essay provides the sharpest account of the consequences of Troeltsch's whole attempt to derive norms from history to be found in the entire dialectical theology. For Troeltsch, not theology but the philosophy of history is said to be the real science for establishing norms.[59] His real norm is the idea of Europeanism,[60] and on his presuppositions the transition from theology to a philosophy of culture, from Christianity to Europeanism was fully justified – however terrifying the prospect might be for theology and Christianity.[61] Since every religion is conditioned by its cultural context it makes sense on Troeltsch's terms to take the question of norms outside the narrow framework of theological questioning and explore general historical, cultural, political, ethical, social, artistic and scientific norms.[62]

This does, says Gogarten, represent one of the possibilities open to theology in the modern world: to surrender the task of establishing norms to the philosophy of history and to restrict theology to the historical investigation of Christianity.[63] This is what has happened in liberalism and all that remains to be done by anyone remaining a liberal protestant is the 'bitter task' of drawing out its implications. But there is another possibility. One might put in question Troeltsch's thesis about the thorough-going historicisation of all our thought; not by

---

[56] The same points are at issue in Bultmann, *Faith and Understanding*, pp. 118, 261.

[57] 'Historismus', *Anfänge*, vol. 2, pp. 171–91; *Beginnings*, pp. 343–58.

[58] *Gesammelte Schriften*, Bd III (Tubingen, 1922; rp. Scientia, Aalen, 1961).

[59] *Anfänge*, vol. 2, p. 178; *Beginnings*, p. 348; quoting *Der Historismus und seine Probleme*, p. 110: 'If we no longer see the norms for shaping life in church dogma or its offspring, rationalist dogma, all that remains is history as our source and the philosophy of history as the solution.' Cf. Bultmann's charge in *Faith and Understanding*, p. 118.

[60] *Anfänge*, vol. 2, p. 179; *Beginnings*, p. 349.   [61] *Ibid.*

[62] *Anfänge*, vol. 2, p. 177; *Beginnings*, p. 347.

[63] *Anfänge*, vol. 2, p. 179; *Beginnings*, p. 349.

denying Troeltsch's accurate analysis of what has happened, but by asking whether it ought to have happened: 'whether the whole happening is not bound to remain hidden and elusive to historical thought because historicised thinking moves in a sphere which is unreal or has been made unreal by it'.[64]

Gogarten takes up Troeltsch's assertion which no theologian should wish to deny, that 'without the idea of God there can be no construction of criteria' for judging history. But he fastens on to Troeltsch's qualification [*Der Historismus und seine Probleme*, p. 184] – without the idea of God 'or something analogous' – to show that Troeltsch's idea of God is not the real God of christian revelation but an idol, the creation of some human conceptual scheme. The scheme in question in these philosophies of history is that of German idealism, and Gogarten attacks it not by a mere assertion of the God of Abraham, Isaac and Jacob, but by a penetrating criticism of the idealist conception of history.

It is the 'contemplative' character of idealism's view of history which Gogarten repudiates in the name of a real and so incomprehensible, unthinkable, non-contemplative confrontation with God which determines everything else and is therefore without analogy. His objection to Troeltsch's idealist philosophy of history is its unreal basis; this unity of ideas is a place of absolute rest, not of historical decision, whatever Troeltsch says to the contrary.[65]

How far Gogarten's criticism of Troeltsch and his own alternative are persuasive may be left open here. His clear recognition of the importance of the debate makes him an exception within the dialectical theology. He

very strongly emphasises that Troeltsch's achievement seems to me to be of the utmost significance and that no theology can hope to make a significant contribution unless it has thoroughly come to grips with it. Since Troeltsch, every theology which fails to tackle the problem of historicism in the full scope of his presentation, is doomed to failure. In this debate with Troeltsch it is necessary to bear in mind that we are not in the first place arguing with a theory of his, by which he tried to gain norms despite and within the historicising of our thinking. The debate is above all one about this general historicising of thinking itself. Again, this is not a theory of Troeltsch but a fact which he

[64] *Anfänge*, vol. 2, p. 180; *Beginnings*, p. 350.
[65] *Anfänge*, vol. 2, pp. 180f.; *Beginnings*, p. 350.

pointed out in all its ramifications and consequences. The debate is made more difficult by the fact that our own thinking is itself part of this historicising. Our entire education is a historical one. No reform of education, however radical, can avoid this basis. All that is possible is a thorough stock-taking. The clear thinking through the historicism and its presuppositions which Troeltsch has left us in his most recent work may help us in this.[66]

The start which Gogarten made was the only significant confrontation with Troeltsch from the side of the dialectical theology – and it fizzled out. Gogarten himself was a man for the present moment and little disposed to argue with dead men. After 1927[67] references to Troeltsch in his writings become infrequent.[68] More immediate questions were presented by the changing political situation. But it can be argued that the sound instinct for historical reality learned in both dependence upon and independence from Troeltsch preserved Gogarten from Marburg varieties of ahistorical theology. He was the first to reopen the question of the historical Jesus – probably he had never closed it.[69] It may also be that the Troeltsch – Gogarten debate contains possibilities for the future of theology which remain to be explored in a generation which has witnessed a renewal of interest in the philosophy of history.[70]

[66] *Anfänge*, vol. 2, p. 181; *Beginnings*, p. 350.
[67] *Theologische Tradition und theologische Arbeit* (Leipzig, 1927) poses the alternative between 'Geistesgeschichte' and theology, i.e. between German idealism and the Reformation. Troeltsch is briefly mentioned. 'Protestantism and Reality', which contains polemic against Troeltsch and 'the idea of autonomous personality' (*Anfänge*, vol. 2, pp. 191–218; *Beginnings*, pp. 359–79) had appeared in 1924.
[68] *Der Zerfall des Humanismus und die Gottesfrage* (Stuttgart, 1937) refers to Troeltsch to indicate the contrast with the post-war 'culture-critical' theology. Gogarten's masterpiece, *Die Verkündigung Jesu Christi* (Heidelberg, 1948; Tübingen, 1965²) barely mentions Troeltsch.
[69] Bk 1 (pp. 25–163) of *Die Verkündigung Jesu Christi* which Gogarten was writing in the 1930s is concerned with this, and I understand from Professor Ernst Käsemann that Gogarten gave a paper (now lost) on the subject to Bultmann's pupils at the end of the 1920s. Appropriately, Ebeling dedicated *Theologie und Verkündigung* (Tübingen, 1962), largely devoted to the question of the historical Jesus, to Gogarten (ET *Theology and Proclamation*, Collins: London, 1966).
[70] K.-G. Faber, *Theorie der Geschichtswissenschaft* (Munich, 1972²), p. 12, notes the revival of interest in methodological questions since the second war and observes that prior to this the most important stimuli came from three outsiders – Dilthey, Max Weber and Troeltsch. See also A. Stern, *Philosophy of History and the Problem of Values* (Mouton: The Hague, 1962).

In the debate about the nature of history, the newly published posthumous manuscripts of Dilthey replaced Troeltsch at the centre of interest as soon as the flood of obituaries had subsided. No theologian paid closer attention to Dilthey than Bultmann, who shared Gogarten's interest in a more existential account of history, but studied this without any debate with Troeltsch.[71] It would be unreasonable to criticise this specialist from another field for not finding time to study the main systematic theologian of his own critical direction, though had he done so he could have learned much.[72] An adequate account of history, which both Bultmann and Troeltsch rightly saw to be vital for christian theology, will need to do justice to both emphases. The whole span of real history, so far as we possess information about this, is as important as reflection upon men's historicity. But Bultmann had been immunised against Troeltsch and when he saw the inadequacies of Herrmann's unhistorical 'inner life of Jesus' he did not correct it by a Troeltschian appreciation for real history but moved in the opposite direction and asserted simply the 'mere that' of the historical Jesus to be theologically relevant.

Like every self-respecting theologian Bultmann had read the *Social Teachings* and was scathing about anyone who had not.[73] He was also of course familiar with Troeltsch's essay on 'The Significance of the historical existence of Jesus for faith'.[74] But he assumed that Troeltsch provided no escape from relativism and saw in him merely a symbol: the great 'Aporetiker' of liberal theology.[75]

E. Brunner was reckoned by Bultmann among the 'pillars'

[71] In *History and Eschatology* (Harper, 1962), p. 123, Troeltsch is explicitly set aside.

[72] H. Ganse Little, 'History, Decision and Responsibility: An examination of a problem central to the thought of Ernst Troeltsch and Rudolf Bultmann' (Diss. Harvard, 1965), has shown convincingly how the views of history in these two philosopher theologians supplement one another.

[73] See *Briefwechsel*, p. 26: 'Rade spoke as though he had never read Troeltsch's *Social Teachings*, and had no grasp at all of the problem.' See also *Anfänge*, vol. 2, pp. 34–6 for his early (1920) criticisms of this work.

[74] 1911, reprinted 1969 (Siebenstern-Taschenbuch); ET in *Ernst Troeltsch: Writings on Theology and Religion* (Duckworth: London, 1976).

[75] *Faith and Understanding*, p. 29. The English translator mistakenly renders *Aporetiker* 'proponent'. The point is that Troeltsch sensed the limits and the difficulties, the *aporia*, of liberal theology.

of the dialectical theology [*Briefwechsel*, p. 113], and although he had little personal contact with the others he qualifies as one who joined the common front and sought to oppose the liberal theology out of which he had come with impulses deriving from the Reformation and Kierkegaard. He did not know much about Troeltsch, having like Barth quite reasonably chosen to settle his account with neo-protestantism through the study of Schleiermacher.[76] But since he referred to Troeltsch less guardedly than any other dialectical theologian it is tempting to recall the asperity of his judgment.[77]

Brunner gave his allegiance to the new movement very early, in the work which qualified him to teach at a university, *Erlebnis, Erkenntnis, Glaube* (1921).[78] The introduction begins by identifying the enemy:

The religious and theological thought of the last decades stands under the signs of *Historismus* and *Psychologismus*. These are the last shoots of that movement which the Renaissance introduced and the Enlightenment carried through and which we may call in a word subjective – anthropological, – a series of variations of world-historical dimensions on the theme: Man is the measure of all things [p. 1].

Modern thought was bound to react against scholasticism and Brunner does not want to return to the middle ages or to protestant orthodoxy. Even historical criticism has had (*sic!*) its day and its justification. But in its concern to show the humanly conditioned and historically accidental element of forms of faith, and under pressure from the spirit of the age *it lost all sense for what is non-human yet objective*. It has totally surrendered the gospel to *Historie* and *Psychologie*. The former is said to have reached its high-point today in the 'icy historical relativism of Troeltsch' [p. 2].

Brunner's posing of the problem virtually demands detailed consideration of Troeltsch's work, even though the complete *Der Historismus und seine Probleme* had not yet appeared. But

---

[76] *Die Mystik und das Wort. Der Gegensatz zwischen moderner Religionsauffassung und christlichem Glauben dargestellt an der Theologie Schleiermachers* (Tübingen, 1924), critically reviewed by Barth in *ZZ* 2 (1924), 8.

[77] A. O. Dyson, 'History in the Philosophy and Theology of Ernst Troeltsch', p. 6, notes the sarcasm of Brunner's reference to Troeltsch in *The Mediator* (1927), pp. 68f., and *The Theology of Crisis* (1930).

[78] Tübingen, 1921, 1923$^{2/3}$, 1933$^{4/5}$.

anyone led by the introduction to expect this will be disappointed. In the second part 'psychologism' is treated at some length [pp. 32–59]. Troeltsch's essay 'Psychologie und Erkenntnistheorie in der Religionswissenschaft' (1905) is mentioned once with approval, though 'Empirismus und Platonismus in der Religions-philosophie' (1912) is ignored in Brunner's discussion of William James. The other evil, 'Historismus', receives a mere nine pages, and the icy Troeltsch is not once mentioned.[79] The argument from near silence has some weight here.

Similar considerations apply with even greater force to Brunner's *Religionsphilosophie evangelischer Theologie*[80] written when he had looked at *Der Historismus und seine Probleme*. As the title suggests this work above all demands a debate with Troeltsch. The page he receives merely repeats without discussion the usual conclusions that Troeltsch is 'the most splendid representative of the history of religions theology, who took *Historismus* consistently to its bitter end and so dissolved theology as such...a specifically christian consciousness of revelation can no longer be maintained here.'[81] In the chapter on 'The element of truth in subjectivism' and even in that on 'The element of truth in Historismus: Revelation and the history of religions', Troeltsch is almost totally ignored.[82]

The most natural explanation is that Brunner's knowledge of Troeltsch's work was rather limited. But the plea of ignorance cannot excuse the polemic of his American lectures delivered in 1928, and published as *The Theology of Crisis*.[83]

[79] Perhaps wisely, since Troeltsch had meanwhile abandoned the evolutionary apologetic which Brunner attacks as a *Greuel* to faith. The structure of the book rather suggests that Brunner may have intended to attack Troeltsch but on investigation discovered that the target was elusive.

[80] (Munich and Berlin, 1927), pp. 99.

[81] *Ibid.* p. 21. Brunner finds an 'irreconcileable opposition' between christian faith and the idealist conception of revelation prevalent in neo-protestantism, and adds that 'radical historicism has performed the great service of making this opposition unmistakeably clear, thus showing that no theology but only a general science of religion, no christian church but only a religious society is possible', p. 22.

[82] *Ibid.* pp. 57–76. Brunner complains that 'for Troeltsch historicism as a principle has so to speak axiomatic validity': p. 58. If, unlike Gogarten who agrees with Troeltsch's analysis (see n. 66), Brunner wished to challenge the thesis of 'the historicisation of all our thought', he should have produced some arguments.

[83] Scribner, London and New York, 1930.

Brunner gives Troeltsch, 'the greatest and most modern of modernists...the credit of having discerned and shown the irreconcilable contradition which modern theology has so long attempted to hide. He saw and confessed, boldly and without equivocation, the chasm which separates modern theology from the theology of the Reformers and of the ancient church' (p. 7). Ignoring the sarcasm and the sneer and the exaggeration, the main point is clear enough and reports correctly the element of newness in neo-protestantism which Troeltsch emphasised. Brunner continues, again more or less rightly[84] that Troeltsch 'introduces also the final stage of the development...The year 1900 marks the approximate date when it began to sink into a sea of relativistic scepticism.' But then Troeltsch is called not only a representative but also an '*advocate* of an almost boundless historical relativism' [pp. 7f.]. From being credited with recognising the implication of modern thought for christian thinking he is now blamed for it. Finally he is cudgelled with a somewhat improbable angel of theological light, borrowed from the American scene with which Brunner was familiar:

A fundamentalist, possessed of a reasonably correct knowledge of Christianity will have little difficulty in proving that the modernist teaches, under the label of Christianity, a religion which has nothing in common with Christianity except a few words, and that these words cover concepts which are irreconcileable with the context of Christian faith. Indeed, in a discussion with his antagonist, the fundamentalist may account on help from the radical left wing of the modernists. For here also the real state of affairs is appreciated – as I have shown in the case of Troeltsch. The left wing recognize that they are not defending or contending for a new interpretation of Christianity. Fundamentalists and extreme modernists are agreed that the real issue at stake is the complete surrender of genuine Christianity [pp. 9f.].

Criteria for 'a reasonably correct knowledge of Christianity' and 'genuine Christianity' are not provided. This question,

[84] Cf. Barth's more substantial account of the *Glaubenslehre* of neo-protestantism's 'last great systematic representative' in *Church Dogmatics* IV 1 (1953); ET Edinburgh, 1956, 383–7. 'Troeltsch was a gifted and, in his own way, a pious man...But it was obvious that with him the doctrine of faith was on the point of dissolution into endless and useless talk, and that for all the high self-consciousness of its conduct Neo-Protestantism in general had been betrayed on to the rocks, or the quicksands. It was because we could no longer take part in this that about the end of the second decade of this century we left the ship': pp. 386f.

which stands at the heart of modern doctrinal discussion, is simply ignored. But it is plainly untrue that the radicals were not, and knew they were not, contending for a new interpretation of Christianity. That is precisely what Troeltsch quite self-consciously *was* contending for.[85] It is also what the dialectical theologians were contending for, and most of them recognised this. It is also what in their day Paul, Marcion, Origen, Augustine, Aquinas, Luther and the rest were contending for, however dimly they were aware of it. The point at issue is not the newness of new theologies but their adequacy; their faithfulness to the christian tradition which Brunner does comment on, and their intelligibility and truth and meaningfulness within contemporaŕy experience which Brunner's fundamentalist ally ignores. But enough has been said to show that Brunner does not take Troeltsch seriously and that there is no reason in this context to pay much attention to Brunner either. He is an extreme case confirming the impression that most of the new generation had long since given up Troeltsch as providing no exit from the liberals' impasse, and therefore did not bother to read him very closely. The important question is whether this is also true of Karl Barth.

Barth was undoubtedly deeply concerned with the question of faith and history[86] and was familiar with Troeltsch's general position. While he was working as editorial assistant on the *Christliche Welt*, Troeltsch's 'name stood at that time at the centre of our discussions'. But though he considered himself very much a liberal protestant – 'witness my contributions to *ZThK* 1909' – nevertheless he had already drawn the line at Troeltsch; he was never *that* much of a neo-protestant! That name 'designated the limits *this* side of which I thought I must refuse to follow the then dominant theology'.[87] It remains to be seen whether any exposition of Troeltsch appears in Barth's *Nachlass*; but he never continued his *Protestant Theology in the Nineteenth Century* as far as Troeltsch, as originally intended.[88]

[85] This is nowhere made clearer than in the essay 'What does "Essence of Christianity" mean?', *GS* ii, 386–451; ET in *Ernst Troeltsch: Writings on Theology and Religion* (London, 1976).

[86] He published an essay on the subject which he later regretted: 'Glaube und Geschichte', *Schweizerische Theologische Zeitschrift* (1912).

[87] 'Autobiographical sketch' (1927) in *Briefwechsel*, p. 305.

[88] The reason given in the foreword is that 'the limits of the academic semester prevented both parts from reaching their intended conclusions', p. 11. But

Around 1909 Barth was reading Schleiermacher 'again and again' [*Briefwechsel*, pp. 305f.] in his attempt to combine idealist-romanticist theology with the Reformation. Had his study of that giant been matched by a study of Troeltsch he would have been compelled to pay closer attention to those aspects of the problem of neo-protestantism which Troeltsch illuminates better than Schleiermacher. Because he is the successor of Hegel and F. C. Baur as well as of Schleiermacher, Troeltsch challenges his readers to penetrate more deeply into the problems of theology and history. But Barth saw in the latter half of the nineteenth century a day of small things. The year 1910 was 'the hey-day of Troeltsch', and one reason why the 'desperate possibility of a revival of idealist metaphysics' mercifully failed was that there was no Hegel or Schleiermacher around at that time, but only 'feeble epigones and eulogists'.[89]

A more substantial indication of Barth's attitude is reflected in a reminiscence of when he heard Troeltsch lecture in Aarau in 1910 'with the dark foreboding that it had become impossible to advance any further in the dead-end street where we were strolling in relative comfort'.[90]

This is more to the point than a consideration of what exactly of Troeltsch he had read.[91] When in 1925 he obtained the posthumously published *Glaubenslehre* it merely confirmed his low opinion of the 'lion's' 'lack of real theology'.[92] As early as 1910 he could see no line of advance along the line of his teachers' generation and struck out on new paths. This bore

at certain points, especially in his discussion of Novalis, Barth clearly has half an eye on 'the last great romantic in theology' (p. 347).

[89] *Church Dogmatics* II, 1 (1940; ET Edinburgh, 1957), 73, hereafter cited as *CD*. There is a sense in which Troeltsch would accept the designation. See E. Lessing, *Die Geschichtsphilosophie Ernst Troeltschs* (Hamburg, 1965), pp. 58ff.

[90] *Theology and Church*, pp. 6of. The essay dates from 1920.

[91] Thurneysen gave Barth the *Social Teachings* as a wedding present in 1913, and we hear Barth requesting a copy of *GS* IV in 1925 (*Revolutionary Theology in the Making*, p. 208).

[96] In *CD* 1, 1, 317f. it is mentioned as a sign of the sorry state of the discipline. *CD* 1, 2, 862 quoted Troeltsch without disapproval – and then adds: 'But by what right is it dared to make the systematic exposition of these assumptions the business of dogmatics?' In *CD* 11, 3, 100 Barth calls Troeltsch's judgment of the older dogmaticians 'barbaric', and says on p. 409 that Troeltsch's not considering the bible and fathers worth a glance on the subject of angels shows his book to mark the depths into which the entire neo-protestant development had led.

fruit in a work of theological interpretation of the New Testament which found a massive echo in the post-war German situation and formed the beginnings of a movement which has decisively influenced christian theology. The question remains whether christian theologians can avoid facing the problem of 'the historian and the believer'[93] in something like Troeltsch's terms. Neither Barth, Brunner or Thurneysen were sufficiently impressed by radical historical criticism[94] to be inescapably confronted with the form of the problem as experienced by Troeltsch. Bultmann and Gogarten, on the other hand, had a far better understanding of Troeltsch's formulation of the questions. It is therefore necessary to speak of two wings of the dialectical theology and to take one representative from each. Barth and Bultmann agreed in rejecting Troeltsch's solutions, but Bultmann's greater sympathy for his questions is a most important indicator of his distance from the author of *The Epistle to the Romans* whom he greatly admired and from whom he hoped to learn [*Briefwechsel*, p. 82].

II

The development of German protestant theology since the first world war justifies a concentration upon the early work of Barth and Bultmann in confronting Troeltsch with the dialectical theology. This is to stage a debate which never actually took place since, unlike Gogarten, these two theologians were barely influenced by Troeltsch and rarely responded to him. However, they were as concerned as he was about the situation of christian theology in a world largely determined by the modern critical understanding of history. Since the notion of revelation became something of a slogan it is important to recognise at the outset that the issue was not for or against revelation. Both sides thought that Christianity had something to do with God's self-revelation. The point at issue was rather

[93] This is the title of Van Harvey's excellent book on the subject (SCM Press: London, 1967) which begins with a consideration of 'the shadow of Ernst Troeltsch'.

[94] See Barth's comment in 1919 on 'the mighty errors of this time from which the treatment of the Acts suffers especially'. *Revolutionary Theology in the Making*, p. 47.

how this should be understood, and on this point the two wings of the dialectical theology themselves varied considerably.

The problem may be posed in terms of the relationship between christian revelation and the modern critical understanding of history which had destroyed the older identification of revelation with the text of scripture. The liberal theology which developed out of this collapse of the older orthodoxy was accused by the new movement of having lost the subject-matter of theology and so of failing to do justice to the christian revelation. It had sought to combine the new historical research with belief in God with the help of German idealist philosophy which allowed it to see in the process of world history God's gradual self-revelation. The historical study of religion was then the appropriate way of doing theology, because on this view God's self-revelation is perceived by the finite mind of spirit of the historian who contemplates the process of world history.

The new generation of theologians, for whom recent history posed more problems than it solved, were not impressed by this metaphysics. The idealist synthesis was discredited, and the question was what could take its place. Barth was in due course to develop a massive new proposal with which to replace the theological ontology of idealism – but that lay in the future. The early dialectical theology was stronger in criticism than in constructive proposals, and the weapon of their theological criticism was Paul's polemical doctrine of justification on the basis of faith alone – a faith which results from hearing the Word proclaimed (Rom. 10.17). Luther's recovery of the pauline gospel was here given a new epistemological twist and turned not against reliance on good works or religious practices, but against metaphysics and natural theology. The continuities which this move can claim with Luther's repudiation of scholastic theology, and his substitution for it of a 'theology of the cross' should not blind us to the novelty of its application in the post-Kantian theological situation. Since one main concern of this essay will be to show what was right in the dialectical theologians' appeal to Paul and the reformers against Troeltsch, it is necessary at once to insist that *this* aspect of their appeal cannot be sustained. Paul and Luther cannot be used as witnesses in the case against natural theology as such, but only against christian theologies which lose sight of the centrality of Jesus as God-given good news. Theologians who concentrate upon natural theology are particularly susceptible to this loss of christology, but the two things do not necessarily go together.

Paul's doctrine of justification was directed against a legalistic version of Christianity; it presented Christ as God's gracious act on behalf of the ungodly. In his attack upon scholastic metaphysical *theologia gloriae*, Luther could legitimately appeal to the pauline gospel or theology of the cross so long as the object of his attack was the scholastic surrender of a christology which presented Jesus as good news, and the transformation of Christianity into a christian nomism. In other words, the validity of Luther's appeal to Paul at this point depends upon his attack being directed against a *particular* metaphysical theology which had usurped the central place of God's free grace in Christ. The appeal to Paul will not support an attack on natural theology in principle – and Luther did not intend it as such.[95] It was given that function later in order to make a virtue of necessity, following the destruction of the old natural theology by Kant.

This opposition to metaphysical theology in the name of the Reformation did not originate with the dialectical theologians, and neither was it an advance on Troeltsch. They inherited it from Ritschl and Herrmann, and Troeltsch had decisively repudiated it in that earlier form in his first book. 'The attempt to prove that an apologetic is neither necessary nor grounded in the nature of the matter is itself an apologetic operation, albeit a very misguided one.'[96] Troeltsch was quite scathing in his attack upon the use made of Kant by the Ritschlians to separate faith and knowledge and make room for a supranaturalist theology.[97] It was inconsistent in the way it judged other religions by different criteria from those applied in its

[95] Neither will it support a defence of natural theology. The echoes of Stoic natural theology in Rom. 1.19f.; 2.14f., are part of an argument for man's need of revelation. The 'Paul' of Acts 17 who engages in it is a very different figure.
[96] *Offenbarung und Vernunft bei Johann Gerhard und Melanchthon* (Göttingen, 1891), p. 2.
[97] See especially, 'Die Selbständigkeit der Religion', *ZThK* v & vi (1895–6); 'Geschichte und Metaphysik', *ZThK* viii (1898).

own case, and it was defenceless against the projectionist theory of religion proposed by Feuerbach.[98] Troeltsch saw the task of theology, 'a kind of necessary evil', in tying the knots between christian faith and the knowledge of the day.[99] The philosophical climate of his day was dominated by positivism, which undercut Christianity by dismissing all religion as illusion. Troeltsch met the beast on its own ground and defended the independence of religion as a necessary prerequisite for defending the rationality of a modern christian belief. He developed, in a more hostile philosophical climate, the work of Schleiermacher, who, in his philosophical ethics, had proceeded from a philosophy of history and of human consciousness, 'and through his analysis of religion and its historical development pioneered the way first to the understanding and then to the justification of Christianity'.[100]

It is important to distinguish between the question whether natural theology as such is legitimate, and that whether the particular efforts made by Troeltsch on a basis of the notion of 'religion' were successful. Since the former question became the issue upon which the dialectical theology finally broke up when Gogarten, Bultmann and Brunner reopened the question of anthropology, it seems likely that there was from the outset a latent disagreement here, and that the distance between Troeltsch and his different detractors varied. It will not be surprising, either, to discover corresponding differences in the dialectical theologians' conceptions of revelation, and to find that Bultmann was closer to Troeltsch than Barth.

Natural theology cannot be banished in principle by appeal to Paul or Luther. It is therefore necessary to consider particular proposals and assess their value. Troeltsch's apologetics were open to criticism from the Ritschlian side. Herrmann could claim that the evolutionary apologetic of his science of religion was bad science because it smuggled in christian presuppositions. Troeltsch himself soon found it necessary to abandon his early quite Hegelian position,[101] and

[98] E.g., *ZThK* VIII (1898), 34, 51, 53.
[99] *Offenbarung und Vernunft*, pp. 2f.   [100] *ZThK* VIII (1898), 28.
[101] In 1902 he explained that 'the strongly Hegelian standpoint that appeared in ['Geschichte und Metaphysik', 1898] has here been transformed into a critical (i.e. Kantian) one, due to the influence of Rickert' [*AC*, p. 168]. What is meant by 'strongly Hegelian' is indicated by his comment in the

he later came to doubt whether the general history of religion would disclose to rational enquiry even the 'supremacy' or 'prime validity' (*Höchstgeltung*) of Christianity.[102] His theory of the 'religion *a priori*' was another attempt to rebuild an apologetic upon the epistemological basis established by Kant.[103] It too was soon agreed to have failed; Troeltsch's development of Kant's thought is not persuasive at this point.[104] But Herrmann's objections to Troeltsch's enterprise[105] were not at the level of Kant interpretation. He considered it misguided in principle on the grounds that religion is not an objectifiable 'thing in the world', and that it cannot, therefore, be investigated by empirical scientific research.[106] The scientific aims and methods of Troeltsch could never do justice to the reality of religion. There is an important issue here concerning the relation of christian theology and the science of religion which for Troeltsch was a normative, and not simply a descriptive task. This issue is still insufficiently clarified and can only be touched on here. Herrmann, and later Barth, were right to insist that theology must have a methodology appropriate to its subject-matter. Troeltsch for his part recognised the difference between the believer's attitude and that of the scientist of religion, and he defined rather carefully the point at which rational argument ceased and personal decision and commitment were necessary.[107] But instead of reserving the notion of revelation for that event in which insight dawns in response to a claim

same year (1898) that it 'needs only to be freed of its metaphysics of the absolute, its dialectic of opposites, and its specifically logical conception of religion' [*GS* II, 747].

[102] In 'The Place of Christianity among the World Religions' (*Christian Thought*, London, 1923), he indicates the shift in his thinking since he wrote *Absoluteness*. See pp. 22ff.

[103] See especially *Psychologie und Erkenntnistheorie in der Religionswissenschaft* (Tübingen, 1905).

[104] See R. Köhler, *Der Begriff a priori in der modernen Religionsphilosophie* (Leipzig, 1920), for a convincing argument that Kant knew only one *a priori*, that it does not *ground* anything, and that Troeltsch's attempt to combine transcendental and psychological methods was a failure.

[105] See especially *Schriften zur Grundlegung der Theologie* (Kaiser, Munich), 1 (1966), 193–9, 258, 284–8, and 2 (1967), 1–6, 32–42, 282–9.

[106] *Ibid.* Teil 2, p. 4.

[107] H. Benckert, 'Der Begriff der Entscheidung bei Ernst Troeltsch', *ZThK* N.F. 12 (1931), 422–42, shows how this is as central in *Der Historismus und seine Probleme* as in his earlier work. See also below, n. 117.

mediated by the tradition, as kerygmatic theology was to do, and as Troeltsch himself was to do in his *Glaubenslehre*,[108] he retained in his early published work traces of the idealist assumption that revelation could be perceived in history.

That was excellent apologetics – for as long as it was plausible. Talk of 'the general revelatory character of all religions'[109] is more credible than the traditional, pre-critical view which identified revelation with a bit of tradition, and on this basis asserted that Christianity (one's own version of it) was true and all other religions false. But once the idealist metaphysics of history no longer seems plausible, the truth of religion in general and Christianity in particular can no longer be read off its history. The relationship between tradition and revelation must then be redefined and one solution is to free the notion of revelation from its idealist associations with the whole span of history and to reserve it to interpret the event of decision and faith in which the tradition is personally appropriated, as involving the reality of God. This distinction between the religious tradition and the revelation event, in which the former is necessary for (but not identified with) the latter, has practical benefits for theology and church. This is one reason for much modern excitement about hermeneutics. It directs theology to the basic task of interpreting the tradition in such a way that the event of revelation may, where and when God wills, occur. Despite his different terminology, this corresponds very closely to what Troeltsch was proposing when he defined the task of christian theologians, as to interpret the tradition critically, to define the 'essence of Christianity' and so shape it anew.[110] The most obvious difference between Troeltsch's proposals and Bultmann's procedure is that the latter concentrates upon the scriptural part of the tradition (without ever adequately explaining why)[111]

---

[108] See especially *Gl.*, §3, 'Offenbarung und Glaube', pp. 39–56. On p. 51 the language of 'word and faith' comes very close to Bultmann and Ebeling. Troeltsch casually lets drop that 'this theory is not new. It is found already in Luther.'   [109] *RGG*¹ IV, Sp. 920.

[110] *GS* II, 431; Eng. tr. *Ernst Troeltsch: Writings on Theology and Religion.*

[111] In *Faith and Understanding*, p. 137, he simply asserts, against Herrmann, the unique position of scripture as the basis for preaching. In 'The Problem of a theological Exegesis of the New Testament' (1925) he raises it as a theoretical question whether other documents might be used. *Anfänge*, vol. 2, p. 67.

and has a preference for Reformation terminology. Their procedure for relating history and theology is very similar. Both theologians do their history according to modern critical norms, and try to draw out its theological significance. They both stand opposed to Barth, whose theological method resists the autonomy of modern critical history.

Granted this account of the relation between tradition and revelation, the 'absoluteness of Christianity' is no longer a problem. Only God, or revelation, is absolute. The believer asserts the absoluteness of Christianity in the act of affirming his faith, as Herrmann insisted.[112] Christianity, in the sense of the human phenomenon or tradition is not absolute. There is, of course, then no apologetic income to be gained from the notion,[113] because other religions' believers can also lay claim to revelation and absoluteness; and the conflicting claims cannot be settled by argument, since this would assume a position from which God can be judged, which is absurd. On the other hand, competing religious *traditions* can be compared and may be evaluated by human ethical and aesthetic criteria. It is meaningful for believers to argue for the superior value of their own traditions, which is what Troeltsch did. A theology which refuses to do this is at a disadvantage in an age of religious pluralism. Even if idealist efforts to dragoon other religions into the service of christian apologetics is a failure, there is surely no evading the patient confrontation and comparison of rival traditions, if religions are thought to contain any cognitive content.

Since Troeltsch is, despite his idealism, rather close to Bultmann in his theological method, it is not surprising to discover that he in fact anticipated the standard objections made by Bultmann and others to idealist theologies of

---

[112] *Schriften zur Grundlegung der Theologie*, Teil 1, p. 199: 'So christian faith not only has but is conviction of the "absoluteness of Christianity". Troeltsch is right only insofar as he is thinking of the apologetic task. We can only perform this if we help other people to test whether Jesus is not greater than all other masters.' This sensible concession to Troeltsch was repudiated by the dialectical theologians, for whom 'apologetics', like religion, idealism, history, etc., was a tainted concept. See *Faith and Understanding*, p. 119.

[113] In 'The Independence of Religion' (1895/6), Troeltsch had argued that only Christianity laid claim to absoluteness: *ZThK* VI (1896), 212f.

history.[114] The argument that history is at best ambiguous and full of human sinfulness does not touch Troeltsch, because unlike advocates of 'salvation history' who glorify the church, Troeltsch is not tempted to identify revelation with christian history. He insists that we never have the christian principle 'neat' in history, but always and only in the form of a creative 'compromise' with the harsh realities of human history.[115]

Secondly, the objection that a Hegelian pantheism of history makes God accessible to the enquiring mind and leaves no room for the venture or leap of faith[116] misses Troeltsch. He never accepted Hegel's apriorism and dialectic, and while rejecting Kierkegaard's pietistic account of the relationship of the christian ethos to the realities of history [*GS* II, 293f.] he did take over, and gave a central place to, the Kierkegaardian concepts of decision and venture in the creative or axiomatic act of adopting a religious and ethical stance.[117] If the matter is considered from the side of decision, rather than from Troeltsch's idealistically determined use of the word revelation, it appears that his correlation of revelation and faith [*Gl*, §3] differs in idiom rather than substance from that of Bultmann's kerygmatic theology. It makes little difference whether the tradition is assimilated through one's ears hearing the Word proclaimed, or one's eyes viewing history. In both cases the crucial matter is that of understanding and decision. Gogarten's exaggerated antithesis of faith and world-views,[118] and Bultmann's insistence that we do not have our destiny at our disposal are both expressions of their firm rejection of idealism. But while he never abandoned an idealist (in the broadest sense) framework,[119] Troeltsch found room for an

---

[114] See *Essays Philosophical and Theological* (SCM Press: London, 1955), pp. 103–7.

[115] An account of Troeltsch's concept of 'compromise' is given by B. A. Reist, *Towards a Theology of Involvement* (SCM Press: London, 1966), pp. 156–68.

[116] *Essays*, p. 105. *Faith and Understanding*, pp. 149, 157.

[117] E.g., *GS* II, 712: 'This "scientific" character (of judgments made on a basis of historical study) does not eliminate the individuality of the decision. Everything historical, in spite of all references to absolute values, remains irrational and individual.'

[118] See his *Weltanschauung und Glaube* (Furche: Berlin, 1937). Also the subtitle of *Theologische Tradition und theologische Arbeit* (Hinrichs: Leipzig, 1927): 'Geistesgeschichte oder Theologie'.

[119] The article on 'idealism' in Hastings' *Encyclopedia of Religion and Ethics* (1913), VII, 89–95, includes almost everything short of materialism.

existential emphasis – despite Gogarten's denial of this [*Anfänge* vol. 2, p. 180]. His opting for a particular material philosophy of history is as genuine a faith-response to the possibilities disclosed by careful attention to the tradition as is Bultmann's response to the kerygma. In both cases a decision is based upon historical study and critical interpretation of the tradition, but goes beyond any deductions which may be made on the basis of this. And in both cases constant renewal is necessary: what Troeltsch calls 'the ever renewed making present of the christian idea',[120] and Bultmann 'new every morning'.[121] The main difference is that as a New Testament scholar Bultmann restricts himself to the canon (or parts of it)[122] and also retains the pauline phrase for this conception of revelation: the Word of God.

The differences between Bultmann and Troeltsch, then, are smaller than is generally assumed. Bultmann's insistence that God cannot be objectified, which Herrmann had expressed through his concept of religion, was better expressed by the dialectical theologians' talk of revelation, since Herrmann's claim that only Christianity is truly religion was plainly unsatisfactory. But Troeltsch's account of how the believer's acknowledgement of revelation or religious truth was related to his historical and scientific study of religious tradition was in substance the same. Bultmann, who had probably not studied the way Troeltsch correlates revelation and faith in the *Glaubenslehre*, asserted that Troeltsch's science of religion has sold christian theology out to the social sciences and 'gained "universal validity" at the cost of no longer mattering to anyone'. It had lost its object and so lost all reason for existing.[123] A science of religion housed with the social and cultural sciences could not be theology; that belongs essentially to faith and can only proceed as itself an act of faith.

From Troeltsch's side the problem was how to move from empirical study to the normative judgments required by theology and intended by his science of religion. The key role given to existential decision suggests that he failed to answer it fully in his own scientific terms, and it was natural for his

---

[120] *Die Kultur der Gegenwart*, IV, I, ed. P. Hinneberg (Berlin and Leipzig, 1906), 397.　　[121] *Existence and Faith*, pp. 65, 85, 267, 351, etc.
[122] Only Paul and John in the New Testament rate as genuine theologians.
[123] *Faith and Understanding*, p. 118.

opponents and successors to start elsewhere. By starting from faith they had no problem about reaching normative judgments. Their difficulty, conversely, was that of relating faith to the real world, a world which includes religions, and amongst them Christianity. It is necessary to ask what positive significance for theology the historian Bultmann can give to the historical and scientific study of religion. The answer that it can only raise human existential questions is curious in view of the fact that all religions do actually offer answers, and it is hard to believe that one's acceptance of a particular set of answers is divorced from some sort of rational assessment of their respective merits. It may, and probably will, somehow transcend rational considerations, but if these play any part it is necessary to allow a point to Troeltsch over Bultmann for his more positive attitudes to the worldly phenomenon called religion. Bultmann's assertion that 'theology does not have to look upon Christian faith as a phenomenon of religious or cultural history'[124] is intelligible as a reaction to the failure of idealism's religion apologetic to prove as much as it set out to prove. In this situation it was worth insisting that the Schleiermacher–Troeltsch procedure for doing theology by starting with a general analysis of religion, is not the only possibility. He associated himself with Barth's repudiation of 'religion' and Herrmann's objections to *Religionsphilosophie* because this line of apologetic appeared unfruitful,[125] and later on he himself explored an alternative anthropological apologetic. But Herrmann and Bultmann paid a heavy price for defending the non-objectifiable object of christian faith by severing the links between christian theology and the worldly reality of religion. Their tendency to reduce Christianity to the personal and private sphere presents a striking contrast to Troeltsch's ontological endeavours and his attempts to come to grips with political, social and economic reality.[126] There can be no doubt which theology takes the more responsible account of the creator's claim to his world.[127]

[124] *Existence and Faith*, p. 340. Cf. *Faith and Understanding*, p. 119.
[125] *Ibid.* and see above n. 105.
[126] This concern is evident in 'Grundprobleme der Ethik', *GS* II (1902), 552–672. It led to the *Social Teachings*, and took Troeltsch to Berlin where he was later mentioned as a possible presidential candidate.
[127] It is this concern for the universal scope of theology which has led W. Pannenberg away from theologies of the Word to learn from Troeltsch.

The question may be raised whether a theology which refuses to identify revelation with a special part of the tradition does not *require* a positive evaluation of religion as a kind of middle term relating revelation to worldly reality while preserving its non-objective character. To ignore the fact of religion, instead of maintaining its dialectical relationship to the notion of revelation, severs the link between God and the world and leads to a 'theology' which declares its bankruptcy with the cry that God is dead.

In the dispute between Herrmann and Troeltsch over the science of religion and its object, Barth also followed Herrmann, while abandoning his 'religion' terminology. His dialectic between religion and the gospel does not, of course, imply a denial that Christianity actually is a religion. But like Herrmann he reflected the believer's sense that a descriptive account of the human phenomenon is not adequate to the reality of religion's object.[128] However, we have seen that a similar dialectic between tradition and 'revelation' in the sense of kerygmatic theology may be found in Troeltsch's work. This is not the important difference between them. Neither is it Barth's exposure of the culture-critical potency of Christianity. Troeltsch was fully aware of this[129] even if he was not himself the prophetic figure to release it. The major difference isolated

---

[128] More recently the phenomenology of religion has attempted to evade this criticism and avoid reductionism by paying closer attention to what believers themselves say. Herrmann claimed that 'No-one can have an understanding of the reality of religion cut loose from his own attitude towards it' (*Schriften zur Grundlegung der Theologie* Teil 1, p. 286). He therefore rejected Troeltsch's model of a science of religion which passes into theology and argued that they were somewhat similar from the outset. A suspicion that some phenomenology of religion is crypto-theology persists.

[129] He insisted that 'the greatness of religion consists precisely in its opposition to culture, in its difference from science and utilitarian social ethics, its proclaiming supramundane and suprahuman powers, its unfolding of the imagination and pointing to what lies beyond the world of sense. A religion reconciled with culture is usually nothing but bad science and superficial morals; it has lost its religious salt' [*GS* II, 100]. This is very different from the Barmen declaration, in which christology is the determining criterion, but it should be remembered that Troeltsch was not among the ninety-three German intellectuals who supported the Kaiser's war policy – contrary to the impression given by Barth, *The Humanity of God* (Collins: Fontana, 1947), p. 12. See also the autobiographical sketch, *Briefwechsel*, p. 306, for Barth's dissatisfaction with neo-protestantism on this score.

in this discussion of the natural theology question concerns the
extent to which Barth and Bultmann stand in the Herrmann
tradition of severing the links between theology and the real
world, a tradition which Troeltsch vigorously, and one must
say rightly, challenged [*GS* II, 552–672]. Even if Troeltsch's
concern with religion failed to yield the apologetic capital
which the idealists expected, it kept his theological thinking in
touch with the real world.[130] It is the dialectical theology rather
than that of Troeltsch which is in danger of establishing its
subject-matter 'at the cost of no longer mattering to anyone,
[having] lost its object and so lost all reason for existing'.
Bultmann knew that 'theology speaks of God because it speaks
of man as he stands before God'.[131] But real men live in the
world.[132]

The argument so far has suggested that Bultmann's objection
to Troeltsch's attempts to find an idealist substitute for the
pre-critical natural theology was simply that it would not work.
It was therefore necessary to look in another direction, and it
was not long before he and Gogarten did so. Related to this, it
has been argued that Troeltsch and Bultmann can be seen to
have shared a very similar conception of revelation, if attention
is paid not to Troeltsch's idealist language, but to the use he
makes of the notion of decision and his emphasis upon
interpreting the tradition to shape anew the essence of
Christianity.

The situation is quite different with the other wing of
dialectical theology. The response of Barth and Thurneysen to
the reopening of the question of natural theology shows that
their repudiation of it was more a matter of principle.[133] Their

---

130 A. O. Dyson, *The Immortality of the Past* (SCM Press: London, 1974), gives an
   excellent evaluation of Troeltsch and Bultmann on this front and finds
   Troeltsch far more satisfactory.   131 *Faith and Understanding*, p. 52.
132 'Contemporary theology is still having to pay for the fact that it is still a
   victim of the heritage or curse of idealism to a greater degree than it cares to
   admit. It could have learned as much from Marxism as it did from
   Kierkegaard and would then have been unable to go on assigning the
   absolutely decisive role to the individual': E. Käsemann, *Perspectives on
   Paul*, (SCM Press: London, 1971), p. 11. This criticism of Bultmann is
   incidentally a partial vindication of Troeltsch – who learned equally from
   Marx and Kierkegaard.
133 Barth refused to come to Marburg to discuss the matter. He stigmatised the
   revival of interest in anthropology as a return to the flesh-pots of Egypt,

repudiation of liberalism was coupled with a new appreciation of 'the strange new world of the Bible'.[134] An element of conservative reaction is unmistakable here. The relish with which Thurneysen reports the failure of the latest attempts at natural theology suggests that its breakdown is welcome because it will (he hopes) force theologians back to a more excellent way of doing theology. The 'inner catastrophe [of modern Religionsphilosophie] from its beginnings in Schleiermacher through Richard Rothe down to Pfleiderer and Troeltsch' frees theology for a new apprehension of the concept of revelation, associated in a Reformation way with scripture [Anfänge, vol. 2, pp. 250f.]. Barth went on to develop sophisticated reasons for his rejection of natural theology;[135] it would therefore be rash to associate him, even in the early days, with his friend's naïveté. Nevertheless, Barth's relation to scripture, like that of the less sophisticated Thurneysen and Brunner, remains problematic for those educated, like Bultmann, in the Enlightenment tradition of historical criticism. His laughter at the difficulties disclosed by Strauss and Feuerbach [Protestant Theology, p. 568] has not made them go away. The way in which kerygmatic theology has accepted radical historical criticism and combined it with a version of the Reformation scriptural principle[136] is closer to Troeltsch's position than to Barth's. This is reflected particularly clearly in their treatment of the Old Testament.[137] It is, therefore, necessary to distinguish between the two wings of the dialectical theology, both in their attitudes to natural theology and in their use of the bible. Gogarten and Bultmann never shared

and no different in principle from the old concern with natural theology. Briefwechsel, pp. 100, 118.

[134] Barth gave an address with this title in 1916: The Word of God and the Word of Man (Harper: New York, 1957), pp. 28–50.

[135] Church Dogmatics, II, 1 (1940; ET 1957), 63–178.

[136] See especially G. Ebeling, The Word of God and Tradition (Collins: London, 1968), pp. 102–47, and E. Käsemann, Essays on New Testament Themes (SCM Press: London, 1964), pp. 54–62, and Das Neue Testament als Kanon (Vandenhoeck: Göttingen, 1970).

[137] Barth (Church Dogmatics I, 2, 79f.) was sympathetic to W. Vischer, Das Christuszeugnis des Alten Testaments. Bultmann (Existence and Faith, p. 271) calls it 'false allegorizing' and compares it with the Epistle of Barnabas. See also Bultmann's negative account of the significance of the Old Testament for christian theology in C. Westermann (ed.), Essays on Old Testament Interpretation (SCM Press: London, 1963), pp. 50–75.

Barth's outlook,[138] and were much closer to Troeltsch than Bultmann realised or Gogarten was prepared to admit in the heat of controversy. Gogarten was attracted by Barth's actual criticism of culture, in which (as a pupil of Troeltsch!) he rightly recognised an authentic function of the gospel; and Bultmann recognised the value of his theological interpretation of Paul. Neither shared Barth's hostility to any form of natural theology on principle, though both realised that the liberals' approach did not lend christian theology the support which Hegel and Schleiermacher had expected of it, and both doubted that Troeltsch's attenuated form of this apologetic was a fruitful line of advance. But neither saw the alternative between an anthropocentric and a theocentric theology so starkly as Barth and Brunner did,[139] and, finally, neither could agree that the exodus from neo-protestantism must lead into the deserts of biblicism. Luther provided them with a promised land which was not so harshly biblicist.[140] All theologies of the Word can be accused of residual biblicism, if this is defined as any theology which accords to the bible a greater authority than can be rationally justified, but their argument over *Sachkritik* shows how far apart Barth and Bultmann were on this matter.

Barth accepted the 'biblicist' label, when explained in his own way,[141] and a case can be made for saying that christian theology must necessarily contain an element of biblicism if the centrality of an adequate christology is to be preserved. What

---

[138] For Gogarten, see *Anfänge*, vol. 2, pp. 329–37. For Bultmann, see above, p. 38f. In 1930 Barth wrote to Bultmann: 'It may well be that what I mean by Word of God was never what you were after.' Far from sharing a common theology, they were simply ships that passed in the night. (*Briefwechsel*, p. 102.)

[139] Cf. *Faith and Understanding*, pp. 29 and 52, where the dialectical theology's objection to liberalism that 'it has dealt not with God but with man' is corrected: 'The subject of theology is God. Theology speaks of God because it speaks of man as he stands before God. That is, theology speaks out of faith.' See also pp. 53–65!

[140] Luther could 'urge Christ against Scripture' (*Weimar Auflage* vol. 39, p. 11; vol. 47, pp. 19f.). For Barth's reservations about this 'new, one might almost say the over-emphasised valuation' of proclamation over the written word, see *Church Dogmatics*, I, 1, 137–40.

[141] *Romans*, pp. 11f.: 'I am prejudiced in supposing the bible to be a good book, and I hold it to be profitable for men to take its conceptions at least as seriously as they take their own.'

constitutes an adequate christology, how central it should be in christian theology, and whether only biblicist theologies can achieve it, are arguable. Without leaving the general theme of revelation and history it is necessary now to turn from the question of natural theology to that of christology. On the former issue Troeltsch must be judged victorious. On the latter it is possible to see real justification for the dialectical theology's rejection of Troeltsch.

The claim that it is on account of christology that the new movement's protest against Troeltsch is justified might seem surprising, because the early dialectical theology, unlike the later Barth, was decidedly weak on christology. If this was their legitimate bone of contention they showed little explicit awareness of it at the time. As they struggled, rightly or wrongly, to break the fatal alliance between Christianity and idealism, it seemed more important to stress the biblical dualism between God and man. But that was a secondary issue. The doctrine of God is the key point at which the biblical witness and contemporary rationality always have to come to terms in christian theology, and the change of philosophical climate after the war necessitated some new thought about God. But the real weakness of liberalism was in its christology. It is because the christology of liberal protestantism in general – and Troeltsch in particular – was so inadequate, that the protests of Herrmann, Kähler and Schlatter were necessary. In each case it was a neo-reformation protest, and in continuing the neo-reformation trend the dialectical theology was heir to this tradition even if it was not at first sufficiently clear about the precise significance of its heritage. The weakness of liberalism here fully justified the vehemence of the reaction, including the bitter hostility of Herrmann to Troeltsch's theology – which he was not prepared even to call theology.

Despite the formal similarity between Paul, Luther, Barth and Bultmann's 'obedience of faith', and Troeltsch's opting for a particular cultural synthesis after careful attention to the tradition, there is one important difference. The object of christian faith is the Lord who is obeyed. So long as it is Christ who is proclaimed on the basis of scripture, the kerygmatic theology of the early Barth and Bultmann remained continuous with the christocentric theologies of Paul and Luther, and with the classical christian tradition which has understood little enough of Paul and Luther, but which has in its own ways focussed upon the same Christ, identified in scripture.

Troeltsch, too, recognised the centrality of christology for christian faith. From the beginnings it has been belief in Christ which has made of Christianity an independent religion, and within the church this has remained the centre both of dogma and cult.[142]

There is no other way to hold together the Christian community of spirit than through the common confession of Jesus; it is impossible to keep alive the distinctively Christian idea of God apart from seeing its life-giving embodiment in Jesus; and all the greatest and most characteristic ideas of Christianity – the idea of a grace that grasps and conquers us, of a certitude available to us, and of a superior power that elevates and overcomes us – depend on a religious appreciation and interpretation of Jesus as divine revelation.[143]

But Troeltsch's passionate belief in God and in the significance of Jesus for faith is 'in no way any longer the christological dogma of the church'.[144] He considered it conceptually impossible to fuse belief in God with the traditional theological evaluation of Jesus as being 'of one substance with the Father', and therefore rejected the doctrines of Trinity and Incarnation. However, while abandoning the traditional christology, he thought he was retaining 'the innermost motif of that dogma' which he defined as 'the Christ mysticism of an inner bond by which the community is united with the head, from whom the members derive life and strength and whose representation and symbol of God constitutes the chief element of a properly Christian cultus'.[145]

It is an open question whether the meaning which Troeltsch here attaches to a phrase like 'the living Christ' is adequate for a viable christian faith, or whether the ontological underpinning provided by the fourth-century church is not still necessary. Troeltsch was aware of the discontinuity between

---

[142] 'Schleiermacher und die Kirche', in F. Naumann (ed.), *Schleiermacher, der philosoph des Glaubens* (Berlin, 1910), p. 28.
[143] 'On the Possibility of a Liberal Christianity' (1910); Eng.tr. in *The Unitarian Universalist Christian*, 29 (1974), 30.   [144] *Ibid.* p. 32.
[145] *Ibid.*

his position and not only Nicea but also Paul and John.[146] He also recognised that it was an open question whether his version of 'free protestantism' would be able for long to support a specifically christian faith and life – 'the fundamental question whether a Christianity thus based on new foundations and presuppositions is at all inherently viable or not...or whether it is merely the last echo of a disintegrating Christian piety.'[147] If Gertrud von le Fort is a reliable witness, he lost at the end of his life his earlier robust confidence and optimism,[148] and thus lent support to the man who as early as 1910 experienced a 'dark foreboding that it had become impossible to advance any further in the dead-end street' represented by Troeltsch. [See above, p. 53.] Whether or not Barth's new theological ontology can help overcome the dualism between time and eternity inherent in modern historical theology remains to be seen. The fact that Troeltsch's religious metaphysics precluded the possibility of his calling a historical figure 'truly God' does not mean that the traditional christology is dead.

The strength of liberal theology lay in its wholesome criticism of a partly moribund tradition.[149] Every critical theologian will want to prune from his theology whatever conflicts with the rationality he accepts. Troeltsch's criticism of Ritschlian residual supernaturalism in the light of the historicisation of all our thinking was in principle justified. Whether it had to involve such a massive critical reduction of the tradition as becomes apparent in his christology remains a question. In interpreting the tradition critically and forging his own account of the 'essence of Christianity', Troeltsch brought to the task whatever help he could find from the science and philosophy of his day. Christian theologians do

---

[146] G. E. Wolfe, 'Troeltsch's Conception of the Significance of Jesus', *American Journal of Theology* xx (1916), 179–204 argues unconvincingly that 'the Christ-mysticism advocated by Troeltsch is *in essence* the same as that of Paul and John': p. 202.

[147] 'On the Possibility', *The Unitarian Universalist Christian*, p. 27.

[148] W. Pauck, *Harnack and Troeltsch* (OUP: New York, 1968), quotes the passage in *Der Kranz und der Engel* (Munich, 1953⁶), in which the disillusioned theologian speaks of 'the sunset of Christianity'.

[149] Even the great conservative theologian Martin Kähler could welcome this effect of the Life of Jesus theology: *The So-called Historical Jesus and the Historic Biblical Christ* (Fortress Press: Philadelphia, 1964), p. 46.

have a *dual* responsibility: to the tradition and to the intellectual climate of their own day; but Troeltsch may be judged to have discharged the latter more successfully than the former. That is the tendency of all liberals, just as the opposite is the tendency of all conservatives. The thinking of the christian church has always consisted of an on-going argument between the conservative majority and the liberals, progressiveness or radicals, some of whose proposals for the development of the tradition are gradually adopted, and others rejected. What is important for the religious community is that the two sides remain in communion and conversation, stimulating and correcting one another.

As well as deferring a decision on the christological questions, acceptance of this 'unfinished' character of theological work, and the inevitability of some theological pluralism, also answers the objection to Troeltsch's mode of theologising by interpreting the tradition, that different interpreters reach different conclusions, and argument between conflicting interpretations is seldom conclusive. The door which must be kept open for creative new interpretations, and for growth and development of the tradition, allows free entry to subjectivism and arbitrariness.

Troeltsch's reply was to acknowledge the element of subjectivity in all interpretation[150] but to deny the charge of arbitrariness. Rational argument can eliminate at least some interpretations and reduce the variety from which it is finally necessary to choose. But it is true that in addition to the variety of theological expression which stems from the different historical situations in which christians find themselves, competing possibilities of doctrinal and ethical response will be found in any situation. The argument continues and only the future can bring a greater degree of clarity. Theologians are not exempt from the risk and uncertainty which is present in all historical experience.

A further corrective to the subjective element in all interpretation is provided by the fact that the individual theologian

---

[150] E.g., *GS* II, 712, 760 and especially 432ff. (Eng.tr. *Writings*), and 'Religionsphilosophie', in W. Windelband (ed.), *Die Philosophie im Beginn des 20en Jahrhunderts* (Heidelberg, 1907²), pp. 447ff. Bultmann also emphasised that every act of critical interpretation was a risk: *Faith and Understanding*, pp. 86, 93, 280.

works as a member of the church. The necessary 'daring to bring a living idea forward out of history for the present time and (with the courage of a conscience grounded in God) to set it within the intellectual world of the present' [*GS* II, 448], must be balanced by the recognition that one's own vision is partial. The individual theologian can hope and trust that in the long run his own one-sidedness will be corrected, and the errors he opposes, if they really are errors, eliminated. When he has made a contribution he will be content for it to be discussed, and for the community critically to test it in its own experience before accepting it into the ever-expanding tradition – or rejecting it. Troeltsch was less self-consciously a 'church theologian' than Barth and the rest, but he had reflected long and hard about the church and its relationship to religion. He saw clearly that his liberal protestant 'religion of the educated' and the conservative 'religion of the people' require each other,[151] and he was strongly aware of belonging to a religious movement, though one which might well leave the church behind.[152]

Since this volume and the renewal of interest in Troeltsch may be taken as a sign that the church has caught up enough to digest what Troeltsch stood for and to decide what must be assimilated it is fair to conclude by recapitulating our judgment in the doctrinal case of Troeltsch *versus* the dialectical theology.

The critical impulses of liberal protestantism have firmly established themselves. No responsible theologian now doubts the necessity of a critical and historical approach to bible and doctrine. Its theological reconstructions, on the other hand, are still struggling for acceptance in a church which remains sceptical about their adequacy.[153] A reaction, such as occurred

---

[151] See 'Religionsphilosophie', *op. cit.* p. 485. See also the comments of Professor Sykes, below. See also n. 163 below.

[152] See especially, 'On the Possibility', *The Unitarian Universalist Christian*, and see below n. 167.

[153] The debate surrounding M. F. Wiles, *The Remaking of Christian Doctrine* (SCM Press: London, 1974), is indicative of the English climate, and of the headway made in the decade since *Honest to God*. Those who were shocked at the spectacle of an Anglican bishop thinking for himself, and in the Sunday newspapers too, were of course pained to see the chairman of the doctrinal commission espousing a classical liberal protestant position.

in the 1920s, was inevitable and right. The nineteenth century was a time for daring new interpretations of the tradition in response to the great advances in modern knowledge. But since the decline of idealism, twentieth-century theology has found so little help from the philosophies of the day that a more defensive attitude has perhaps been appropriate.[154] It is necessary to 'guard the deposit', or preserve the tradition from dissipation by a merely destructive criticism which is not complemented by successful constructive systematic endeavours.[155] Even 'biblicism' of the refined sort found in Käsemann, Ebeling, Moltmann and Jüngel is legitimate as a holding operation. Each of these leading contemporary theologians is heir to the recovery of Reformation theology in the 1920s. The Paul–Luther strand in the christian tradition is particularly effective in criticism of and polemic against interpretations of Christianity which fail to present Jesus as gospel. As such it resists jewish Christianity's making Jesus into a new law, confessional catholicism's subordinating him to the church, and liberalism's loss of christological substance. The development of dialectical theology's left wing from Bultmann to Braun and Ogden has shown that kerygmatic theology also is compatible with a loss of christological substance no less drastic than that of Troeltsch. For all its other failings the Barthian wing of the theology of the Word of God has maintained the centrality and the substance of christology more consistently than the existentialist wing. Where within the kerygmatic theology the centrality or 'primacy' of christology has been recovered, this has been achieved in part[156] through a reassessment of the theological significance of the historical Jesus that has little in common with what Troeltsch had to say on this topic.[157] Whether some of the so-called New

---

[154] Present indications are that Hegel may yet prove to be *the* philosopher of modern Christianity.

[155] Barth's sly comment on Strauss' critical endeavours, that 'blessed with a little impudence, any child can do the same, and we really have no occasion to worship such people as great theologians', makes a point (*Protestant Theology*, p. 566). But Troeltsch, like F. C. Baur and Barth himself, attempted to be constructive, whether or not successfully.

[156] Only in part: Käsemann's pauline interpretation is also a sustained attempt to correct Bultmann's systematic theology.

[157] For comparison, see G. Ebeling, *Theology and Proclamation* (Collins: London, 1966), the 'New Quester' who in many respects stands closest to Troeltsch.

Questers' christology is more adequate than that of Troeltsch may be doubted. They seem equally remote from the homoousion which remains a serviceable criterion of orthodoxy, and one which is in principle as compatible with a Troeltschian style of theologising as with Barth's *Church Dogmatics*.[158]

That christology should be singled out as the point at which Troeltsch's doctrinal substance is unsatisfactory is not surprising. Idealist theologies generally face difficulties here.[159] It is also the point at which pauline–Reformation theologies are strongest. It is therefore natural that the dialectical theology should be able to press Troeltsch here – even though it did not in fact do so. As mentioned at the beginning of this section, we have been constructing a debate which never actually took place. But Troeltsch's weakness (if discarding the Nicene Creed be considered a weakness) should not have blinded his successors to his very considerable strengths. His openness to the real, social and economic, historical, world, makes him a more helpful guide to christian thinking at the end of the twentieth century than are either the followers of Herrmann who privatise religion and morality,[160] or those who seek to evade the radical consequences of historical thinking and preserve a massive biblicist fortress in the midst of a secular world.

Troeltsch's idealism looks curiously dated today. But there is very much more to his thought than that. The historical realism which made him a pioneer in sociological theory and 'the most eminent sociologically oriented historian of Western Christianity'[161] also mark his significance for the future of christian theology. The critical aspect of the historical movement within theology has established its legitimacy and

---

[158] See W. Pannenberg, *Jesus God and Man* (SCM Press: London, 1968), for an affirmation of the incarnation concept within the framework of a historical view of reality and an enlarged view of historical method.

[159] Despite his polemic against idealism, there is a strongly idealist residue in Bultmann's theology, which is probably a reason for his unsatisfactory christology. The same might even be said of Barth, who has not integrated the historical Jesus into his christology.

[160] For astute criticism of Bultmann on this front see the work of a Gogarten pupil, D. Sölle, *Political Theology* (Fortress Press: Philadelphia, 1974).

[161] So Talcott Parsons, quoted by James Luther Adams, 'Why the Troeltsch Revival?', *Unitarian Universalist Christian*, 29 (1974), 15.

remains an indispensable tool. The extravagant hopes about the constructive significance of the movement were greatly muted from Hegel to Troeltsch and have been further dampened since then. But Hegel and Troeltsch were right to see the significance of the historical movement in anchoring theology within the one reality known to us, within a world characterised by religious pluralism and haunted by the ambiguities facing moral man in immoral society. The church may yet have a more distinctive role to play than Troeltsch, the disciple of Richard Rothe, acknowledged. There was a positive side to the dialectical theology's emphasis upon the church. But to allow the idea of the church to fill the role occupied by history in the thought of Troeltsch and the liberals[162] was no solution. Insofar as the new movement involved a flight from history, that was no more satisfactory than the idealists' divinisation of it.

Troeltsch himself was too well aware of the ugliness of ecclesiastical politics to be guilty of any such idolatry. He wrote of 'protestantism's insight into an inner antinomy between religion and church. They cannot dispense with each other, neither can they endure each other. In this conflict only the ever-renewed making present of the christian idea can get us anywhere, so as to keep the life of the fellowship free from the dangers of ecclesiasticism.'[163] He was personally inclined to the mystical or 'spiritualist' type of Christianity, and traced the roots of German idealism there.[164] But he realised that institutions were necessary if anything was to be achieved in the real world. Corresponding to the awareness of the necessary involvement of religion with society, Troeltsch allowed his thinking to relate positively to the intellectual world of his day. During his period as professor of systematic theology in Heidelberg (1894–1914) the most significant fruit of this openness was his advocacy of a science of religion which

---

[162] See Trutz Rendtorff, *Kirche und Theologie. Die systematische Funktion des Kirchenbegriffs in der neueren Theologie* (Gütersloher Verlagshaus, Gerd Mohn: 1970²), pp. 194ff.

[163] *Die Kultur der Gegenwart* IV, 1, 397.

[164] *Ibid.* p. 305. He considered modern protestantism to stand closer to Sebastian Franck than to Luther. The dialectical theologians drew different conclusions from this insight.

took seriously the empirical evidence without abandoning the question of truth.[165] The inadequacies of his account of religion and religions at a time when the discipline was in its infancy are less important than the fact that he took a realistic account of them, whereas most of his theological opponents did not, and some still do not.

Towards the end of his life this same attempt to hold together the claims and values of Christianity and the modern world led him out of the more narrowly ecclesiastical concerns of the German theological faculties, to work to overcome the wider cultural crisis of the west – which he perceived just as clearly as, and much earlier than, any dialectical theologian.[166] In an autobiographical sketch written towards the end of his life he observed [GS IV, 12] that he had outgrown the theological faculty – not that he had outgrown theology. Theology, or a philosophy of religion concerned with establishing norms, is concerned with reality as a whole, and so in principle with the whole of modern knowledge. Troeltsch was understandably impatient with a church which was failing to meet the intellectual challenge of a new age, and felt himself alienated from it.[167] He was scathing, too, about much of the activity of the theological schools which he called 'a harmless conventicle game – the petty squabbles of children in the nursery who do not realise that the house is on fire' [GS II, 238]. His final answer to the younger theologians who thought he had abandoned the church's theological task[168] was given in

165 'What theology is concerned with is not the history of religion in general but *normative* knowledge acquired through the scientific study of religion' (*AC*, p. 25]. This concern led to the attempt to combine 'psychology and epistemology in the science of religion' – see above, n. 103.
166 No essay on Troeltsch would be complete without a recollection of his dramatic appearance before the 'Freunde der christlichen Welt' in 1896. 'Meine Herren, es wackelt alles!' ('Gentlemen, everything is tottering!') Cited by W. Köhler, *Ernst Troeltsch* (Tübingen, 1941), p. 1.
167 W. Köhler (*op. cit.*, pp. 389f.) records a part of his *Selbstbekenntnis*, 2 May 1916: 'The church is a way of stopping faith from becoming extinct and a means of educating the lower middle class. We have to use this means, and equip it for its task. But in itself it is an institution with all the hardness, and stupidity of a bureaucratic institution.' He had no hopes for its future, nor of its ever changing. Intellectuals were bound to maintain a critical distance; the old opposition between humanism and the Reformation continued.
168 Barth read symbolic significance into his transfer to the philosophical faculty. See *The Humanity of God* (Collins, Fontana: London, 1967), p. 12.

advance, in 1913: 'However, should anyone conclude from these tasks that I have become basically more interested in the general analysis of culture and religion than in specifically christian theological issues, my comment would be that the question of course is what we take theology and its task to be' [*GS* II, 227].

Part II

3. Ernst Troeltsch and the possibility of a systematic theology

A. O. DYSON

I

Many of Troeltsch's critics, in his own day and more recently, have cast him in the role of a demolisher rather than a builder, an opponent of christian theology rather than its ally. Many have argued that he represented a low-water mark in the history of modern theology.[1] On this view, our interest in him can only be antiquarian; there is nothing to be gained by exploring his theological 'bad conscience' in relation to current tasks. In this essay, on the other hand, I shall argue that Troeltsch's principal concern was in fact theological rather than historical, his intention positive rather than negative. I shall also suggest that his approach deserves attention from theologians of the present generation, not least on account of the many conflicting factors (still in circulation in our own day) which Troeltsch, painfully and with differing degrees of success, sought to hold together in a coherent and intellectually responsible understanding of theological practice.

II

There is today a much greater willingness to allow that, if nothing else, Troeltsch perceptively identified and boldly confronted the problem of the relationship between history and theology, as this came to the fore amid the general uncertainty and confusion of intellectual life in the late nineteenth century,[2] Furthermore, whatever the precise suc-

[1] Cf., E. Spiess, *Die Religionstheorie von Ernst Troeltsch* (Paderborn, 1926), p. 3; K. Barth, *Church Dogmatics* IV, 1 (Edinburgh, 1956), 387; E. Brunner, *The Mediator* (London, 1934), pp. 68f.
[2] See H.-G. Drescher, 'Das Problem der Geschichte bei Ernst Troeltsch', *ZThK* N.F. 57 (1960), 186f.

cess or failure of Troeltsch's own analyses and proposals, many
would now agree that he uttered a solemn warning to later
generations of theologians that this problem cannot be solved
by tactical manoeuvres, nor evaded by appeal to authorities
which are themselves undermined by critical history. In
drawing attention to the effects of the revolution in historiography upon theological science, Troeltsch certainly wanted to
claim that christian theology, in its contents and methods,
could never be quite the same again.

But when all this has been said, not much credit has been
accorded to Troeltsch for his own constructive ventures in
theology. Indeed, it may be argued that Troeltsch's intentions
have not been understood. His intellectual enterprise is
many-sided and complex. It consists of a succession of frag-
ments, sometimes detailed analyses, sometimes grand sweeps
in the history of ideas, but nowhere coming together into a
whole.[3] His theological yield has its roots in this kind of
material. But, in a simple-minded way, Troeltsch is often
grouped among those German liberal theologians of the
nineteenth century who, according to Tillich, had no real
systematic theology. More dramatically, but along similar lines,
Reist has written of the 'collapse of Troeltsch's theology' and
of its 'ruins'.[4] Whatever may have been Troeltsch's achievement in other spheres, there is little disposition to place
confidence in him as exponent or herald of a new systematic
theology. Yet, in his own life-time, Troeltsch was fully aware
of, and critically responded to, the principal objections and
alternatives to his own point of view. With the passage of time,
the articulation of these objections and alternatives may have
changed in details. But little that is noticeably different in
substance has appeared which might justify such dismissive
attitudes to his work.

The twists and turns of theology since Troeltsch have
instead only served to confirm the accuracy of his general
analysis. In one way or another, it has been a period marked by
strenuous attempts to grapple with, or evade, the historical

---

[3] See K. Bornhausen, 'Ernst Troeltsch und das Problem der wissenschaftlichen Theologie', ZThK N.F. 4 (1923), 196–223.
[4] B. Reist, Toward a Theology of Involvement (London, 1966), pp. 154,
201.

question, even if a host of other problems have also crowded in upon the theologian. On the one hand, the evasions have meant a move *behind* Troeltsch as if his searching questions about history and revelation had never been put. On the other hand, there has been an increasing sense of reserve about the very possibility of systematic theology. The number of ventures which have broken new ground in this area have been few indeed over recent decades. But in this overall situation it is now no longer especially instructive to welcome Troeltsch's work in general terms, whether as a theological lighthouse telling theological sailors of nearby rocks and sandbanks, or, if one prefers, as itself a lighted wreck warning others against a similar fate. If Troeltsch's endeavour is to be regarded as more than a monument of the past, however significant, we need to ask more precise questions about his legacy. For example, if his general analysis is correct, how do we account for his supposed failure as a systematic theologian? Or does that failure, if it be a failure, point to inadequacies in the analysis? Or can we judge that Troeltsch's theological effort points us towards a better understanding of the scope and methods of theology? Or are we to learn from him that systematic interests must in fact give way to historical, phenomenological and other forms of enquiry which used to be seen as no more than preparatory to the central theological task? To deal effectively with questions such as these requires more than a summary estimate of Troeltsch's work.

There are two ways of approaching Troeltsch's writings with these questions in mind. In this paper I adopt a *formal* method, looking at the structure and relationships of Troeltsch's closely argued historical, philosophical and theological standpoints with a view to exploring their implications for the task of systematic theology. This approach enables us to situate Troeltsch's work within the nineteenth century's theological history of which he was a conscious heir, and to grasp the main alternatives which are presented to us today. The second, *material* approach proceeds much more directly by critical exposition of Troeltsch's own productions in systematic theology. The two approaches are of course complementary and a full treatment of my theme would require both. This would however involve an enquiry far beyond the scope of a single essay. The possibilities of this second, material approach are fortunately indicated in Dr Gerrish's essay. Thus the formal approach adopted here should in no way be construed as a negative judgment on the *Glaubenslehre*,[5] the articles in *Die Religion in Geschichte und Gegenwart*,[6] and other material. I do not think that in these writings Troeltsch always fulfilled in a material way the formal possibilities of his position. But they certainly illustrate in a pertinent and concrete manner the methodological questions with which I am primarily concerned.

III

In the first place, it is important to give more exact definition to the notion of 'systematic theology'. In the history of theology, the term covers a multitude of different theological undertakings. Thus the charge that the German liberal movement was weak in systematic theology can only be elucidated and assessed if more exactness in definition is attained. I shall adopt as a working definition, 'by understanding, expression, and criticism, to formulate christian beliefs in a comparatively systematic manner'.[7]

The business of *expression* or exposition relates to the nature of theology's subject-matter. Does theology expound a nucleus of truth authoritatively given in the bible, in the church, or in personal religious experience? Or does it make deductions from this nucleus of truth? Or does theology treat a subject-matter whose claims to authority are less bold? By what criteria are these validating authorities, of whatever kind, judged? The notion of *criticism* indicates that the theologian bears responsibility for ordering his material according to certain canons of rationality and for testing its claims with some kind of critical equipment. His task is not simply one of rehearsal and repetition.[8] He has to face up to the demanding question as to how we judge where the tradition which is being expressed has prior rights over the theologian's understand-

---

[5] *Glaubenslehre von Ernst Troeltsch* (Munich and Leipzig, 1925).
[6] Vols. 2–5 (1910–13).
[7] In making this definition I am indebted to phraseology from H. R. Niebuhr, *The Purpose of the Church and its Ministry* (New York and Evanston, 1956), and M. F. Wiles, *The Remaking of Christian Doctrine* (London, 1974).
[8] Cf. G. Sauter, *Theologie als Wissenschaft* (Munich, 1971), pp. 70f.

ing, or where the understanding has prior rights over the tradition.[9] Here too the theologian must encounter the problem of adjudicating between rival critical conclusions. The question of *understanding* highlights the relationship between faith and theology. Has the theologian an in-built sympathy for the standpoint of faith, without which the understanding will always be distorted? Can this connect easily, or at all, with his critical responsibilities? Does the standpoint of faith rob theology of all claims to possession of a scientific character? I shall now apply these three features of expression, criticism and understanding to Troeltsch's distinctive approach to theology.

IV

I make a provisional distinction between two understandings of theology in Troeltsch's writings. The first may be called 'applied historical theology' and the second 'confessional theology'. Both are profoundly influenced, but in different ways, by *Historismus*.[10] It seems, however, that only the first may properly claim the title of a 'science'. I shall comment first on 'applied historical theology'.

Vermeil writes as follows: 'theology is a living science which, far from confining us to transmitting the traditional affirmations or to engaging in apologetic, orientates us across the intellectual life of the present, reconstructs the religious idea, and works for the reform of its institutions'.[11] Such a view of theology's task springs from two connected premises, namely the critique of revelation and the understanding of historical reality. Troeltsch held that the phenomena of the historicising and naturalising of thought – both central and irreversible features of the rise of the modern world – undermined and destroyed three principal foundations of the earlier ecclesiastical culture. These were the claim that divine truth resided in a unique revelation, the claim that this divine revelation was concentrated in a single, redemptive incursion into the world,

[9] Cf. F. Buri, *Theology of Existence*, quoted in A. O. Dyson, *Who is Jesus Christ?* (London, 1969), p. 120.
[10] For a fuller account see A. O. Dyson, 'History in the Philosophy and Theology of Ernst Troeltsch' (Diss., Oxford, 1968), pp. 32–68.
[11] E. Vermeil, *La pensée religieuse de Troeltsch* (Strasbourg and Paris, 1922), p. 4.

and the claim that (because of original sin) the way was blocked for an appeal to general and necessary truths of reason.[12]

On the other hand, the picture of historical reality demanded by *Historismus* is such that theology can no longer take as its subject-matter certain normative, absolute, unique events of a supposed objective salvation-history. For no historical event can be abstracted from those events around, before and after it. Thus to no historical event can be ascribed a special and private divine causality. So Troeltsch can conclude that 'historicism is a leaven which transforms everything and finally explodes the entire form of theological method as known hitherto' [*GS* II, 729ff.]. In particular, historicism 'renders impossible a separation of natural and supernatural elements, a distinction between what is humanly conditioned and what is directly divine'.[13] This leads Troeltsch to distinguish very sharply between supernaturalism and historicism. He insists that 'supernaturalism was a way of thinking which had closed, inviolable, generally valid, and firmly grounded ideas', whereas 'historicism knows the ideas of all ages, and even its own ideas, to be historically conditioned'.[14] In this context, it is important to notice that Troeltsch is not rejecting supernaturalism as such, but only an exclusive supernaturalism tied to certain supposedly historical events. Nonetheless, the implications for christian theology are formidable.

The history of religion is being drawn far more deeply into the stream of events, and into the varying conditions within the fundamental elements in life. Thus it becomes still less possible to find an unchangeable and absolute point in the Christian ethic, since this also only means the mastery of an existing situation and the establishment of an ideal which corresponds to the situation [*STCC*, vol. 2, p. 1003].

These passages summarise the presuppositions with which Troeltsch approaches the questions of theology's subject-matter and expressive function. The only kind of theology which he could envisage was one which respected the limitations imposed by *Historismus*. But, more positively, such a theology could be open to the rich profusion of life which the historical method disclosed. The key to expressing coherently

[12] Troeltsch, *Protestantism and Progress* (London and New York, 1912).
[13] Troeltsch, *ZThK* VIII (1898), 6.   [14] *Ibid.* p. 68.

this rich profusion lay in the individualising method of his historical logic.

The theologian must grasp the individual totalities of christian religious history, draw out their characteristic traits, determine their value, and relate this to the existing situation. It is along these lines that the theologian can respond to the challenge to 'construct theology on the basis of an historical...method' [*GS* II, 738]. It follows, however, that in a theological enterprise so conceived no single historical expression can ever lay claim to absoluteness and finality. For 'each factor is relatively conditioned as a synthesis which cannot be repeated, and as a spiritual-ethical mastery of the particular situation' [*STCC*, vol. 2, p. 1003]. The concluding pages of *The Social Teaching of the Christian Churches* provide an example of this 'living science' in action. Having explored by historical enquiry the varied nature of the christian ethos, Troeltsch relates this exposition to current questions about ecclesiastical organisation and to current social problems. Thus, by this method, we are always 'thrust back again into history itself and to the necessity of constructing from this history a religious world of ideas which shall be normative for us'.[15]

It is particularly important to recognise that, for Troeltsch, the deployment of this method is rendered extremely difficult because, as we look at the history of the christian religion, 'a genuinely historical point of view reveals to us such a variety of interpretations, formulations and syntheses that no single idea of impulse can dominate the whole'. This means that the theological expressions at which we arrive are 'actually the subjective, personal interpretation and synthesis which present thinking derives from the entire situation with reference to actual living issues and for the purpose of directing future activity'.[16] They are not inviolable and generally valid ideas. If, then, we were to examine any one expression of religious ideas, we should always find that it was marked by this personal and subjective character, itself moulded by previous religious ideas, and – perhaps even more significantly – by sociological and other contemporary factors. I shall return at a later stage to consider the implications of this personal subjective ele-

[15] Troeltsch, *American Journal of Theology (AJT)* XVII (1913), 8.
[16] Troeltsch, *op. cit.*, pp. 12f.

ment. In the next section I go on to examine what I have called
Troeltsch's 'applied historical theology' in relation to the
critical function of systematic theology.

                                  V

This 'applied historical theology' has a scientific and critical
character. But Troeltsch regards it as scientific and critical in a
way which is congruous with the nature of historical life, not by
analogy with the methods of the natural sciences. It is
important to observe how Troeltsch came to accommodate the
subject-matter of religion to that of historical life in general. At
an early stage in his career Troeltsch opted for a largely
psychological explanation.[17] This is later dropped in favour of
a more formal explanation, namely the religious *a priori*.[18] But
this in turn gives way to the more historical approach. When
Historismus is taken as the chief presupposition, it becomes
impossible to separate religious and cultural history given the
'interwovenness of all human events, religious and extra-
religious, christian and non-christian'. Thus the methods of
enquiry and description set out in the early pages of *Gesammelte Schriften* III in relation to general cultural history are
found to be entirely suitable to deal with the phenomena of
religious life and history. This leads Troeltsch to the important
conclusion that 'in the face of the real passage and correlation
of things, it is impossible to ascribe to the religious element a
different mode of formation and realisation than that which is
ascribed to the life of the spirit with which it is endlessly
entwined' [*GS* II, 754].

   This entire openness of religious phenomena to being
treated in terms of the individuality and development of the
historical logic inescapably raises the question as to the kind of
understanding involved. Is the applied historical theology in no
way related to faith? Does faith play any part in the process of
understanding which is involved?

---

[17] Troeltsch, *Psychologie und Erkenntnistheorie in der Religionswissenschaft*
(Tübingen, 1905).
[18] See R. J. Jelke, *Das religiöse Apriori und die Aufgaben der Religionsphilosophie*
(Giessen, 1917).

VI

The quotation from Vermeil made clear that in Troeltsch's view the purpose of theology is not to transmit the traditional affirmations nor to engage in apologetic. How is such a view of theology to relate to *piety*, about which Troeltsch speaks so positively? By piety Troeltsch means 'a living creative movement of the present day'. Piety is the expression of what Troeltsch elsewhere calls 'a definitely earnest, warm and practical religious life'. While it appears to have nothing to do with the intellectual dogmatic assertions which derive from supernaturalism in the narrower sense, it is closely related to a belief in God and in his presence in the world. Piety, in Troeltsch, has affinities with the idea of creativity which the Romantic movement bequeathed to the German tradition and which finds bold expression in the work of Fichte. But if the totally unscientific character of piety is emphasised, is there not a danger of Troeltsch falling into an extraordinary dualism – a dualism to which many of the later critics of Troeltsch themselves succumbed in the search for assured positions in theology? Can the intellectual and theological bases of piety be wholly ignored? If applied historical theology depends in no small measure upon personal interpretation and decision, must there not in principle be some relationship between the religious ideas implicit in the applied historical theology and the piety of the christian man? These questions can be formulated in a more precise and positive way as follows. Granted the view of reality to which Troeltsch's historical logic points, is there not a congruous religious view of reality which both respects the nature of the world disclosed by historicism and can adequately contain the implicit assertions of christian piety? This raises the question of the place of religious metaphysics in Troeltsch's approach to theology. At this point, in my judgment, we draw close to the heart of Troeltsch's legacy to the world of systematic theology. Troeltsch's treatment of the nature of the *understanding* involved in theology turns out to be more complex than might at first be supposed.

VII

If *Historismus* marks a true and irreversible gain in our understanding of the world, it follows that the central features of a historicist view of the world must be incorporated into our religious view of reality. Or, to change the emphasis, if the historicist view is true, it should contain within itself a theological conceptuality. Thus, in an important phrase, Troeltsch speaks of the 'latent theology of *Historismus*'.[19] Moreover, he sees it as the task of religious metaphysics, as a component in the science of religion, to explore the possibilities of such a 'latent theology' as an up-to-date framework for the main christian ideas. I wish to argue that full weight has not been given to the considerations which Troeltsch puts forward in this regard. In footnote 14 on page 28 of *Gesammelte Schriften* III, Troeltsch introduces the conception of a 'metalogic' which, in his view, has been ignored on account of the pressure which the natural sciences have exercised upon modern thought. Later in the same volume Troeltsch elaborates the foundations upon which a metalogic must rest. At first sight all this seems inconsistent with Troeltsch's defence of the scientific and critical character of an historicised theology. But a charge of inconsistency along these lines rests, I believe, on a misunderstanding of what is involved in the historical logic.

I referred earlier to Tillich's critique of liberal systematic theology. In full the passage reads: 'my criticism of the whole liberal theology, including Harnack, is that it had no real systematic theology; it believed in the results of historical research in a wrong way'.[20] Tillich has in mind, I suppose, that many of the liberal theologians hoped, with the help of historical-critical method, to get behind the 'religion about Jesus' to the 'religion of Jesus'. Having once arrived there, they found that there was not too much to report. In that sense their systematic utterances were comparatively poor because it was not that kind of material that they found. In fact, it seems more likely that the procedure of these theologians was not

[19] Troeltsch, *ZThK* VIII (1898), 69.
[20] P. Tillich, *Perspectives on Nineteenth and Twentieth Century Protestant Theology* (London, 1967), p. 223.

really related to historical-critical questions but was rather indebted to Kant (as they interpreted him) and so expressed their intention to reduce dogmatic formulations to an immanent ethic. But Troeltsch himself was quite unwilling to pursue this path to the extent that, for example, Ritschl did.

Troeltsch's immensely high estimate of the richness of cultural history prevented such a restriction of religious reality. Here he was deeply indebted to Wilhelm Dilthey whom he called the 'philosopher of *Historismus*'.[21] Dilthey was concerned to rescue social and cultural reality from the thraldom of the methods of the natural sciences. To achieve this he developed a form of evolutionary pantheism. So Troeltsch could write of Dilthey:

The old narrow relations of German thought to history were set in a new light. Dilthey, above all, was active in this. In his own way he achieved the break with the naturalism which was at work in historiography in the form of sociology. He taught a purely historical intuition of the great, fundamental, supra-rational experiences in which, in a kind of inner vision, the great cultural tendencies of history are received and from which they spread and intersect in great historical developments [*GS* IV, 657].

Thus, alongside the Kantian tendencies in Troeltsch's thinking there is an impulse in another direction towards the sphere of religious metaphysics in order adequately to ground those ethical and religious movements which are disclosed in an historicised world.

We can in fact discern in Troeltsch's work another manifestation of that tension which can be found in all the post-Enlightenment theology which attempted the enterprise of mediation. It is a tension between rarified abstraction in the form of supernaturalism or speculative metaphysics and naturalism in a historical or ethical form. In Troeltsch's case, the religious metaphysics is an essential element in the attempt to work out this tension in a way which is faithful to the christian gospel and to the world of individuality and development disclosed by the historical logic.

Troeltsch's own effort already stands some distance in time from the Hegelian synthesis and its collapse. He had absorbed in a critical way the strengths of this movement but had also

---

[21] Troeltsch, in *Harnack Festgabe* (Tübingen, 1921), p. 288.

found much to value in the work of those who had turned away
from Hegel to right and left. He was also conscious that new
problems had to be faced, especially those arising from the
influence of the natural sciences, and, even more, of scientism,
over many areas of thought and life. But in Hegel and others
there had been a notable attempt to cope philosophically with
what was also a major theological problem – namely the
relationship between finite and infinite. Despite different
presuppositions, Enlightenment philosophy and supernaturalist theology shared the conclusion that finite and
infinite must be kept apart. Thus supernaturalism had to
depend upon special revelation and miracle in a special
salvation-history. With this standpoint it was impossible to face
effectively the full force of those philosophical, theological and
political radicalisms which followed Hegel. In theology, one
popular reaction involved a return to classical Lutheran
orthodoxy or biblical fundamentalism. Another attractive
option was to follow through the supposed consequences of
Kant's philosophy in confining theology to the realm of
finitude. Tillich correctly observes that Kantianised theology is
built upon only two foundations: historical research and the
moral imperative. On this view, the basis of religious certitude
lies chiefly with our sense of moral personhood; specifically
christian faith is built upon the fruits of historical research
about Jesus. But, notwithstanding the presence of many
neo-Kantian motifs, Troeltsch is both philosophically and
theologically a synthesiser – as ambitious even, but by no
means as tidy, as Hegel. In this venture the religious
metaphysics is vital.

Troeltsch's treatment of religion is very similar to that of
Schleiermacher, namely that theology is primarily concerned
with the factually given reality of religion. But neither
Schleiermacher nor Troeltsch is content to treat religion
simply as the product of finite experience. Their empirical
approach to the phenomenon of religion is grounded in an
immediate awareness of the impact of the divine spirit upon us
in the ground of our being. In other words, this universe is the
kind of universe where the infinite is immanent in the finite,
and immanent in such a way that it individualises itself in every

phenomenon.[22] Here we observe Schleiermacher's profound indebtedness to the Romantic movement. A similar standpoint is found in Troeltsch. It offers a basis for christian piety in and through the relativities of history. It provides a basis for the sympathetic and constructive handling of the religious past, inasmuch as there the infinite individualises itself in the individual totality to be grasped by the religious historian and brought forward into the present. It yields a basis for treating cultural history as an arena of genuine religious and cultural creativity. In the case of both Schleiermacher and Troeltsch, the charges of subjectivism and doctrinal thinness fail if the full weight of the religious metaphysics is realised. Troeltsch writes approvingly of Schleiermacher as follows:

At the height of German idealism the weighty theological problems of modern protestantism were gathered up in a remarkable way by Schleiermacher, the great theological master of neo-protestantism. He belonged to both worlds and set out a theological programme of mediation in the fullest and highest sense of that word. On the basis of a general philosophy of spirit and of culture, an equally general critical philosophy of religion was to emerge which affirmed, psychologically and epistemologically, the autonomous nature of religious events and of religious knowledge.[23]

From this programme there arises for the theologian a two-fold task. Theology 'must first investigate historically the rise and history of Christianity; second, it must mould dogmatically into a *Glaubenslehre* what is presented by history with reference both to inner personal experience and to the modern scientific world-view.[24] In relation to these comments on Schleiermacher, Troeltsch observes: 'This indeed formulates the programme as it arises from the modern situation and the programme must remain like this as long as there is to be an independent christian *Glaubenslehre*.'[25]

In considering Troeltsch's approach to theology, we now begin to see the emergence of an organic relationship between 'applied-historical' and 'confessional' interests. Troeltsch

---

[22] Cf. A. Frohne, *Der Begriff der Eigenthumlichkeit oder Individualität bei Schleiermacher* (Halle, 1884).

[23] Troeltsch in *Die Kultur der Gegenwart*, ed. Hinneberg, Teil I, Abt. IV. i, ii Hälfte (Leipzig and Berlin, 2nd edn, 2nd impression, 1922), 725f.

[24] *Ibid.*   [25] *Ibid.*

accords great importance to mysticism, piety, and what he calls 'spiritual religion'. In *Die Absolutheit* the relation of these to historicised religion is clearly expressed.

Piety requires the absolute, the incursion of a world of eternal forces and ultimate values. This means nothing other than the need for God. The absolute is possessed only in God, the source of all historical life, and not in a single historical phenomenon. Only in piety do we know as a certitude that there is in fact an ultimate, eternal, value-full end. Only in piety do we have a guarantee of the future, through the present knowledge of God. In the life-process of history a man participates in the absolute only in an historical way, only in a way conditioned by the context at any one time, only in historically individualised revelations of the absolute which point to the future, to an eternal and unconditioned value which transcends history.[26]

The understanding of piety in this passage is clearly not arbitrary. It is rooted in the christian doctrines of creation and redemption; it respects the kind of world disclosed by *Historismus*. It is a theological standpoint deeply rooted in a long and independent tradition – in Nicholas of Cusa; in Leibniz and Malebranche; in the mystical-theosophical tradition of Boehme and Oetinger; in Schleiermacher, Schelling and Rothe; and later in Tillich and Teilhard de Chardin. So Troeltsch can refer with evident approval to the way in which for Leibniz the interconnections of life of finite spirits are continuous movements grounded in the ontological and teleological unity of the divine life. Malebranche too approaches the inner relationships of the process of becoming in terms of the participation of the finite spirit in the inner unity and movement of absolute spirit. Troeltsch comments: 'The real and individual identity of finite spirits with the infinite spirit and, with this, the intuitive participation in the infinite spirit's concrete content and living unity of life, is the key to the solution of our problem' [*GS* III, 675–9]. Troeltsch recognises the danger of this approach, namely that it can lead to a purely speculative conception of God. This danger led Kant to confine this participation in the divine spirit to the sphere of morality. But Troeltsch maintains that these dangers can be avoided if the historical standpoint is consistenly

[26] Troeltsch, in *Die Absolutheit des Christentums und die Religionsgeschichte* (2nd edn, Tübingen, 1912), p. 98.

maintained and full recognition given to historical contingency.

VIII

I have given special attention to Troeltsch's treatment of religious metaphysics because it is an important feature of what has the potential of being a subtly connected theological structure. *First*, there is applied historical theology, theology as a living science, using an individualising historical method, and relating christian ideas to the present for the purpose of transforming culture. Here the constraints and possibilities of *Historismus* are fully acknowledged. But without a basis in religious metaphysics this portion of the structure is threatened with dissolution by various forms of reductionism. *Second*, there is the confessional theology, the *Glaubenslehre*; reflecting the deliverances of piety and the religious metaphysics; helping to shape the power of interpretation which must be employed in applied historical theology; subject in its self-articulation to criteria imposed by *Historismus*; and, finally, needing adjustment in the light of changing scientific world-views. *Third*, there is the religious metaphysics, licensed by the view of reality emerging from *Historismus*, and grounded in the practical religious life.

When however we come to examine Troeltsch's declared theological intentions, it seems that some of the potential of his position is lost. In an article written in 1913,[27] Troeltsch outlines three tasks: 1. to establish, on the basis of an historical and philosophical comparison of religions, the fundamental and universal supremacy of Christianity for our own culture and civilisation; 2. to determine the meaning of Christianity; 3. to expound the content of this essential Christianity. It will be clear that, in Troeltsch's view, 1 and 2 belong together as essentially historical undertakings. But he treats 3 as of an entirely different character and insists that it must be kept separate. He describes it as the 'task of setting forth the christian faith in God, or in other words, the conceptions involved in essential Christianity in complete self-dependence without any intermingling of historical elements. It sets forth our faith in God as something existing in present experience

[27] Troeltsch, *AJT* XVII (1913), 1–21.

and renewing itself with each individual in the experience of redemption.' Troeltsch stresses that a dogmatics so conceived can proceed in a 'free and unembarrassed fashion'. For it is not a science but a 'confession of faith and a systematic exposition of this confession for the guidance of preaching and of religious instruction'. He concludes that 'dogmatics is a part of practical theology', whereas philosophy of religion and the history of Christianity have a 'purely scientific character'.

At first sight, this sharp demarcation between 'historical' and 'dogmatic' suggests a rather impoverished neo-Kantian liberalism. But my own exposition has shown an interdependence of philosophical, historical, theological and religious interests offering a far richer yield and demonstrating that Troeltsch's demarcation is inadmissable on his own premises. This false distinction between a scientific historical method and an unscientific dogmatic method is too crude on both sides. It has helped to give rise to what are, in my view, equally false distinctions between theology and religious studies, and, more recently, between contextual and dogmatic approaches in theology.[28]

In conclusion, I shall try to relate some features of the foregoing discussion to the contemporary theological task.

IX

1. Troeltsch's account of the impact of *Historismus* upon theology shows decisively that a systematic theology may not, with legitimacy, appeal to a single primary authority but always and only to a plurality of (often competing) secondary authorities. Moreover, since historically conditioned authorities always require interpretation, it follows that interpretation (despite its own standpoint of faith) must always exercise control over the sources if theology is to be any more than repetition and translation. Following Troeltsch, I should therefore claim that the effect of systematic theology is to orientate us in relation to the intellectual life of the present and to reconstruct the religious idea, with all the thorough historical and scientific enquiry which these tasks imply.

[28] A. O. Dyson, 'Dogmatic or Contextual Theology?', *Study Encounter*, VIII (1972).

2. We cannot however pursue such goals with the confessional element standing in complete self-dependence, as Troeltsch prescribes. Present-day religious convictions are inextricably interwoven with other convictions and are conditioned by many factors. Only as these convictions are fully tested can we begin to understand and evaluate the presuppositions which we bring to our interpretation of past and present. Thus present-day convictions about God and Christ must be compared with former convictions and the latter often allowed to reshape the former.

3. A systematic theology must always be critically grounded in a religious metaphysics if it is to have the freedom both to respond to and reject the world-views implicit in the different sciences. Without continual attention to the metaphysical element, theology finds itself either bound to prevailing non-religious metaphysics or obliged to reject metaphysical systems on principle. I think that the elaboration of an evolutionary metaphysics in which the infinite is present in the finite by a process of individuation is, in some form or another, an essential requirement for a theology which would be properly responsive to historical and scientific versions of reality. The long tradition to which Troeltsch belonged in this regard deserves much closer attention than it has received.[29]

4. It is obvious that systematic theology is, in no small measure, subjective and confessional in character – though in a much broader sense than Troeltsch had in mind. He overstated the distinction between historical and dogmatic method since, on his own admission, the individualising historical method involves much by way of personal selection and judgment. Moreover, to move from a historical logic to a historical view of reality is no simple deduction but involves many other presuppositions. Nonetheless to acknowledge the confessional element as integral to systematic theology is not to deny its scientific character, though the choice and use of criteria is made more difficult.

[29] See S. M. Daecke, *Teilhard de Chardin und die evangelische Theologie* (Göttingen, 1967); A. O. Dyson, 'Christ and Man's Place in Nature', *Theology* LXXII (1969), 98ff.

X

Troeltsch may properly be regarded as a figure of great resourcefulness for our thinking about the ways and means of systematic theology. Throughout his lively intellectual career, he was always on the move towards a synthesis of important factors. To this extent he belongs to the classical German tradition of mediation and synthesis. Where that tradition had got into difficulties, Troeltsch brought new resources in the form of a strong historical and sociological grasp which took him beyond Hegel and Schleiermacher as far as theology is concerned. I see Troeltsch's analysis and constructive work as pointing authentically to the comprehensive task which awaits the systematic theologian. T. Kaftan described Troeltsch as 'condemned to the labour of a Sisyphus'.[30] Less dramatically, H. Frei observes that 'all his life Troeltsch looked towards a synthesis in which formal philosophy, the interpretation of culture and history, and theology would all cohere without undercutting one another's autonomy. He did not attain the goal of his vision, but he developed a breadth of interest and sympathy probably unmatched by any other theological contemporary.'[31] Kaftan and Frei are closer, in my view, to a sound judgment on Troeltsch than Reist with his talk about the 'collapse of Troeltsch's theology' and his 'faltering, failing steps toward a theology of involvement'.[32]

Troeltsch was aware that to be a responsible theologian in his time meant more than simply taking account of the impact of historical science upon christian thought in a situation dominated by the growing prestige of the natural and social sciences. It meant also a new persistence in exploring and developing the theme of finitude and infinity in the wake of a tradition which included Schelling, Hegel, Novalis, Schleiermacher, and Dilthey. To those who hanker for a certain kind of authority in theology, Troeltsch marks the end-point of an exhausted tradition. But for those who are prepared to accept a certain vulnerability in the theologian's work, Troeltsch represents new possibilities of speaking creatively about the

[30] *Ernst Troeltsch: Eine kritische Zeitstudie* (Schleswig, 1912), p. 71.
[31] In *Faith and Ethics: The Theology of H. Richard Niebuhr* (ed. P. Ramsey, New York, 1957), pp. 53f.   [32] See note 4 above.

concrete relationship between transcendence and historical existence.[33] The impoverishment of systematic theology (with honourable exceptions) in the half-century since Troeltsch's death has not come about through the following of Troeltsch, but through the sundering of finitude and infinity for the sake of supposed tactical victories. There is a real case for taking Troeltsch as a starting-point (for 'he was one of the clearest thinkers that we had')[34] and even for beginning all over again.

[33] For a fuller treatment see A. O. Dyson, *The Immortality of the Past* (London, 1974), chs. 2 and 5.
[34] Bornhausen, *ZThK* IV (1923), 199.

4. Ernst Troeltsch and the possibility of a historical theology

B. A. GERRISH

I know myself at one with these friends in the wish that the Heidelberg theologian not be quite forgotten in the Berlin philosopher of culture.[1]

For the great generation of protestant schoolmen, whose names today are scarcely remembered, dogmatics was a deductive, biblical science. Whatever initial aid they may have found in a natural theology, they derived the fundamental teachings of their church strictly from the written Word of God; and the indispensable prolegomenon to this enterprise was simply to establish the exclusive claims of scripture. The oracles of God had been distributed to his people with a largesse which overflowed the bounds of mere order. It was the task of the theologian to bring them, with due humility, into a coherent system, which, precisely because it contained no more than the faith delivered once for all to the saints, had the character of an enduring and irrefutable body of divinity. Within the limits of such a scheme, historical study could scarcely be more than a branch of confessional apologetics, by which one's own party could be shown to have preserved the truth without adulteration or alteration.[2]

Friedrich Schleiermacher, by contrast, identified dogmatics as a part of historical theology. Protestant scholasticism did

---

[1] Marta Troeltsch, in her foreword to Ernst Troeltsch's lectures on dogmatics, posthumously published at the request of 'friends and students' [*Gl.*, p. vi]. Translations from this and other German works are mine, unless otherwise stated.

[2] See Heinrich Schmid, *The Doctrinal Theology of the Evangelical Lutheran Church*, trans. Charles A. Hay and Henry E. Jacobs, 3rd ed. (1899; reprint ed., Augsburg Publishing House: Minneapolis, Minn. [1961], introduction and part I, ch. i, esp. pp. 27–8. Cf. the parallel discussions in Heinrich Heppe, *Reformed Dogmatics Set Out and Illustrated From the Sources*, rev. ed., ed. Ernst Bizer, trans. G. T. Thomson (George Allen & Unwin: London, 1950), chs. i–iv.

not, of course, constitute the entire background to his enterprise; but, whatever may have been the contributory factors,
past or contemporary, the move he made was nothing less than
revolutionary. It meant that the heart of theology, its essential
business, was now seen to be the explication of the life of the
church (or of one aspect of it). Dogmatics has for its subject-
matter the same datum as church history: the christian
community as a phenomenon of change, growth, development. The difference between the two disciplines is that
church history is directed towards the church in its past,
whereas dogmatics deals with the church in the present. And
since the past is pregnant with the future, and the present is the
issue of the past, the dividing line is little more than a
pragmatic convenience. So Schleiermacher presented the
scope and task of dogmatics in his *Brief Outline* (1811 and
1830).[3] His own dogmatic system, *The Christian Faith* (1821–2
and 1830–1), must be understood as the implementation of this
same programme: it is a contribution to historical theology, in
that it offers historical knowledge of the (then) present
condition of the evangelical church. It is no longer a deductive,
biblical theology in the old protestant style.[4] Even what
Schleiermacher calls 'philosophical theology' is inextricably
bound up with the historical task, since it is constantly to test
the language of the church by reference to a distinctive
'essence' of Christianity (or of protestantism) which can only
be grasped in its historical manifestations.[5] Plainly, in Schleier-

---

[3] *Kurze Darstellung des theologischen Studiums zum Behuf einleitender Vorlesungen*,
3rd critical ed., ed. Heinrich Scholz (1910; reprint ed., Wissenschaftliche
Buchgesellschaft: Darmstadt [1961]), abbrev. *KD* and cited by numbered
paragraph: pars. 26–8 (the concept of 'historical theology'; cf. par. 188), 81–5
(its three divisions), 94–7 and 195 (its two aspects; cf. pars. 90 and 166–7). Par.
33 of the first ed. (cited by Scholz in a footnote on p. 11) makes the essential
point in these words: 'Die christliche Kirche als das zu Regierende ist ein
Werdendes, in welchem die jedesmalige Gegenwart begriffen werden muß
als Produkt der Vergangenheit und als Keim der Zukunft.'

[4] *Der christliche Glaube nach den Grundsätzen der evangelischen Kirche im
Zusammenhange dargestellt*, 7th ed., based on the 2nd ed. of 1830, ed. Martin
Redeker (2 vols., Walter de Gruyter: Berlin, 1960); abbreviated *Chr. Gl.* and
cited by paragraph and, where appropriate, sub-paragraph: esp. pars. 19
and 27.

[5] *KD* 39–40 (the task of philosophical theology; cf. par. 21), 252–6 (the relation
of philosophical and historical theology; cf. pars. 29, 35, 37 and 65).
Schleiermacher's definition of the essence of Christianity is given in *Chr. Gl.*
11.

macher's programme the theological task is thoroughly 'historicised' – made into a function of history. Not sufficiently, however, to satisfy some of his critics and successors!

The dogmatics of Schleiermacher was subjected to relentless criticism, from the side of historical thinking, by F. C. Baur, D. F. Strauss, Wilhelm Dilthey, and others.[6] It was pointed out that the *content* of Schleiermacher's system – indeed, at its christological centre – violated historical modes of thought. It appealed to an absolute moment of history, a fixed point to which theology had constantly to refer back as the unblemished norm and the unique centre of mankind's history.[7] Further, the questionable content was traced to defective *method*. The method of the system, despite the explicit historical turn, remained incurably 'dogmatic' (in a pejorative sense). And this was most notably the problem just at the place where the profession of historical-critical principles was most dutifully made: in Schleiermacher's lectures on the life of Jesus.[8] Schleiermacher was by no means unaware of the alleged inconsistencies his critics urged, and were later to urge, against him. But he did not believe it possible to surrender the absoluteness of Christ.[9] Now, the desire of some of his successors, including Baur, was to make dogmatics more consistently historical by erasing vestigial blemishes in Schleiermacher's programme. Others, like Franz Overbeck,

---

[6] Ferdinand Christian Baur, *Die christliche Gnosis oder die christliche Religions-Philosophie in ihrer geschichtlichen Entwicklung* (C. F. Osiander: Tübingen, 1835), pp. 637–56 (including, in an extended note on pp. 646–52, refs. to the earlier exchange between Schleiermacher and Baur); David Friedrich Strauss, *Der Christus des Glaubens und der Jesus der Geschichte: Eine Kritik des Schleiermacher'schen Lebens Jesu* (1865; reprint ed., Texte zur Kirchen- und Theologiegeschichte, no. 14, Gerd Mohn: Gütersloh, 1971), which refers also to Strauss' earlier criticisms of Schleiermacher in the popular version of his own life of Jesus (1864); Wilhelm Dilthey, *Leben Schleiermachers*, I, 2nd ed. enlarged, ed. Hermann Mulert, (Walter de Gruyter: Berlin, 1922), 765–98 (on Schleiermacher's *Die Weihnachtsfeier*); II: *Schleiermachers System als Philosophie und Theologie*, ed. Martin Redeker (2 part-vols., Walter de Gruyter: Berlin [published simultaneously by Vandenhoeck & Ruprecht, Göttingen, as Dilthey's *Gesammelte Schriften*, vol. XIV], 1966), 473–507 (on the significance of Christ esp. in *Chr. Gl.*).

[7] See, e.g., *KD* 108; *Chr. Gl.* 89, 93, 98.

[8] Posthumously ed. for the *Sämmtliche Werke* of Schleiermacher, div. I, vol. VI, by K. A. Rütenik: *Das Leben Jesu: Vorlesungen an der Universität zu Berlin im Jahr 1832 gehalten* (Georg Reimer: Berlin, 1864). Publication of these lectures was the occasion for Strauss' detailed critique in his *Christus des Glaubens*.

[9] See esp. *Chr. Gl.* 93.2; cf. pars, 7.3, 8.4, 11.5, 86.1, 89.3.

were persuaded that historical method and dogmatic theology were, in the end, simply exclusive.[10] Here, then, is the question that was asked of Schleiermacher: Is a historical theology (in his sense) possible? And this is also the question addressed, in his own day and since, to Ernst Troeltsch.

I

Characterising his own theological programme in his *Glaubenslehre*, Troeltsch remarks: 'No theologian of the present keeps so close to the method and intent of Schleiermacher, or feels himself in such inward agreement with him' [*Gl.*, p. 130]. As his very next words demonstrate, Troeltsch was by no means an uncritical disciple of the man he elsewhere calls 'our great master'.[11] In the course of the *Glaubenslehre*, he reproduces the more or less standard objections to Schleiermacher's system: that it is entangled in a monistic world-view, borrowed chiefly from Spinoza; that it obtrudes historical propositions about Jesus into the main body of dogmatics, where they do not belong; that it describes Jesus by means of predicates which cannot be derived from history [*Gl.*, pp. 130, 79, 86].[12] A similar stance of critical discipleship is adopted in others of Troeltsch's writings. One further example may suffice. In his essay on the dogmatics of the 'history of religions' school, Troeltsch judges that the programme of Schleiermacher's *Brief Outline* 'simply needs to be carried out consistently' and that 'hardly any change is necessary'. This,

---

[10] Against what he considered the incurably apologetic motives of theology, Overbeck stood for history *nach Möglichkeit ohne Tendenz: Über die Christlichkeit unserer heutigen Theologie*, 2nd ed. (1903; reprint ed., Wissenschaftliche Buchgesellschaft: Darmstadt, 1963), p. 181; cf. pp. 3–4, where Overbeck acknowledges the influence of F. C. Baur. But he considered it equally an error of 'our present-day theology' that by *historical* interpretation it sought access to Christianity as a *religion* (*ibid.* p. 36).

[11] 'Rückblick auf ein halbes Jahrhundert der theologischen Wissenschaft' (1908), *GS* II, 226. Cf. also *Gl.*, p. 56.

[12] It is, of course, the third objection – that Schleiermacher's Jesus was *kein eigentlich geschichtliches Faktum* [*Gl.*, p. 86] – which links Troeltsch most closely with the criticisms of Baur, Strauss, and Dilthey. Cf. 'Weiterentwickelung der christlichen Religion', *Die Religion in Geschichte und Gegenwart* (henceforth *RGG*), ed. Friedrich Michael Schiele and Leopold Zscharnack (5 vols., J. C. B. Mohr [Paul Siebeck]: Tübingen, 1909–13), V, 1882. We shall find reason to doubt Troeltsch's claim that his own *Gl.*, by contrast, 'will show not the slightest inclination to monism' [*Gl.*, p. 130; cf. pp. 68–9, 77].

however, is to endorse only the programme. For although Schleiermacher indicated the contours of a genuinely modern theology, the historical interpretation of Christianity has made enormous strides since his time, and his *Life of Jesus* is simply dated. So, too, in the light of progress in the history of religions, his theory of religious development appears as 'a completely antiquated exercise of the imagination'.[13]

What Troeltsch learned from Schleiermacher was a 'theology of consciousness',[14] which could appropriately be designated a 'historical theology', although Troeltsch did not, in fact, adopt this feature of the master's peculiar terminology. Schleiermacher is singled out as the pioneer in modern dogmatics, first of all, because he built his theology on the double foundation of a comparative philosophy of religions and a historical-critical (therefore *religionsgeschichtlich*) investigation of Christianity itself. In other words, he made theology rest on a 'philosophy of the history of religions', which, in turn, was rooted in what he called 'ethics' (that is, the philosophy of history and of the human spirit). The design of such a philosophical approach is not, as in the old natural theologies, to prove the reality of the religious object, but to furnish an analysis of religion, its distinctive character and its historical development. Troeltsch identifies himself with Schleiermacher's general programme, so understood. He

[13] 'The Dogmatics of the "Religionsgeschichtliche Schule"', *American Journal of Theology*, XVII, no. 1 (Jan. 1913), 1–21 (German in *GS* II, 500–24); esp. p. 17, n. 1 (*GS* II, 515, n. 39) and pp. 8–9 (*GS* II, 507–8). The former remark is not quite identical in the German version, which, however, gives a reference (without page number) to a similar statement in 'Rückblick'. The reference is doubtlessly to *GS* II, 225–6, where Troeltsch adds that of Schleiermacher's actual teachings scarcely one stone is left standing on another. Cf. also Troeltsch's important piece, 'Schleiermacher und die Kirche', in *Schleiermacher der Philosoph des Glaubens*, essays by Ernst Troeltsch and others (Moderne Philosophie, no. 6, Buchverlag der 'Hilfe': Berlin–Schöneberg, 1910), p. 34.

[14] In a *Bewußtseinstheologie*, the divine object may be had only indirectly, through the veil (*Schleier!*) of subjective experience. But this is a real 'having' since the subjectivity is thought of as 'God-filled' [*Gl.*, p. 132]. See also *Gl.*, p. 14 ('Wie Schleiermacher, so bauen auch wir auf dem gegenwärtigen Bewußtsein der Gemeinden') and the methodological remarks on the doctrines of God [*Gl.*, pp. 127–8] and redemption [*Gl.*, p. 356]. A *Bewußtseinstheologie* is distinguished from a *Theologie der Tatsachen*, which supposes it possible to assert objective theological facts (cf. 'Heilstatsachen', *RGG* II, 2066–7), and its method is said to be 'historical-psychological' instead of the old 'dogmatic' method ('Prinzip, religiöses', *RGG* IV, 1843).

differs, however, where revisions are required by advances, since Schleiermacher's time, in the historical-phenomenological foundations and in the analysis of the concept of development. Further, he judges that Schleiermacher's somewhat minimal philosophy of religion was cramped by an exclusive interest in laying the groundwork for dogmatics. What, for Schleiermacher, was merely the introduction to *Glaubenslehre* has since become a separate discipline. But the path opened up by him remains the right one.[15] It is easy to see why Troeltsch is willing to understand it as a programme for a 'dogmatics of the history of religions school'.

Dogmatics, then, is intimately connected with philosophy and with the history of religions through a distinct discipline which Troeltsch calls 'philosophy of religion' or 'fundamental theology'.[16] It is simply the grown-up child of Schleiermacher's introduction to his own *Glaubenslehre, The Christian Faith*. But dogmatics necessarily passes beyond the scope of its initial partners insofar as its proper business is to present a normative system of specifically christian beliefs or (to follow Schleiermacher once again) a system of the essential christian ideas which radiate out from the personality of Jesus. Troeltsch distinguishes three dogmatic tasks: first, by a comparison with other religions, to establish the supremacy of Christianity for our civilisation; second, to trace the church's entire historical course and to draw out the essence of Christianity for the present; third, to explicate the content of this essence in appropriate concepts. It is clear that the first two tasks are closely related to Schleiermacher's two foundations of dogmatics, and that the third is its 'real and specific business'.[17]

There are several senses in which this dogmatic enterprise may be considered 'historical'. To begin with, the first and second tasks both proceed from historical data; and the third, more strictly dogmatic, task evolves out of the second. Hence

[15] 'Dogmatics', pp. 6, 15 [*GS* II, 505–6, 514]: 'Geschichte und Metaphysik', *Zeitschrift für Theologie und Kirche*, VIII (1898), 27–9; 'Rückblick', pp. 221–6. For the shift from natural theology to history of religions as theology's frame of reference, cf. *Gl.*, pp. 1, 128, 135; 'Logos und Mythos in Theologie und Religions-philosophie' (1913), *GS* II, 805–6.

[16] German, *prinzipielle Theologie* [*Gl.*, p. 1]. Cf. 'Dogmatics', p. 5, where the phrase 'theology in the distinctive sense of the word' mistranslates *prinzipiell-theologische* [*GS* II, 504].

[17] 'Dogmatics', pp. 6–7, 10–15 [*GS* II, 505–6, 508–14].

Troeltsch can assert that the entire conception of dogmatics as the unfolding of Christianity's essence is conditioned by a history-of-religions viewpoint. Moreover, the actual ordering of the essence into its conceptual content, so Troeltsch claims, simply appropriates the common categories discovered by the history of religions in every higher religion. For every religious principle signifies a practical relationship of God, world, and man; and always associated with this fundamental relationship is a religious community and the hope for a final consummation. This yields the six concepts of Troeltsch's dogmatics, each of which presents the whole content of the christian principle, but from a different perspective, and each of which receives a separate chapter in his *Glaubenslehre*: God, world, man, redemption, church, and consummation. The consequences of this history-of-religions orientation, Troeltsch adds, extend still further into the execution of the dogmatic task since they require that the critical standards of historiography should be brought to bear on the christian story, which is not exempt from the relativity of all historical events nor from the uncertainties of all historical testimony. In this regard, the special standpoint of the history of religions only strengthens the earlier claims of historical criticism.[18]

There is at least one further respect in which dogmatics is a historical task: because it is itself a part of religious growth and becoming. Troeltsch's interpretation of Schleiermacher is at no point more fascinating than here, where the functional-ephemeral character of dogmatics comes into view. What does the theological student actually possess once he has mastered Schleiermacher's *Glaubenslehre*? Troeltsch replies that he will be equipped to nurture the religious sensibility of his future pastoral charges. *The Christian Faith* is a guide to preaching. It is a 'technical-theological' book, and therefore unpalatable to laymen, not in the sense of being academically esoteric, but rather because its end is knowledge of the 'technical' means by which religious feeling is represented and stimulated. Precisely as such, the *Glaubenslehre* of Schleiermacher takes on a strictly ephemeral character: it does not fix dogmas, but only

---

[18] *Ibid.* pp. 13–14 [pp. 512–13]. Cf. 'Prinzip', col. 1846; 'Über historische und dogmatische methode in der Theologie' (1898), *GS* II, 729–53. See further n. 67 below.

expresses, in forms suited to the moment, the religious strength that radiates from Christ. The means of expression have their source in Christ, but they are shaped by the situation of the present. Hence theology's task is essentially to mediate between old forms and new for the sake of practical ends.[19] Pursuit of this strand in Schleiermacher's dogmatics leads Troeltsch to his repeated insistence that *Glaubenslehre* is not a science, but rather 'a confession of faith and a systematic exposition of this confession for the guidance of preaching and of religious instruction'. It is, he argues, a part of practical theology. The most that can be claimed for the scientific status of dogmatics is that it retains contact with science through its relationship with the philosophy of religion and church history, both of which bear a purely scientific character.[20]

It is hard not to judge that Troeltsch here develops Schleiermacher's thoughts one-sidedly. He claims that to classify dogmatics with practical theology is the intent of Schleiermacher's *Brief Outline*. And yet it is obvious that he has at least made a shift in Schleiermacher's *language*, since the *Brief Outline* in fact presents dogmatics as a part of *historical* theology, and practical theology as the crown or goal of theological studies in general.[21] Perhaps the verbal difference betrays a material shift as well. But it is not our purpose to assess the justice of Troeltsch's claim to be Schleiermacher's disciple at this point; only to comprehend Troeltsch's own theological programme. And whereas others have sought to defend Schleiermacher against his apparent debasement of theology's scientific status,[22] Troeltsch develops the practical aspect fully and approvingly. He was convinced that dogmatics, because it deals with the confession of faith and from the standpoint of commitment to it, could not pretend to scientific status. Indeed, he speaks of it in language which invites comparison rather with the free, creative activity of the artist.

---

[19] 'Schleiermacher und die Kirche', p. 27; 'Dogmatics', p. 15 [*GS* II, 514].
[20] 'Dogmatics', pp. 16–18 [*GS* II, 514–17]. Cf. Schleiermacher, *KD* 28.
[21] The phrase *die Krone des theologischen Studiums* comes from the first ed. (see Scholz, p. 10, n. 2). Of great importance for assessing Troeltsch's interpretation at this point are Schleiermacher's balancing of 'ecclesial' and 'scientific' interest and his location of historical theology on the scale: see, e.g. *KD* 9–13, 66, 193; *Chr. Gl.* 17.
[22] Heinrich Scholz, e.g., in his intr. to *KD* (p. xxviii).

Dogmatics is production out of the resources of christian history; and its products, because they are values with an ineradicably personal stamp, resist incorporation with the uniform and universally valid objects of science.[23] We must surely ask, however, not only why Troeltsch classified dogmatics with practical theology, but also why, after all, he did *not* classify it as historical theology. Does this represent a substantive departure from Schleiermacher, one more germane – indeed, crucial – for our own theme?

Since no German theologian, with one solitary exception, had adopted Schleiermacher's inclusion of dogmatics under historical theology, it is hardly surprising if Troeltsch did not do so either.[24] Schleiermacher's terminology was apparently felt to be eccentric, and even theologians who titled their systematic work *Glaubenslehre* omitted to take the further step of calling it *historische Theologie*. Still, the question remains whether something material was lost or gained by the omission. As far as Troeltsch is concerned, my own judgment is that the terminological departure from Schleiermacher really does signify a material point, but not such as to question Schleiermacher's design in calling dogmatics 'historical theology'. Between Schleiermacher and Troeltsch, historical theology had become the secure fortress of those who wished to affirm the scientific character of their business, and the term frequently implied a clear repudiation of church dogmatics.[25] Besides, there really was (at that time) something eccentric in speaking of the present as 'historical'. Schleiermacher, of course, was moving towards the notion of man's 'historicity' as a description of his temporal existence, and this was a notion whose time had not quite come. Troeltsch was not merely acquiescing in current usage, however, but himself acknowledging the need for differentiation when he declined to follow Schleiermacher's lead. This, admittedly, is an inference, since I am not aware of any place where he directly explains his own usage. It is clear, however, that he was impressed by the logical

---

[23] 'Dogmatics', p. 18 [*GS* II, 516–17]. Cf. 'Glaube, IV: Glaube und Geschichte' (*RGG* II, 1447–56), where Troeltsch speaks of the 'poetic liveliness and freedom without which *Glaubenslehren* are unthinkable' (col. 1456).
[24] The exception was Richard Rothe: see Heinrich Scholz, intr. to *KD*, pp. xxii–xxiii.   [25] Troeltsch traces this development in 'Rückblick'.

difference between strictly historical and strictly dogmatic functions. What historical enquiry discloses can never be more than a historical reality until it is changed by a judgment into a valid truth. The logical transition from the historical to the constructive theological task lies here – in an act by which a value is lifted out of mere fact.[26] But this could hardly be interpreted as a material *criticism* of Schleiermacher, since Troeltsch is not denying what Schleiermacher sought to affirm by his admittedly unfamiliar usage: namely, that dogmatics is directed to the present consciousness of the church, and that this can only be understood in continuity with its past.

Where Troeltsch does offer his most emphatic criticism, it concerns neither the raw-material, nor the general method, nor the function of dogmatics, which we may fairly distinguish as the elements that warrant the appellation 'historical theology'. It concerns, rather, the end-product, which Troeltsch understands as strictly conceptual in character. The concepts comprised in the essence of Christianity are to be presented 'without any intermingling of historical elements', so that dogmatics, in the end, contains 'purely present-day religious' or 'purely metaphysical-religious' propositions. The criticism of Schleiermacher is that he mixed the historical and the metaphysical propositions. Troeltsch has chiefly in mind the way in which Schleiermacher mingled dogmatic propositions concerning the present experience of redemption with historical propositions about Jesus. In Schleiermacher's *Glaubenslehre*, the historical-religious propositions, he maintains, are the sorest point because they are forced dissonantly into the section where only present-day religious propositions belong [*Gl.*, p. 79; cf. *Gl.*, pp. 329, 348]. Accordingly, Troeltsch thinks he improves on Schleiermacher by dividing his own *Glaubenslehre* into two parts. The first deals with Jesus Christ in the light both of his prophetic forerunners and of his subsequent interpreters. The second seeks to formulate the conceptual content of christian faith understood as strictly a present experience. Still, the logical segregation of historical

---

[26] 'Prinzip', col. 1846. The particular *historisch-psychologische Wirklichkeit* intended in this passage is the 'essence' or 'principle' of Christianity, which only a 'deed' can transform into a *geltende Wahrheit*. See further section III below.

and metaphysical propositions, Troeltsch points out, is but one side of the matter. Not only are the present-day formulations attained solely at the end of a historical enquiry, but present religious experience continues to receive its life and power from the vital world of history: this it is, and particularly the prophets and Jesus, which leads us to God.[27] And that was a particular insight of Schleiermacher's – indeed, from the early time of his *Speeches on Religion* (1799).[28] Even here, then, we come back again to the historical and to Schleiermacher as the great master of a historical theology. So decisive was the new direction he gave to protestant theology that Troeltsch, while not adopting the term 'historical theology' in Schleiermacher's sense, does hold that in principle Schleiermacher did away with the other term 'dogmatics'. Henceforth, *Dogmatik* was superseded by *Glaubenslehre* [*Gl.*, p. 10], though in practice Troeltsch was no more able than Schleiermacher to dispense with the more traditional word. The new dogmatics is dogmatics no longer, since it knows no dogmas.[29]

---

[27] 'Dogmatics', pp. 14–15 [*GS* II, 513]. (Note Troeltsch's cautiousness here in using the term 'metaphysical', which belongs more properly to philosophical than to religious discourse.) The historical-religious propositions have a mediating function, and in this sense Troeltsch can call the historical elements in faith 'foundations of revelation and knowledge for present faith': 'Glaube und Geschichte', col. 1456.

[28] See Troeltsch's remark concerning the *Reden* in 'Adolf v. Harnack und Ferd. Christ. v. Baur', *Festgabe von Fachgenossen und Freunden A. von Harnack zum siebzigsten Geburtstag dargebracht* (J. C. B. Mohr [Paul Siebeck]: Tübingen, 1921), pp. 284–5.

[29] 'Dogmatik', *RGG* II, 109; cf. 'Dogmatics', p. 17 [*GS* II, 516]. Although he does not use *historische Theologie* in Schleiermacher's sense, Troeltsch does speak of a *Theologie des Historismus* ('Geschichte und Metaphysik', p. 69; see also 'Adolf v. Harnack', p. 287) and of a *religionsgeschichtliche Theologie* ('Über historische und dogmatische Methode', p. 738). It should be noted that Troeltsch considers it a 'travesty' if some theologians after Schleiermacher turned his mediating theology into a 'churchly-biblicistic dogmatics' ('Dogmatics', p. 7 [*GS* II, 506]), even though he himself frequently spoke of the 'ecclesiasticising' (*Verkirchlichung*) that marked the work of the later Schleiermacher (see, e.g., 'Rückblick', p. 225, no. 10). 'Dogmatics' (in the old sense) exists today, he thinks, only in the narrowest theological circles (*Die Bedeutung der Geschichtlichkeit Jesu für den Glauben* [J. C. B. Mohr (Paul Siebeck): Tübingen, 1911], p. 21), notably in America [*Gl.*, p. 7]. Perhaps the reason why the old term persists nonetheless is not merely custom, but the inflexibility of the new term, which lacks German cognates as well as a convenient English equivalent ('doctrine of faith'?): see 'Dogmatics', p. 17 [*GS* II, 516], where the translator may have missed the sense of the German *gewisse sprachliche Vorteile*.

It would, no doubt, be fruitful to turn next to some leading themes of Troeltsch's dogmatics and to compare them with some of Schleiermacher's. My purpose, however, is not to move from the methodological to the material concerns, but rather to raise some questions about the viability of the method. Such an exercise may well appear gratuitous in view of the scorn that a whole generation of theologians have heaped upon Troeltsch's theology. We have become accustomed to the verdict that Troeltsch led theology into a blind alley. No progress was possible, we are told, along the path he marked out. Hence his own departure from a theology chair at Heidelberg for a chair in philosophy at Berlin was a kind of symbolic or symptomatic act.[30] Either the theological task had to be taken up from another, fresh standpoint; or else it would dissolve into philosophy and the social sciences, and so cease to be theology.[31] In Germany, Bodenstein has given currency to the image of Troeltsch as a 'tragic' figure, who represented in his own career the general tragedy of a whole era in German theology.[32] Similarly, in the English-speaking world, Reist has expressed the common sentiment that Troeltsch's theology simply 'collapsed'.[33] Bodenstein and Reist represent something close to a mainline consensus which stood, during the second and third quarters of our century, under the shade of

---

[30] Karl Barth, 'Evangelical Theology in the Nineteenth Century', *God, Grace and Gospel*, trans. James Strathearn McNab (*Scottish Journal of Theology Occasional Papers*, no. 8, Oliver & Boyd: Edinburgh and London, 1959), pp. 57–8; 'The Humanity of God', *ibid.* p. 34. In the *Church Dogmatics*, IV: *The Doctrine of Reconciliation*, pt 1, trans. G. W. Bromiley (Charles Scribner's Sons: New York, 1956), 386–87, Barth remarks that some of those who left the foundering ship took the route to catholicism: e.g., Gertrud von le Fort immediately after she had seen Troeltsch's *Gl.* through the press!

[31] Friedrich Gogarten, 'Historicism', in *The Beginnings of Dialectic Theology*, I, trans. Keith R. Crim and Louis de Grazia, ed. James M. Robinson (John Knox: Richmond, Virginia, 1968), 349; Hermann Diem, *Dogmatics*, trans. Harold Knight (Oliver & Boyd: Edinburgh and London, 1959), pp. 4–9; Gotthold Müller, 'Die Selbstauflösung der Dogmatik bei Ernst Troeltsch', *Theologische Zeitschrift*, XXII, no. 5 (Sept.–Oct., 1966), 334–46. Cf. also Thomas W. Ogletree, *Christian Faith and History: A Critical Comparison of Ernst Troeltsch and Karl Barth* (Abingdon Press: New York and Nashville, 1965), p. 60.

[32] Walter Bodenstein, *Neige des Historismus: Ernst Troeltschs Entwicklungsgang* (Gerd Mohn: Gütersloh, 1959), p. 17. Cf. p. 207: Troeltsch was a 'wrecked theologian'.

[33] Benjamin A. Reist, *Toward a Theology of Involvement: The Thought of Ernst Troeltsch* (SCM Press: London, 1966), esp. ch. VI.

neo-orthodoxy (or perhaps one should better say 'neo-
orthodoxies', in the plural). Although signs of a fresh interest
in Troeltsch's theology have begun to accompany the decline
of neo-orthoxy itself, reappraisal of the Heidelberg theologian
has scarcely begun.[34]

Did Troeltsch bequeath to christian theology anything more
than a problem or a budget of problems? Did he perhaps offer,
in addition, something like the groundplan for a historical
theology? The obstacles to an affirmative answer are forbidding. It would not do simply to consider the neo-orthodox
chapter closed and to reopen the books at 1923. There can be
no question of merely reproducing either the content or the
idiom of Troeltsch's dogmatics: that would violate his own
sense of the passage of time. Besides, formidable theological
objections were raised against Troeltsch's enterprise: that he
surrendered theology's own internal norms; that he placed at
the centre of his theology, as its cardinal motif, an outdated
idealistic metaphysic of spirit; that, for all his emphasis on
history, he had, in the end, no appreciation for truths of fact;
that his entire enterprise founders on the problems of individuality and relativism.[35] (I say nothing of the further
objection, which weighs less heavily in the Anglo-Saxon world
than in Germany, that Troeltsch failed to appreciate the
genius of Martin Luther.)[36] Small wonder, then, if Reist judges
that it would be simply pointless to set out Troeltsch's theology
in its full breadth and unpardonably stupid to reduplicate his
errors.[37] Obviously, one takes something of a risk if one

[34] See, e.g. Wilhelm F. Kasch, *Die Sozialphilosophie von Ernst Troeltsch* (Beiträge
zur historischen Theologie, no. 34, J. C. B. Mohr [Paul Siebeck]: Tübingen,
1963), esp. ch. VIII and pp. 85, 250. Dyson has similarly called for an
approach to Troeltsch suited to a post-neo-orthodox scene, but he has
assigned only a very minor place in Troeltsch's career to the dogmatic
writings and accordingly did not make use of them in his dissertation:
A. O. Dyson, 'History in the Philosophy and Theology of Ernst Troeltsch'
(unpubl. diss., University of Oxford, 1968), pp. 7–10, 289–90.

[35] Besides the literature already cited, see, on the question of *Tatsachenwahr-
heiten*, Ignacio Escribano Alberca, *Die Gewinnung theologischer Normen aus der
Geschichte der Religion bei Ernst Troeltsch: Eine methodologische Studie*
(Münchener Theologische Studien, II, 21, Max Hueber: Munich, 1961), pp.
89, 121, 126, 188ff.; esp. p. 190.

[36] This is the source to which Bodenstein, in the final analysis, traces the
shortcomings of Troeltsch (*Neige des Historismus*, p. 56; cf. pp. 59, 99–100,
133), and he finds the failure to be connected with the deficient religious
experience of this 'all too modern man' (*ibid.* p. 135).

[37] *Towards a Theology of Involvement*, pp. 191–2, 202.

proposes a serious reappraisal of the *Glaubenslehre*. But, at the least, I should like to move beyond the condescension with which the *Glaubenslehre* was addressed from the very first days of its publication. Erich Seeberg, for instance, treated it patronisingly in his review as a document of Troeltsch's personal piety and so of a religiousness from a bygone day.[38] I should like, by contrast, to take it seriously as a theological document. And, although Reist's call for caution is well taken,[39] I cannot believe either that there is a very grave problem with the authenticity of the text or that there has been any great risk of too much dependence upon it as a source for Troeltsch's theology. On the second point, I need only remark that had there been *more* dependence on Troeltsch's *Glaubenslehre*, some of the objections alleged against his theology would be infinitely harder to sustain.[40] What we have really had too much of, if anything, is the endless summaries of *Der Historismus und seine Probleme* (or certain favourite portions of it). On the first point, the transcript of the lectures, though admittedly not published by Troeltsch himself, was approved by him, incorporated his own dictation, and was the work of a highly competent assistant who aimed at fidelity to the spoken word.[41] No objection can be brought against the authenticity of the dictation (clearly distinguished in the text), and it would be over-fastidious not to use the freer portions of the lecture, which amplify the sense of the dictated paragraphs and are a

---

[38] *Deutsche Literaturzeitung*, XLVII [n.s. III], no. 43 (23 Oct. 1926), cols. 2131, 2133. It must be admitted that Marta Troeltsch's foreword invited precisely such an interpretation of the *Gl.* as 'ein menschliches Dokument, in dem der Schwerpunkt auf dem spontanen und lebendigen Bekenntnis liegt' (*Gl.*, p. v).

[39] *Toward a Theology of Involvement*, pp. 155–6; cf. p. 251, n. 103.

[40] So, for instance, Bodenstein's objections to Troeltsch's conception of God (*Neige des Historismus*, pp. 66–8; cf. pp. 32–3) take no account of the two-sidedness of the *Gottesbegriff* presented in *Gl.*, pp. 266–78. Similarly, the notion of a *Tatsachenwahrheit*, supposedly lacking in Troeltsch's thought, seems to be expressly affirmed in *Gl.*, p. 93; but Escribano Alberca neglects both *Gl.* and the other most pertinent discussion, *Die Bedeutung der Geschichtlichkeit Jesu*.

[41] See the introductory remarks to *Gl.* by Marta Troeltsch and Gertrud von le Fort (pp. vi, ix). Even after the point where the pressures of time caused the lectures to be broken off (Gertrud von le Fort indicates that it was in the chapter on the soul, but this seems to be a slip for ch. IV, on redemption), the *Gl.* is completed by materials from other lectures (ch. IV) or by drafts made earlier for undelivered lectures (chs. V and VI). See pp. ix–x and 351 as well as the chs. concerned.

remarkable testimony to the vividness of Troeltsch's speech. From Gertrud von le Fort's observations, we may conclude that the transcript is not so much a complete stenographic report as an accurate single-track abstraction from Troeltsch's multi-track discourse, in which he conveyed the same idea in a rich variety of formulations.

An adequate appraisal of the *Glaubenslehre* would certainly be obliged to meet in detail the various criticisms that have been advanced against Troeltsch's theology. (We should, indeed, not overlook criticisms from the left, so to say, any more than those from the right.)[42] For the moment, however, I do not wish to confront such favourite problems as historical relativism and historical knowledge of Jesus (though both are important, and I have addressed myself to them elsewhere).[43] Rather, I have selected three other themes from the *Glaubenslehre* which seem to have the merit of illustrating both the promise and the embarrassment of a historical theology. I need make no claims about their importance or unimportance in Troeltsch's total career. Even were it true (which I doubt) that the *Glaubenslehre* represents only a minor deviation in Troeltsch's own development, it would not necessarily follow that it had only a minor importance for the development of dogmatic theology.[44] On the contrary, particularly for those of us who still consider Schleiermacher the 'great master' of modern dogmatics, the *Glaubenslehre* of Troeltsch is a fascinating and significant work, important both for the history of theology and for the construction of a viable theological method at the present time. My three themes are all methodologically oriented; and, although they could be documented from others of Troeltsch's writings, I confine myself chiefly to his treatment of them in the *Glaubenslehre* and the closely related articles in *Die Religion in Geschichte und Gegenwart.* It will be clear that, for each theme, I have further

[42] For instance, the six objections of the 'modern world', listed by Troeltsch himself, against connecting faith and history: 'Glaube und Geschichte', cols. 1450–2.

[43] B. A. Gerrish, 'Theology and the Historical Consciousness', *McCormick Quarterly*, XXI, no. 2 (Jan. 1968), 198–213; 'Jesus, Myth, and History: Troeltsch's Stand in the "Christ-Myth" Debate', *Journal of Religion*, 55 (January 1975), 13–35.

[44] *Pace* Dyson, 'History in the Philosophy and Theology of Ernst Troeltsch', p. 290.

confined myself to the preliminary historical task of entering sympathetically into Troeltsch's own world of thought, so that the questions I raise are presented as internal to his own system. (Naturally, the further, systematic or constructive task would call for the presentation of another standpoint in the vastly different idiom of the present day.) The themes have to do, respectively, with religious sensibility, the uses of the past, and the reality of history; or, we may say, with the materials, the method, and the premiss of a historical theology.

II

The advantage of the new dogmatics, in Troeltsch's eyes, is that it enables the theologian to address himself to the feelings and instincts of his own age, appropriating the strength and the blessing of the past without making history a burden to be borne. The essence of Christianity for any age is always a 'synthesis', which brings together the present situation and the historical resources. But what are the particular needs of the present which Troeltsch himself is anxious to address? He confesses that his dogmatics is not designed for missionary expansion, which can safely be left to the conservatives, but rather for the needs of the old Christianity, which finds itself in a severe internal crisis. How is religious clarity to be gained amid the perplexity of modern life? Every age has its peculiar problem. For ours, the problem is posed by the depersonalisation of self and society. It arises from diverse changes which belong to the respective domains of historical thinking, natural science, and sociology. But it is, at bottom, one problem: how to regain possession of the soul. 'We do not ask, How do I get a gracious God? We ask rather, How do I again find the soul and love?' A genuinely free dogmatics has the opportunity to articulate the question of the present, and not to discourse laboriously about dogmas inherited from an alien past. And yet it is free to appropriate the past in a manner the old dogmatics could never have allowed.[45]

Modernity thus enters into dogmatics as one of its major

[45] 'Dogmatics', pp. 13, 19 [*GS* II, 511, 517–23]. Note that the positive advantages of the new theology, which in the German [*GS* II, 519–23) follow the answers to objections, do not appear in the English.

coefficients. And this is not merely a matter of dealing externally with modern ideas, but of consciously coming to terms with influences which have flowed in upon us quietly and unobtrusively [*Gl.*, pp. 30–2] and which *must* materially affect a theology of consciousness.[46] The religious consciousness of the present is cumulatively conditioned by history [*Gl.*, p. 20], even though it is the connection with the prophets, Jesus, and the bible that remains determinative.[47] And it is not revelation itself which is the immediate object of theology, but the expression of it in forms which are always shaped by the spirit of the time [*Gl.*, pp. 42–3, 51].

Troeltsch's own profound grasp on the change in religious sensibility is nowhere more strikingly displayed than in his frequent meditations on the post-Copernican world-picture. This is not, by any means, to pass out of history into natural science, since it is the movement of history which demands the adjustment in the first place and the problem of the modern scientific world-picture is in part its meaning for man's historicity. The sun and the stars are no longer there just for us to set our watches by. The sense of intimacy with God has vanished, and we perceive ourselves as day-flies or as mere toys in the immensity of the universe [*Gl.*, pp. 33, 177]. We need only to pass through the prehistoric collection of a museum, with its endless rows of relics from time immemorial, and the question must force itself upon us whether our own civilisation, too, will have its day, perhaps sinking back into a new ice-age. 'A massive impression of the nothingness of all historical existence (*der Nichtigkeit alles geschichtlichen Seins*) comes over us at such possibilities' [*Gl.*, p. 94]. 'What will the

---

[46] Commenting on Schleiermacher's theological method, Troeltsch observes that the treasure of inherited ideas must be saturated with the inner unity of the religious sentiment (*Gesinnung*) which fills the present moment: 'Schleiermacher und die Kirche', p. 27. In *KD*, at any rate, Schleiermacher speaks more narrowly of the prevailing *philosophy* as the coefficient (along with the utterances of primitive Christianity) in the articulation of the religious consciousness: see pars. 166–7, 177–82 (with the parallels in the first ed.).

[47] 'Dogmatik', cols. 108–9: note the phrase 'substantial [and not merely formal] transformations of the religious and ethical sensibility (*Empfindens*)'. In the *Gl.* Troeltsch distinguishes three (or perhaps four) theological norms: beside bible and tradition he places 'modern life'. But all of these are 'synthesised' only in personal experience, which is thus the 'decisive source and authority' [*Gl.*, p. 24].

end be? Presumably, a waning of solar energy and, with it, ever-increasing difficulties of nutriment, until finally the last man roasts the last potato on the last ember' [*Gl.*, p. 292].

We obviously cannot lock out the consequences of a Copernican system. We may not shrink from the immensity of the All, in which we, together with our whole solar system, are swept upon paths which defy thought. In view of the uniformity of the entire universe opened up by spectral analysis, the geocentric and anthropocentric view of things must vanish. Man has to adapt himself to no longer being able to establish a physical centre of the universe. But from here there arise new, quite definite tinges of the religious feeling. The world of unspeakable grandeur which stands before us is another one than that of the bible's seven-day work. A current of immense majesty streams into our religious feeling from this world that has been extended into infinity. We know that the formation of our earth arose by detachment from another heavenly body, and our entire organic life on this earth seems, in comparison to the duration of the world, like breath on cold window panes, which disappears the next moment. But what the world is without organic life, we do not know. At a certain point we emerged from the development, at a certain point we will disappear again. More science does not say. As the beginning was without us, so will the end also be without us. Transferred to religion, this insight means: the end is not that of the Apocalypse [*Gl.*, p. 64].

A historical theology, we may say, is a theology of man's historicity – his confinement within the 'nothingness of historical existence'. Troeltsch found the new sensibility crushing, but not paralysing, since he grasped it (characteristically) as a task. It sets before *Glaubenslehre* the distinctive form of its present assignment. Negatively, it requires surrender of the churchly doctrine of redemption, since the old divine interventionism cannot be harmonised with the immensity of the world-process or the unbroken continuity of its working.[48] Positively, it opens up once more the duty of rethinking the christian heritage. We do not become sceptics or materialists, but cling all the more firmly to the revelation of God which we possess in our hearts. We must transfer the old ivy-stock to the new wall [*Gl.*, pp. 64–5]. A part of what this means – not the whole of it[49] – is that the distinctive christian message for the

[48] See, e.g. 'Erlösung, II: Dogmatisch', *RGG* II, 484; 'Theodizee, II: Systematisch', *RGG* v, 1188–9.

[49] It also means rethinking the doctrine of God [*Gl.* pt II, ch. 1] and speculating on the probability that the universe must have other goals than the redemption of man [*Gl.*, pp. 179–80, 255–6].

day is shaped by the new question. And Troeltsch boldly – perhaps even defiantly – affirms that the God of the whole, whom none can name, is also the God who knows me in all my littleness and chooses to deal personally with me [*Gl.*, pp. 274–5]. Nothing falls from the hand of God. I am summoned to grow into his divine life, and so to overcome the threat of infinity. Troeltsch does not argue the point; he holds it out as an affirmation of faith against the sole alternative of being crushed [*Gl.*, p. 250]. He was deeply aware of the elements of immensity, mystery, terror in the idea of God [*Gl.*, p. 161]. Religious awe before the vastness of the cosmos does indeed belong to the religious sensibility, and Troeltsch can pronounce the somewhat melancholy aphorism, 'The *Whole* is our fate' [*Gl.*, p. 259]. But faith in the immediate activity of the living God is no less a datum of the religious sensibility. Though a distinctive trait of theistic faith, it obtrudes itself even into the less congenial worlds of Stoicism, neo-Platonism, and Buddhism [*Gl.*, p. 269].

It could well be argued that Troeltsch here reverses the movement of pauline Christianity from transience to sin as the cardinal religious problem.[50] But his solution lay, not so much in a quantitative extension of human life, as in the affirmation of its worth despite transience; and he expressly distinguishes the modern problem, not only from the Reformation's concern with legalism, but also from antiquity's preoccupation with death. Our problem is broader: it concerns the worth of the soul [*Gl.*, pp. 285ff.] – despite transience, yes, but also despite cosmic anxiety and the mechanisation of modern life [*Gl.*, pp. 177, 298]. Here, however, there is a difficulty in Troeltsch's theology. It is not merely that the infinite value of the soul appears to be professed as a mere fideistic affirmation; nor that the value of the soul admittedly remains unrealised for the masses of mankind.[51] The diffi-

---

[50] On the contrast between the pauline and hellenistic ideas of salvation, see Wilhelm Bousset, *Kyrios Christos: Geschichte des Christusglaubens von den Anfängen des Christentums bis Irenaeus*, 3rd ed., unaltered reprint of the 2nd ed. (Forschungen zur Religion und Literatur des alten und neuen Testaments, no. 21 [n.s. no. 4], Vandenhoeck & Ruprecht: Göttingen, 1926), p. 140.

[51] With the discussion of the particularity of divine love in *Gl.*, pp. 215ff., cf. the arts on 'Theodizee', v, 1186–92 *RGG* and 'Prädestination, iii: Dogmatisch', *RGG* iv, 1706–12.

culty, rather, is that the gospel of the soul's infinite worth is jeopardised by an ambiguity in Troeltsch's doctrine of God and a corresponding indecision in his eschatology.[52]

The initial line Troeltsch draws between theism and pantheism is, in the course of his presentation, virtually erased. The distinction is strongly affirmed in principle: the only live religious options are christian theism and buddhist monism, and the issue at stake is the value of personality. Only the theistic conception of God is capable of supporting personal worth and moral activity [*Gl.*, pp. 73–6, 141–2, 169–70, 184–5, 196–7, 357–9]. Schleiermacher is sharply criticised because, having rightly stated the choice in principle,[53] he was unable in practice to resist Spinozist monism [*Gl.*, pp. 68–9, 130]. For his part, Troeltsch is willing to pursue the supposed advantage of theism over monism even to the point of affirming that the development of finite persons has its meaning also for the life of God. The redemption of man is an enrichment of the divine being – indeed, it is God's redemption of himself [*Gl.*, pp. 218–19, 236–8, 344]. And yet one must ask: Was Troeltsch any more successful than Schleiermacher in affirming ethical theism in practice as well as in principle? Though he warns us that it is not possible to be a Spinozist with the head and a theist with the heart [*Gl.*, p. 67], he apparently is tempted to try the impossible himself.

It is with respect to the ultimate destiny of the finite person that Troeltsch finds himself speaking an appreciative word for pantheism. He can both affirm the infinite worth of the soul and yet entertain the probability that the epic of human freedom will end in free surrender of selfhood to God. Certainly, the pantheistic notion of God provides the more natural counterpart to the dissolution of finite consciousness, whereas theistic hopes are for perfected communion of the finite spirit with the Spirit of God [*Gl.*, p. 327]. The relative freedom of man to make the world's purpose, which is the will of God, his own moral task is antipantheistic. It invites an eschatology of continued moral growth, in communion with God, beyond the grave [*Gl.*, pp. 190–1, 298–300, 321, 362–3,

---

[52] Besides the relevant passages in *Gl.*, see the encyclopaedia art., 'Eschatologie, IV: Dogmatisch', *RGG* II, 622–32; cf. 'Erlösung', cols. 482–3.
[53] 'Dogmatics', pp. 6–7 [*GS* II, 505–6].

380].[54] But it cannot go on forever [*Gl.*, p. 382]! The thought
that it might, Troeltsch finds horrifying.[55] Hence, though
declining to speculate overmuch on the content of the
eschatological symbols, he finds himself bound to speak of a
last stage, at which the finite self is 'consumed', 'returns to
God', 'sinks down into the divine life', 'dies from the final
perfection of blessedness'.[56] Freedom thus attains its goal in
the act of total surrender to God, even, it may be, to the point of
dissolution of the separate consciousness [*Gl.*, p. 297]. And so
we stand simultaneously before the elements of truth in theism
and in pantheism, even if we cannot combine them in a unified
conception of God; and a measure of right is to be granted to
pantheistic feeling [*Gl.*, p. 220]. Troeltsch concludes: 'For the
practice of the present, we hold on to theism; and only in the
sequel does the pantheistic notion emerge' [*Gl.*, p. 239].

Plainly, there is a problem in this seemingly happy solution.
Is it any safer to be a theist in your ethics and a pantheist in
your eschatology than to be a Spinozist with your head and a
theist with your heart? Is the affirmation of the person and its
worth a kind of interim-ethic (*zwischen Grundlage und Ziel* [cf.
Gl., p. 297]), pending the return of the creation into the
Creator?[57] And if, as Troeltsch suggests, the fate of the wicked
is plausibly thought of as a dissolution of the self [*Gl.*, p. 210],
are 'Heaven' and 'Hell' diverse names for the same destination? Well, we should not chide Troeltsch if he could give no
clear answer to the Buddha's question: Where does the flame
go when it goes out? The point, rather, is that Troeltsch's

---

[54] The buddhist doctrine of reincarnation, though hard to conceive, is found
attractive by Troeltsch because, like the catholic doctrine of purgatory, it
holds out the hope of further growth and purification [*Gl.*, pp. 216, 231, 382].
Occasionally, there are also hints of a qualitative eternity – present in every
historical moment, but mythically represented as lying in the future [*Gl.*, pp.
321, 325].

[55] 'Eschatologie', col. 630.

[56] *Ibid.* cols. 627, 628, 630.

[57] Troeltsch makes explicit use of the neo-Platonic theme of emanation and
return, though it cannot denote a merely natural process [*Gl.*, pp. 364, 381].
But even the surrender of the self, in his eschatology, retains its roots in the
personal variety of mysticism: the self does not sink down into a lifeless
cosmos, but into God and along with others [*Gl.*, pp. 362–3]. Although the
final moment is inconceivable, high points of religious experience afford a
foretaste: 'The mysticism of love, which lets the self-will sink into the
Universal Will, is the final word' [*Gl.*, p. 382].

theology was a theology of historicity, of human finitude and temporality. He affirmed this to the very end, to eschatology as the final chapter of *Glaubenslehre*, even though it could well be said to have challenged the very heart of his gospel and not merely to have posed its central problem. Adjustment to the modern world-view, of which natural science and historical thinking are the main arbiters, changes the religious sensibility that produces the materials of dogmatics. Against modern man's sense of his own temporality – his sense of the 'nothingness of all historical existence' – Troeltsch sets his revisionist gospel of the infinite value of the soul. It is the methodological move that chiefly concerns us, for something like it must surely be risked by any modern theology whatever. Still, the intrinsic defiance of Troeltsch's own execution of the move is made even more problematic by the ambiguity in his eschatology, in which pantheistic piety, ruled out initially and in principle, reasserts itself. And, whether or not Troeltsch's eschatology is correct, it obviously poses yet another methodological problem: the nature of dogmatic norms.

III

Naturally, Troeltsch's flirtation with monistic eschatology was pointed out disapprovingly as a betrayal of christian thought. Normally sympathetic, R. S. Sleigh protested: 'It is bad enough to lose God in man, as Hegel did, or tended to do [!], but it is worse to lose man in God.'[58] Within the framework of Troeltsch's own attitude towards tradition, however, it is peculiarly difficult to hold him accountable. The method of dogmatics, like its material, is historicised; and this means a radical rethinking of the old problem of scripture and tradition. The tradition acquires a new status which it could not have had for protestant orthodoxy. And yet the turn to christian history cannot furnish conveniently fixed points of reference such as the old orthodoxy had (or thought it had) in scripture. Once again, though in a quite different manner, the historical perspective is both liberating and disquieting.

A favourite canard during the heyday of neo-orthodoxy was that protestant liberalism lacked theological norms and there-

---

[58] *The Sufficiency of Christianity* (James Clarke: London [1923]), p. 228.

fore could do little more than underwrite existing social values. It might well be supposed that Troeltsch's insistence on adaptation to modernity formalises just this error. In actual fact, however, he constantly reaffirms the theologian's duty to test the spirit of the times. A distinction has to be drawn between the latest novelty and 'the total intellectual structure which shaped the last two centuries'. Coming to terms with the spirit of the times cannot mean simply taking over everything that is modern. Polemic is one way of confronting the modern world. True, it would be futile to repudiate the settled habits of thought which constitute the modern, as distinct from the ancient and medieval, world-view and which do in actual fact shape the consciousness of us all [*Gl.*, pp. 18–19, 22–3]. But the attunement of religious sensibility to the new world-picture cannot mean endorsing the petty little wishes of the bourgeoisie [*Gl.*, pp. 145–6, 150]. Although, then, Troeltsch recommends adjustment as the only feasible way to affirm Christianity in the modern world,[59] he still insists on an inner discontinuity between cultural goals and the religion of redemption. The possibility of the higher life is opened to mankind as revelation and gift, which call for decision and a break with man's natural limits [*Gl.*, pp. 332–3]. Troeltsch has no doctrine of inevitable progress. 'Development', he admits, is the magic word of the day, but by it untold mischief is done. Though in fact a quasi-religious belief, it is speciously clothed with the respectabililty of a natural law. The truth is that Nature knows no inevitable progress, but only a never-ending struggle; and it is just as easily possible that we should one day clamber up the trees again from which we came down [*Gl.*, 323–4].

If, then, the theologian has the means for judging, and not merely endorsing, the spirit of the times, whence does he derive them? Certainly not from his bible alone. The sufficiency of scripture, which had served as a fundamental principle of the old dogmatics, is firmly rejected. The New Testament, too, is a historical, time-bound entity, severely limited by its eschatological expectations, its demonology, and its anthropomorphic view of God. Not even Jesus can provide the sole religious norm. Rather, bible and Jesus alike must be

[59] 'Weiterentwickelung', col. 1885.

viewed in the light of their historical effects over two millennia of the church's history [*Gl.*, pp. 11–13, 27–8].[60] The gospel of Jesus is not the exclusive norm, but the primitive and seminal form of christian life. Subsequent church history is the development of this life, and its principal carriers have been outstanding personalities like Augustine and the protestant Reformers.

If one seeks a common name for all this, what commends itself for this end is the name coined in catholic dogmatics: 'tradition'. Only, this tradition is not a legal authority, but a body of material to be worked through in freedom (*ein frei durchzuarbeitender Stoff*). Herein lies the difference between the protestant conception of tradition and the catholic; and the modern concept of development has pushed this version of tradition into the foreground, whereas it is a concept lacking in the Reformers, who thought to refer exclusively to the bible... [*Gl.*, pp. 21–2]. Catholicism, thinking more practically and realistically than we, recognizes in the gospel only the germ out of which everything else has taken shape. The development of Christianity is not a matter of deviations (*Entfremdungen*), but of growth (*Gewordenes*) [*Gl.*, p. 28].

It hardly needs to be stressed that this represents a remarkable break with the old protestant dogmatics (though it is not exactly 'catholicising', either). Dogmatics is shaped by the history of Christianity, no longer by the bible alone. And history, so far from being an instrument of defence for a system which itself transcends history, now enters constitutively into the dogmatic task. Such a 'constitutive historicism' (if we may venture the phrase) is alien both to the old orthodox dogmatics and to the newer dogmatics of neo-orthodoxy, whose leader found merely historical questions 'frightfully indifferent' (*schrecklich gleichgültig*).[61] It is also alien to any individualistic 'theology of the present moment' which presumes itself liberated from the past. For Troeltsch, it is not individual autonomy, but history – as the common work of entire generations – that has first word. A strong and vital faith comes out of history as a revelation which initially leaves little

[60] Cf. 'Dogmatics', pp. 11–13, 20–1, [*GS* II, 510–12, 518–19].
[61] Karl Barth, letter to Thurneysen (1st Jan. 1916), in *Antwort: Karl Barth zum siebzigsten Geburtstag* (Evangelischer Verlag: Zollikon-Zürich, 1956), p. 845. He has always conceived of criticism, Barth explains, as a means of liberation from tradition, not as constitutive of a new, liberal tradition (*ibid.* p. 846).

room for a man's own inventiveness (*Produktion*). Autonomy is not the starting-point, but the highpoint of religious growth; and even from here there is need to turn back repeatedly to the historical resources which awaken and reassure faith. Autonomous insight is not so much productive of spiritual content as it is the mode of its appropriation.[62]

All of which may be very well said. But if one asks less for inspiration and strength than for dogmatic norms, it is obvious that the appeal to 'tradition' has its difficulties. Hard enough if we confine ourselves to the complexities of the New Testament! What guidance can possibly be had from an additional two millennia of church history? The old, secure check-points of pauline theology and ecclesiastical creeds dissolve into a forbidding torrent of historical data.[63] Troeltsch admits that the 'body of material to be worked through in freedom' is indeed 'an enormous one' [*Gl.*, p. 29]. So complex and diverse is it, that it is extraordinarily hard to trace the continuity through the centuries or even to be sure that it is ultimately one thing which is the subject of the endless mutations. Certainly, neither transformations nor reformations, even when they sacrifice much of the inherited symbolism, necessarily break the continuity. They may even make it clearer.[64] But this cannot be asserted as a universal rule. Troeltsch thinks that there is work here for church historians and historians of dogma, who must locate the continuity in christian history [*Gl.*, p. 48]. Now, he does affirm that we can 'set our compass' by Jesus and Paul [*ibid.*]; and, although he dignifies the entire history of Christianity with the name 'revelation', he does assign a certain priority to the primitive revelation.[65] But, when

---

[62] 'Glaube und Geschichte', cols. 1452–5.

[63] Hence one of the four 'needs' for a dogmatics is simply to order and reduce the luxuriant growth of *Glaubensvorstellungen* [*Gl.*, pp. 45–6, 55]. The other needs are for drawing out the logical unity of the religious concepts, establishing their relationship with non-religious knowledge, and formulating them suitably for practical use.

[64] 'Prinzip', col. 1844; cf. 'Weiterentwickelung', cols. 1881–3.

[65] The personality and proclamation of Jesus are the *eigentlich klassische Quelle* [*Gl.*, p. 20]. Again, the bible has decisive normative rank because it offers the picture of Jesus and the means for understanding it [*Gl.*, p. 21]. These affirmations must therefore qualify Troeltsch's repeated claim that the christian revelation is to be found in 'the totality of Christianity's historical manifestation': 'Dogmatik', col. 108; cf. *Gl.*, pp. 39–40 and the art. 'Offenbarung, III: Dogmatisch', *RGG* IV, 918–22, esp. col. 921. However, two

all is said and done, the attempt to extract dogmatic insight from the convolutions of tradition drives inexorably to the conclusion that pure historical science has its limits. Historiography is not dogmatics. The theologian is summoned, in the end, not just to *write* history, but to *make* history. Concern with the past thus acquires for Troeltsch what may appropriately be called a strongly 'ethical' character: it achieves its finality in a deed to be done.

It is the problem of the 'essence of Christianity' or the 'christian principle' which now confronts us. But I am concerned with it only so far as to make a methodological point. It is here that the limits of history (*qua* historical method) are most clearly seen and most frankly acknowledged – here that *Glaubenslehre* ceases to be a strictly demonstrative science and calls for personal impression, the taking of a stand, the risk of decison [*Gl.*, p. 14].[66] In general, no doubt, progress of the christian principle beyond the original biblical form, admits of periodisation, and Troeltsch's penetrating historical sketches of the several concepts implicit in the principle generally move from the primitive stage, through the catholic and 'old protestant', to the 'new protestant' stage. And it is the 'new protestant' form of the christian principle which is presupposed in present-day *Glaubenslehre* [*Gl.*, pp. 2–3]. Pattern in the story is by no means lacking.[67] Nonetheless, the adoption of the principle (in any form) and the determination of its content for the present are results of a decision. The synthesis of past

further points must be noted if the place of scripture in Troeltsch's *Bewußtseinstheologie* is to be correctly stated. (1) The bible 'receives its due', not directly, as though it were a formal dogmatic norm, but indirectly: because it influences the present-day christian life which furnishes the immediate data of dogmatics [*Gl.*, p. 3]. (2) The essence or principle of Christianity, derived only in part from the biblical sources, itself serves as the foundation of the third, most proper task of dogmatics; hence it tends, in practice, to occupy the place held in the old dogmatics by scriptural authority. See *Gl.*, p. 2; 'Dogmatics', pp. 12 and 20 [*GS* II, 511, 519]; 'Prinzip', col. 1846.

[66] Troeltsch adds, though without argument, that 'for Schleiermacher, too, *Glaubenslehre* meant a decision'.

[67] And it contributes materially to the constructive task, *pace* Seeberg [*Deutsche Literaturzeitung*, XLVII, no. 43 (23 Oct. 1926), col. 2130], who suspected that Troeltsch's fondness for historical surveys betrayed a deficiency of systematic talent. The constitutive role of *Dogmengeschichte* in Troeltsch's *Gl.* makes his dogmatics even more markedly a 'historical theology' than Schleiermacher's and brings him somewhat closer to the method of F. C. Baur.

and present occurs in personal religious experience, and it therefore remains ineradicably personal and individual. The selection and shading of the historical materials can never be strictly demonstrated. *Glaubenslehre* therefore remains a religious confession;[68] and the determination of what is essential in the changing religious forms is an ever-new task, in which each must determine the divine for himself, as it has attested itself to him.[69]

'Certainly', Troeltsch remarks in one place, 'we feed on the tradition; but this tradition would be dead if the production of those who feed on it did not keep it alive' [*Gl.*, pp. 38–9]. The remark tersely conveys the strength of his idea of tradition. But no one will have any difficulty in pointing out its weaknesses. Initially invited to the grandiose historical task of establishing the essence of Christianity from its total development [*Gl.*, p. 13], we are finally summoned to introspection of our own religious experience. The obvious perils of such a method are perhaps most painfully betrayed in Troeltsch's recommendation that we should seek in the bible such texts as knock at the door of our own soul [*Gl.*, p. 27]. Naturally, one would not object to a devotional exercise of this sort did not one suspect that it is continuous with the theological method of Troeltsch. But, in fairness to him, his theology should be approached rather from the other side, on which it is continuous with *historical* method. The quest for essence, he insists, is simply a common enough exercise of modern historical thinking, which must reduce a complex of endlessly manifold phenomena to a central formula. The task can only be accomplished through utter surrender to the historical data. If a certain subjectivity is also requisite, Troeltsch characterises it as *historical* intuition: that is, as something indispensable to the equipment of a historian. Hence the very method of history in dealing with the past already hovers on the margin of the axiological judgments by which the future is shaped. Nor can there be any question of bringing to the data a fixed and

---

[68] 'Glaube und Geschichte', col. 1456.
[69] 'Offenbarung', cols. 921–2. The inescapability of individual decision is reaffirmed with respect to specific dogmatic issues: e.g., the particularity of grace [*Gl.*, pp. 228, 231] and the choice of one religion rather than another [*Gl.*, p. 159].

ready-made standard, for the standard must itself emerge in the course of the enquiry [*Gl.*, p. 71].[70]

It would, I suppose, be possible to retort that even cultivated taste is still taste, nothing more. But I myself am inclined to locate the problems less in subjectivity as such, more in Troeltsch's apparent neglect (in this context, at least) of intersubjectivity. He is more eager to justify individual variety – by pointing out that variety has always been there in christian history [*Gl.*, pp. 331, 354] – than to recall that the theologian does his work along with others. It may be true that the historical task culminates in a judgment that transcends history, an act which is simultaneously the coronation and the abdication of historical theology.[71] But even when he moves beyond historical science, the theologian is not on his own. We must grant Troeltsch's point that Schleiermacher's theology of consciousness is infinitely more difficult today, when the unified national or territorial communions have dissolved still further into pluralism [*Gl.*, pp. 14–16]. We may further agree that the problem of theological diversity is not to be resolved by doing away with professors of theology [*Gl.*, p. 17]. We may agree, finally, that dogmatics nowadays can only claim advisory, rather than coercive, status.[72] And yet, when all of that is granted, we may still wish that Troeltsch had carried his profound sense of the social character of *religion* into a more explicit recognition of the corporate character of *theology* (as of any other academic discipline). His most characteristic sentiment on the subject is that the collective consciousness will take care of itself, automatically controlling the individual judgment and restraining the proliferation·of divergent views.[73]

---

[70] See further 'Prinzip', cols. 1842–4 (where Troeltsch uses the terms 'intuition', 'divination', 'depth and refinement of perception'); 'Dogmatics', pp. 17–19 [*GS* II, 516–17]; 'Logos und Mythos', pp. 820–1. The locus classicus, of course, is the essay, 'Was heißt "Wesen des Christentums"?' (1903 [*GS* II, 386–451]), in which Troeltsch argues that the task of *Wesensbestimmung*, though it rests upon history, must pass beyond the historical task as normally conceived (p. 398). The question is not what the essence *was* (even in the teaching of Jesus), but what it *is* for us (p. 420) – indeed, what it *is to be* (pp. 424, 429).

[71] The metaphor is suggested by one of Troeltsch's own phrases: 'Was heißt "Wesen des Christentums"?', p. 433.

[72] 'Dogmatik', col. 109.

[73] 'Offenbarung', col. 922. In response to the charge of subjectivism, Troeltsch *could*, on occasion, provide what the *Glaubenslehre* appears to lack: a strong

His position would, I think, have been strengthened – and even made more consistent with its own principles – had he argued that dogmatics is a collective *task*. But in the lectures on *Glaubenslehre*, perhaps for autobiographical reasons, he appears to have spoken of it as essentially an *individual* task.

IV

'Nowhere does autonomy produce the contents of our modern thought and life. Everywhere they rest, for the most part, on tradition and authorities...In religious thought, this is simply the case in greater degree.'[74] It would be hard to think of a sentiment that more perfectly summed up the major premiss of Troeltsch's programme. Indeed, it conveys a psychological trait as much as a logical premiss – a pervasive attitude, a frame of mind, not just the beginning-point of an argument. It embodies, we may say, the protest of the 'romantic' against the spirit of enlightenment. In theology, it requires that we begin, not by pretending we know nothing, in order to see what we can prove on this unpromising supposition; but rather by receiving the heritage of faith in all its richness and asking what it all means. Faith goes before *Glaubenslehre*, whose task it is to order the luxuriant growth of faith – its images and ideas – into a systematic whole. Though not able to qualify as an exact science, *Glaubenslehre* is a 'scientific treatment and regulation of faith'. As such, it must be content to take faith for what it is, not trying to transform it into scientific and rational knowing. Even at the end of the theological task, faith retains a practical and symbolic character [*Gl.*, p. 46]. It is faith, we may say, *as a reality of history* that is the primary datum for a theology of consciousness.

'We come to the ever-repeated new birth', so Troeltsch maintains, 'through the mediation of history' [*Gl.*, p. 79]. This, in large part, is the meaning of divine 'grace'. Knowledge of God is not simply the result of reflection on the contents of consciousness, but rather something acquired historically (*ein Erwerb der Geschichte*). It comes to the individual only through

plea for the dual corporate context of dogmatics in both academy and church. See esp. 'Was heißt "Wesen des Christentums"?', pp. 436–9.
[74] 'Glaube und Geschichte', col. 1452.

history, and therefore it lays hold upon him as a gift of God, a power that grasps and transforms him. True, even as a 'power of history' (*geschichtliche Macht*), it is not the result of an immanent dialectic, but is always a new and creative revelation of God [*Gl.*, pp. 338–9]. Nonetheless, the divine activity is historically mediated, so that grace – the 'gift-character' of redemption – is a thoroughly historical idea. Indeed, it coincides with the idea of the church.

Christian redemption does not spring from religious autonomy. We have received it from history. This does not only mean looking to the person of Jesus as transmitted in history, the one in whose name we take heart towards God. It also means resorting to the pauline–johannine doctrine of spirit, by which the death of Jesus wins back its meaning for the idea of redemption. The death of Jesus is the overcoming of what was merely time-bound in his person. It is the great liberation of his spirit through suffering and death, and it makes possible a lively, continuous flow and an enduring contemporaneity from generation to generation. Hence redemption, in trust toward Jesus, is not turned backwards. It acquires its connection with history only because the community which is imbued with the spirit of Christ and which mediates redeeming faith to the individual soul has its origin in the historical figure of Jesus and inwardly regulates and strengthens itself from there [*Gl.*, pp. 360–1].

To receive redemption from history means to receive it through the christian community. It does not mean simply believing in a once-for-all saving deed, recalled by an effort of the memory. The significance of Jesus' death is that it transformed the individual historical manifestation into a continuing principle which adapts itself to time and circumstance and is the actual driving force of the christian community [*Gl.*, pp. 346–7]. It is precisely here that Troeltsch discovers the abiding truth of the idea of the 'church' as distinct from that of the 'sect'. The resources of grace are prevenient, antecedent to the individual, in that they are embodied in a historical organism (a *Lebenszusammenhang*) which proceeds from Jesus.[75] The concept of the church, then – the community centred upon the figure of Christ – is

---

[75] 'Kirche, III: Dogmatisch', *RGG* III, 1153. But this does not prevent Troeltsch from discarding the term 'church' because of its institutional and supernaturalist overtones (*ibid.* col. 1155).

one of the ways in which a connection is established between
faith and history [*Gl.*, pp. 81–2].

Now, the primacy of history over personal insight, of
collective over individual faith, is carried into theology as a
methodological principle. A *Glaubenslehre* takes Christianity in
its historical givenness. Just as the religious sense itself has
precedence over rational argumentation, so the phenomenology of faith has precedence over any theology of proofs. The
religious sense articulated by theology in its specifically christian form is, of course, submitted to 'scientific' scrutiny by
Troeltsch's philosophy of religion. But this is a far cry from the
old natural theologies which sought rational demonstrations
for the existence of God. Troeltsch is a 'romantic' theologian
(my term, not his), who starts from the vitality of the individual
forms of life; and he warns against the rationalistic theologies
which put religious sensibility at the mercy of their own frigid,
meagre, and colourless spirit.[76] Dogmatics, Part I, deals,
accordingly, with the realities of history. In other words, the
primacy of the historical determines the very structure of
dogmatics. Here is Troeltsch's version of a *christologischer
Ansatz*. He begins his dogmatics with an appraisal of christian
history, centred upon the personality of Jesus, since this
history is the vital power by which the christian relationship to
God is attained, strengthened, and anchored. The con-
tinuance of the peculiarly christian organism (or *Lebenswelt*)
depends on constantly bringing the historical into the present
[*Gl.*, pp. 72–3; cf. *Gl.*, p. 85].

The historical point of view enters, further, into the treatment of particular dogmatic themes as well as into the
structure of the whole. Here the two most obvious examples
are Troeltsch's handling of the trinitarian and christological
dogmas. The Trinity can only be interpreted, not immanently
as describing internal relations in the being of God, but
economically as claiming (more modestly) that the self-
disclosure of God in history has its ground in the divine being.
We have no need of the philosophical framework by which the

---

[76] 'Offenbarung', cols. 918–19. 'Romantic' is, of course, a word of many
meanings. The limited sense I intend should be clear. The debate over the
'new romanticism' of Stefan George and his circle focussed on other issues:
see, e.g., Friedrich Gogarten, 'Against Romantic Theology: A Chapter on
Faith', in *The Beginnings of Dialectic Theology*, pp. 317–27.

christian conception of God was once differentiated from neo-Platonic emanationism and made into an object of speculation [*Gl.*, pp. 122–4]. Similarly, Troeltsch detects in the ancient christology an understandable effort to determine the relationship of Jesus to God, and so to furnish a metaphysical grounding of his person. But he himself is content to keep close to the historical data and to inquire only after Jesus' meaning for faith. 'Lord' he finds an acceptable title, but he shows a marked reserve about 'Cosmic Redeemer' [*Gl.*, pp. 116–17].

Jesus was the possibility of redemption. The actual redeemer remains God...For us personally, this is how things stand: we keep to what is within reach. We place ourselves under the spell of this personality and acknowledge in him our mystical Head. Anyone who in good conscience is able to move beyond the psychological significance, should do so. He will then find it easier to make the connection with orthodoxy, since he will be able to speak (in a certain sense) of the 'deity' of Christ. With respect to metaphysical interpretations, we owe one another nothing except toleration [*Gl.*, p. 117].

Winsome though many of us may find such metaphysical reserve, it raises at least two problems. And as the historical-experiential starting-point is close to the heart of Troeltsch's theology, so the problems touch the heart of the revolt against him. In the first place, does it not appear as though the reality of man's religiousness has become a surrogate for the reality of God? And, in the second place, what becomes of the historical standpoint when the reality of man's religiousness itself suffers attrition?

The former problem reflects the difficulty which many have detected in the entire design of a *Glaubenslehre* as inherited from the 'great master'. Recall, for instance, Schleiermacher's serious posing of the question whether dogmatics could dispense with propositions about the attributes and operations of God, since the primary dogmatic propositions have to do with the religious affections.[77] Following in Schleiermacher's

---

[77] *Chr. Gl.* 30. See also *Über die Religion: Reden an die Gebildeten unter ihren Verächtern*, 5th ed., revised, ed. Rudolf Otto (Vandenhoeck & Ruprecht: Göttingen, 1926), pp. 77–82; *Schleiermachers Sendschreiben über seine Glaubenslehre an Lücke*, new ed., ed. Hermann Mulert (Studien zur Geschichte des neueren Protestantismus, no. 2, Alfred Töpelmann: Gießen, 1908), pp. 47–51.

footsteps, Troeltsch can bluntly assert that 'in *Glaubenslehre* we only acquire information about ourselves' [*Gl.*, p. 132]. And he refers approvingly to Rothe's judgment that we analyse, not God, but our own idea of God [*Gl.*, p. 131]. It is not difficult to see why Erich Seeberg detected in Troeltsch's theology a weakened interest in the question of truth. Amidst the display of ideas, Seeberg thought, reality and objectivity had fallen into the background; and he seems to have recognised that the alleged retreat from the question of truth had its roots, not only in Troeltsch's epistemology, but also in the historical mode of thought.[78] We could very well press the problem beyond the limits of the God-question and point out that, for Troeltsch, faith cannot give objective knowledge about history, nature, or the self either. Faith is a way of looking at the world, a stance towards the world, an interpretation of things [*Gl.*, pp. 52, 241–2]. With respect to history, it is interpretation of facts and cannot be supposed to establish facts [*Gl.*, p. 100].[79] With respect to the self, we are to understand, when faith speaks of the 'soul', not an object of cognition, but an inward attitude of a man towards himself, a seeing of himself in a new light [*Gl.*, pp. 282–3]. Should it be pointed out that faith does not always seem to *know* that this is what it is doing, and that it *appears* to be making factual assertions, Troeltsch would presumably reply by referring to his striking, if problematic, notion that the language of faith is the product of the fantasy or imagination and therefore hardly to be confused with scientific judgments.[80] This, too, he believed himself to have learned from Schleiermacher.[81]

It requires a much more thorough investigation than I can attempt here if a just verdict is to be obtained on this apparent subjectivism run riot. Suffice is to point out, for now, that Troeltsch no more than Schleiermacher *believed* himself

---

[78] *Deutsche Literaturzeitung*, XLVII, cols. 2130–1; cf. col. 2128.

[79] Part I of *Gl.* is, accordingly, not historiography, but 'religiously interpreted history': *Gl.*, pp. 78–9; cf. *Gl.*, pp. 85, 346, 348–9.

[80] Troeltsch affirms this notion both as a general principle (*Gl.*, pp. 44–5, 52–4) and with respect to particular christian symbols, such as creation (*Gl.*, p. 242) and the last things (*Gl.*, pp. 190–1, 299).

[81] Schleiermacher's theory of religious language, which Troeltsch characterises as 'agnostic', treats the inherited christian symbols as pictorial and pliable expressions of 'incommensurable experience': 'Rückblick', pp. 200–1, 207–8.

merely to have exchanged the reality of God for the actuality of faith. 'We have', he admits, 'only the ray which falls upon our own soul' [*Gl.*, p. 131]. But the admission is not to be taken for scepticism about the existence of the sun. Even though the craving for proof cannot be gratified, this cannot of itself prevent the conviction that our idea of God comes from God [*Gl.*, pp. 131, 133–4].[82] And although faith's language is supplied by the fantasy, faith is still 'cognitive' in the sense that its referent is a 'revelatory impulse' [*Gl.*, pp. 42–44]. A strong conviction of reality distinguishes faith from the free play of a merely artistic imagination. Against positivism, Troeltsch allows symbols a cognitive value, the measure of which is their adequacy to the religious experience and not their conformity to the model of objective knowing [*Gl.*, pp. 44–5]. In short, Troeltsch's essentially phenomenological method cannot get beyond the *conviction* of reality – plus a reasonable confidence in the normalcy of the religious consciousness. He grants the impossibility of taking a strictly scientific look 'from the other side'. But it simply is not the case that he surrenders the question of truth. Rather, as he expressly argues, the claim to religious truth calls for another apologetic, different in kind from the old natural theology [*Gl.*, pp. 134–5].[83] Apologetics, however, does not properly belong to *Glaubenslehre*, whose business is with 'positive, direct proclamation' [*Gl.*, pp. 135–6].

Even if we take this as a satisfactory answer to the first problem, can Troeltsch turn aside the force of the second? Troeltsch was himself a pioneer in the exploration of modern secularism, the drift of western culture away from its religious heritage. What, then, happens when the drive of our religious history seems to lose its force? One thinks of the remarkable letter the youthful Harnack wrote upon embarking on the study of theology. Even if Christianity were a mistake, he asks, would it not still be fascinating to trace the history of this mistake, of the earth-shaking events it has brought about, of the manner it has penetrated our entire civilisation?[84] The

---

[82] It is in this passage [*Gl.*, p. 132] that Troeltsch speaks of subjective experience as 'God-filled' (see p. 104, n. 14 above).

[83] See also 'Geschichte und Metaphysik', p. 28; 'Glaube, III: Dogmatisch', *RGG* II, 1441–5.

[84] Quoted by Agnes von Zahn-Harnack, *Adolf von Harnack* (Hans Bott: Berlin-Tempelhof, 1936), pp. 39–40.

invited reply may well be affirmative. But it would be only a call
for what Schleiermacher distinguished as 'historical theology
in the narrower sense or church history'.[85] And this was not
for Troeltsch! For him, history always meant a task, not mere
contemplation of the past. When Spengler's *Decline of the West*
was published, it was greeted with a chorus of approval by the
theological prophets of impending doom. Troeltsch remained
as loftily indifferent to the author's thesis as he was contemptu-
ous of his learning. It was, he announced, a matter of no
importance whether our civilisation was moving uphill or
downhill. All that mattered was the ethical task that history sets
before us.[86]

Troeltsch's *Glaubenslehre* is filled with a lively sense of the yet
unexhausted possibilities of Christianity for meeting the
summons of history. To describe this buoyant confidence was,
after all, the very circumspect use to which the Heidelberg
theologian put the old – and, surely, already inappropriate–expression 'the absoluteness of Christianity'.[87] But was
the confidence not lost in the deepening gloom of Troeltsch's
later years, the profound pessimism that has been documented
by his biographers? Well, it is surely possible to attach too much
weight to the moods of the moment, evoked (at least in part) by
non-theological factors. The supposed nemesis that visits
'historicism' has been far too freely seized upon as the

[85] *KD*, the title to Pt II.
[86] *GS* III: *Der Historismus und seine Probleme*, Bk 1: *Das logische Problem der Geschichtsphilosophie* (1922; reprint ed., Scientia Verlag: Aalen, 1961), ix.
[87] Besides the classic discussion in Troeltsch's *Die Absolutheit des Christentums und die Religionsgeschichte* (J. C. B. Mohr [Paul Siebeck]: Tübingen, 1902; 2nd ed., 1912), see also, from the Heidelberg period, 'Dogmatics', pp. 9–11, 21 [*GS* II, 508–9, 519]; 'Rückblick', pp. 224–5; *Die Bedeutung der Geschichtlichkeit Jesu*, pp. 47–51. In addition, Troeltsch constantly returns to the problem of absoluteness in the *RGG* articles: 'Kirche', col. 1155; 'Offenbarung', cols. 920–1; 'Theodizee', col. 1191; 'Weiterentwickelung', col. 1885; etc. Although the superiority of Christianity is the express presupposition for christian theology and for the existence of theological faculties ('Rückblick', p. 225), and although Troeltsch holds on to the notion of Christianity as 'high point' and even 'point of convergence' of mankind's religions, the 'absoluteness' means no more than best *for us* and *for now*. One can see why Barth, already before Troeltsch's last thoughts on the question, could represent him as holding only a 'temporary social significance' for the church pending the next ice-age. 'Unsettled Questions for Theology Today' (1920), *Theology and Church: Shorter Writings 1920–1928*, trans. Louise Pettibone Smith (SCM Press: London, 1962), pp. 60–1.

theological explanation of his supposed *aporia*. Paradoxically, perhaps, the Heidelberg theologian had already offered historicism as an *antidote* to despondency over the future of Christianity. In one of his keenest observations on the passage of history and its wealth of individual formations, he had indicated how flux and relativity afford reasonable security against the loss of faith in our religious estate. The relativising of all historical forms implies a relative truth in them all. And no conceivable new religious formation, even though it presupposed the decline of Christian-European culture, could make untrue what was once true, but would rather have to assimilate it.[88] This, too, is a principle of historical development. Perhaps it represents too modest a confidence to satisfy the critics. But is there sufficient reason to believe that nostalgia for something more was bound, in the end, to drive Troeltsch into despair?

[88] 'Glaube und Geschichte', cols. 1454–5.

Part III

5. Ernst Troeltsch and Christianity's essence

S. W. SYKES

The discussion of the problem of Christianity's essence has a much longer history than is generally recognised. In theological studies it is universally associated with the work of Adolf von Harnack; many know that Schleiermacher made the definition of the essence of religion and of Christianity one of his central themes; but of the antiquity and diversity of the discussion before 1800, opened up by a recent piece of research, relatively few are aware.[1] The discovery of this problem's antiquity may, it is hoped, do something to abate the discernible tendency in some theological circles to be impatient with the term 'essence'. This impatience has a variety of grounds. One may be the feeling that essence-definition was so much linked to the presuppositions of idealism that recent philosophical developments necessarily make it redundant. But from the history of the term it can be readily shown that men were speaking of the 'essence' of Christianity in wholly non-idealist contexts. Or it may be alleged that there have been too many and too divergent views of the essence of Christianity for a claim to have defined it to be intrinsically probable. This objection, however, loses much of its force if it can be shown that some idea of Christianity's essence is a necessary part of the constructive theologian's intellectual equipment. Variety here would accordingly be no more surprising than in systematic theology itself. But perhaps the most persistent and deep-rooted objection derives from the element of *hybris* implicit in claiming to have distilled Christianity in some sentence or formula. This is neatly referred to by Newman,

---

[1] See Hans Wagenhammer, *Das Wesen des Christentums, Eine begriffsge-schichtliche Untersuchung* (Mainz, 1973). Here the commonly-held view, which Troeltsch shared, that the quest for the essence of Christianity began with the Enlightenment is conclusively disproved.

commenting on the attempt to determine the 'leading idea' of Christianity – 'an ambitious essay as employed on a supernatural work, when, even as regards the visible creation and the inventions of man, such a task is beyond us'.[2] Nonetheless even Newman was prepared to acknowledge the convenience of a 'central idea' when it came to organising the content of christian doctrine, provided that no other aspect of revelation was obscured or excluded in so doing.

The attempt to express Christianity in brief compass is by no means the sole motive for the attempt to define the essence. Another reason may be found in the desire to recall Christianity to its heart or centre, and thereby implicitly to pass criticism on deviations. Many institutions, of course, have the capacity for conservative revolutions, in which members are recalled to a state more closely resembling that of their original time or their founder's intentions. The natural capacity of the christian church to undertake such revolutions is strongly reinforced by the very example of Jesus and Paul. Just as Jesus had criticised the Pharisees, so Paul criticised the legalists within Christianity itself; and from that time onwards, reform movements within the church, drawing upon resources internal to the christian tradition, have constantly referred both to Jesus and to Paul in justification of their attempts to purify the christian body from creeping conformity to non-christian standards.

It is with this long-standing tradition that those who sought to reform the church in the period of the Enlightenment connected. But here, of course, there was an important difference. In this context it became controversial whether the criteria for the criticism of the church were derived from within or without the christian tradition. Was the new programme of purification merely attempting to render Christianity more acceptable to educated persons in a culture rapidly becoming de-christianised? Or could it be represented in some way that Christianity was striving once again to become fundamentally truer to itself? The discussion of this question in the seventeenth, eighteenth and nineteenth centuries involved two crucial areas where ambiguity about the criteria of criticism was at its most acute. These were, the morality of

[2] *An Essay on the Development of Christian Doctrine* (New York, 1960), p. 59.

the traditional christian picture of salvation, and the understanding of the relationship of natural and supernatural.
Could it honestly be said that the christian tradition had
generated out of its own resources the criteria for the
upheavals which were taking place in these areas of its
intellectual life? Opinion at the time varied dramatically, and
the longer view of the matter which we are able to take can
scarcely be said to have settled the issue with any finality. On
the one hand it could be argued that many of the men who
offered the most searching critique were covertly or openly
agnostics or atheists; on the other hand it could be replied that
their education had been in christian cultures. On the one
hand, as in the thirteenth century, many of the newer ideas
had their origin in pre-christian, classical sources; on the other
their assimilability in the christian west depended on the
specific attitude to knowledge characteristic of, at the very
least, one long-standing aspect of the christian tradition.

The fascination for us of Troeltsch's work on the essence of
Christianity consists very largely in the fact that we can see the
different considerations in this still current problem struggling
for preeminence. Thus we observe the theme of the necessity
for brevity and simplicity, which he recognised, though by
instinct a complexifier, as a legitimate practical requirement in
christian life. Christianity, he conceded, was not originally a
system of thought appealing to the intelligentsia, but something simple and imaginative, appropriate to the non-
reflective mind. Moreover, no matter what developments this
religion might undergo, its liveliness always depended upon its
very naïveté – 'simplicity is manifestly superior to speculation,
for it produces a driving force and imparts a deep spiritual
experience without which no religious movement can live'
[*STCC*, p. 45]. But, in his own prescriptions for the appropriate apologetic stance of the church of his own day, he felt
unable to commend the simplicity of the traditional form of
Christianity, urging rather (in words echoing Schleiermacher's
self-understanding) 'a scientifically informed restoration of
the naïve outlook now raised to a higher level' [*AC*, p. 136].

Or again, as we consider his grappling with the problem
there is a manifest tension between his desire, as a historian, to
be objective and impartial in his presentation of those aspects

of the christian past to which the strongest objection had been taken at the Enlightenment, and his desire as a christian, to contribute to the urgent task of apologetics in his own day. This was a tension which grew, rather than diminished, with the years. In 1913, as he was editing for publication in the second volume of his collected works an early essay on the apologetic situation of Christianity ('Die christliche Weltanschauung und ihre Gegenströmungen', 1894), he admitted how increasingly problematic he found the task of demonstrating the truth and uniqueness of Christianity. He admitted further that his later work might give rise to the complaint that his interests had shifted from christian theology to general culture; but the validity of this objection depended, he felt, on one's conception of the range of responsibilities implicit in the task of christian theology. In any case he was prepared to defend the view that he had 'devoted the closest attention to the very stuff of christian living itself' in his attempt to 'immerse himself in its essence as impartially as possible', and offered as evidence his work on the history of protestantism and the social teachings of the christian churches [GS II, 227].

The purpose of this study is to unfold these diverse elements in Troeltsch's thought in their historical development. Their unravelling is a far from tidy process, and I have done nothing to schematise his work on this subject into periods. Troeltsch was a prolific and in some ways rather casual scholar, whom it is not difficult to catch in the act of contradicting himself. In such an exercise, however, there is very little point unless it can also be shown that the contradictions arise from a fundamental antinomy in the approach to the subject. Hence ultimately of far greater importance will be found to be Troeltsch's conception of his responsibilities as a philosopher of history, and the question it raises concerning the relation of that assiduously cultivated discipline in late nineteenth- and early twentieth-century Germany to the content of christian theology and the daily life of the christian church. From the problematical nature of his presuppositions on these points a great deal can be learnt, at which, however, it is possible to do no more than hint. The material forming the bulk of the essay presents the reader with the discipline of entering with Troeltsch into his various attempts to explore the structure of the problem, a discipline which, it will be found, has much to teach the christian theologian concerning the way in which assertions of what is specifically christian ought to function in christian discourse.

Troeltsch's principal contribution to the discussion of the essence of Christianity consisted in an article he published in six instalments in *Die christliche Welt*, the weekly christian magazine edited by Martin Rade in Marburg. The article was a further contribution to the debate aroused in Europe by the publication of Harnack's epoch-making lectures, *Das Wesen des Christentums*, which had already been extensively reviewed and discussed in that eminently liberal-minded periodical. Although the tone of the magazine was, broadly speaking, Ritschlian, it was Rade's policy to encourage theologians from the younger, history-of-religions circle – a policy with which the appearance of Troeltsch's article is consistent. Whether or not Troeltsch felt under any constraint to moderate his tone is impossible to say, but seems rather doubtful. What is, however, significant is that when he revised the article for publication in the second volume of his collected works [*GS* II, 386–451], he made in all about seventy alterations (excluding grammatical changes), without making any reference to them in the text. Thus the text printed in the collected works cannot be used, without careful checking, as evidence for Troeltsch's attitude to the quest for the essence of Christianity in 1903. The alterations vary very widely in substance. Some consist merely in the omission of references to his earlier, superseded essays, or in slight expansions or illustrations of original material; other alterations provide interesting examples of changes in Troeltsch's thinking on important matters; and most significant of all is the addition of nine pages of new material at the end of the essay. An attempt to elucidate the meaning of these changes will be made below.

But it is far from the case that the essay of 1903 provides us with the first literary evidence of Troeltsch's concern for this topic. The early apologetic essay of 1894, of which mention has already been made, contains numerous references to the 'essence', 'spirit', 'kernel', 'heart' and 'fundamental idea' of Christianity in contexts which treat the problem of the continuity of the christian *Weltanschauung* in the post-

Enlightenment world. This context is significant. For Troeltsch was convinced that a radical rupture separated the genuinely modern period of European culture and history from the pre-modern period; and that since what was achieved by the Enlightenment was a total alteration of modern thought in every department, nothing less than a total reconstruction of theology could meet the situation [GS II, 325–7].[3] The 'old supernaturalism' is referred to with a variety of opprobrious designations, such as 'superficial', 'anthropomorphic biblico-ecclesiastical', 'ancient naive biblico-ecclesiastical' and so forth, and those who continue to trade in such coin are contemptuously dismissed [GS II, 239, 247, 271 and 317].

Such over-emphatic judgments are not simply symptomatic of Troeltsch's youth (he was, it should be remembered, 29 years of age); they also reflect the insecure sense of superiority felt by a whole group of theologians who had taken over the Kantian and Hegelian analysis of the situation of the churches in the modern world. In the vivid phrase, reminiscent of the early correspondence of Hegel and Schelling, Troeltsch compares the disputes of standard learned theology to children's squabbles in a burning house [GS II, 238]. The theologians simply do not seem to be aware that Kant, Goethe, Hegel, the historical school and scientific theology have laid a completely new foundation [Aufklärung, RE II, 241]. Naturally enough, those who, like Troeltsch considered themselves alive to the new context of theology, faced the grave question whether an identifiably christian faith could persist despite the necessary radical changes. It was precisely to meet this situation that Troeltsch, as an apologist for neo-protestantism, availed himself of the already conventional 'essence of Christianity' argument. It is as easy, he maintained, to conceive of 'the spirit of Christianity' apart from its original historical form, as it was to conceive of the spirit of hellenistic culture without the trappings of Greek mythology [GS II, 239]. The following is typical of his position: 'The salvation of persons, united with the holy and loving will of God in a kingdom of love is the innermost

---

[3] Compare also the article on 'Aufklärung', Realencyclopädia für protestantische Theologie und Kirche (RE) II, 225–41, published in 1897; and 'Über historische und dogmatische Methode in der Theologie', published in 1898, and reprinted in GS II, 729–53, esp. p. 730.

kernel of the gospel. The special nature of Christianity is determined by the formulation of its purpose alone' [*GS* II, 261]. In the modern context, however, this fundamental characteristic of Christianity can only be presented with the help of idealism, the intellectual tradition with which Christianity was inextricably fused in its earliest centuries. In achieving this, two difficulties have to be met. In the first place, the new emphasis on development from within (as distinct from supernatural interference from without) tends towards an optimistic moralism, whereas Christianity is basically a religion of redemption. In the second place, a purely immanental notion of development has no room for a final and unsurpassable revelation, which is, Troeltsch asserts, 'of the innermost essence of the christian principle' [*GS* II, 301]. In other words, he recognised as the terms of the problem he had to solve, a particular view of what is integral to Christianity. The obvious question is why he chose to stick at these points. Was it anything other than sheer assertion that distinguished what he strives to preserve as 'fundamental dispositions' from what he is ready to dismiss as mere 'passing form'? These were the issues which Troeltsch was having to face before Harnack's contribution to the debate, but which the remarkable response to Harnack's lectures forced him to take up with greater urgency.

Before we consider Troeltsch's article in detail, a word must be said about his understanding of Harnack's theological position. Troeltsch, together with most commentators to the present, interpreted Harnack as a disciple of Albrecht Ritschl, in as much as both saw the essence of Christianity to lie in the idea of the kingdom of God [*GS* II, 403, in a passage added in 1913]. In this respect Harnack's work is set in contrast to the Hegelian school, which takes the idea of incarnation as central. But the matter is not quite so simple. In the *Absoluteness of Christianity* (1902), Troeltsch used Harnack's *Das Wesen des Christentums* as an example of that type of 'evolutionary apologetic' which ultimately stemmed from Hegel. As evidence he quoted the sentence: 'It is evident, then, that the gospel is not a positive religion like the others, that it has nothing legalistic or particularistic about it, that *it is therefore religion itself.*' [*AC*, p. 169; citing the fourth edition of Har-

nack's work (Leipzig, 1901), p. 41]. The importance to
Troeltsch of evolutionary apologetic was considerable, since it
represented the attempt to rule out every means of isolating
Christianity from the rest of history on the basis of miracle
[*AC*, p. 60]; and that was the presupposition of the
religionsgeschichtliche Schule of which Troeltsch was a
member.[4] Thus, although it is convenient to regard Harnack
and Troeltsch as respectively a supporter and an opponent of
the Ritschlian theological tradition, the truth is more complex.
Although Harnack was less radical theologically than some of
the 'Kleine Göttinger Fakultät' including Troeltsch himself,
and although Troeltsch made clear that he regarded his own
work on the social context of christian teaching as an improve-
ment on Harnack's *History of Dogma*, nonetheless their work
belonged recognisably in the same problem-complex and
shared many presuppositions.

Troeltsch's starting point in his essay, 'Was heißt "Wesen des
Christentums"?' is the sheer variety of the standpoints from
which Harnack's work had been assessed, attacked and com-
mended. Such variety called, Troeltsch felt, for a methodological investigation into the presuppositions involved in the quest
for the essence of Christianity [*GS* II, 390]. He observed that
the quest in its modern form had arisen together with the
labours of modern historiography. German idealists and
Romantics had assumed the habit of surveying an historical
phenomenon in its totality and of attempting by abstraction to
grasp its driving Idea (*triebende Idee*). Their use of the
expression, 'essence of Christianity', presupposed the view,
'that large coherent complexes of historical events are the
development of an idea, a value, or a line of thought
(*Gedankenkreis*) or purpose (*Zweckgedanken*), which gradually
develops in detail and consequence, which assimilates and
subordintes alien materials and which continually struggles
against aberrations from its leading purpose and against
contradictory principles threatening from without' [*GS* II,
393].[5] This form of abstract thought Troeltsch considered to be

[4] Cf. H. Gunkel, 'Die Richtungen der alttestamentlichen Forschung', *Christliche Welt*, 36 (1922), 66, cited by W. Klatt, *Hermann Gunkel* (1969), pp. 26–7.
[5] I wish to acknowledge the great assistance of Michael Pye in making available
in typescript a translation of Troeltsch's essay, on which I frequently relied
in my own rendering of the passages quoted below.

quite unavoidable in history, and wholly proper provided it remained in close contact with the study of detail. He pointed to other examples in contemporary historiography where other cultures and religions had been submitted to a similar analysis. Christianity is no different in principle from any of these; the same methods apply to all. He therefore endorsed Harnack's proposal to view Christianity in a purely historical manner, though, as we shall see, this in fact constitutes only the first step of the total task.

For the moment, however, Troeltsch wished to press home the proper significance of accepting the presuppositions of the historiography of German idealism. Consistently with all his previous writing he insisted that this meant the end of the dogma of Christianity's normativeness, accredited and recognisable on the basis of divine authority or miracle. Christianity cannot preserve inviolate its own internal criteria of interpretation. It must now be viewed in its totality, and within the whole of human history (i.e. not as a self-sufficient entity). With a reference, added in 1913, both to Schleiermacher's *Glaubenslehre* and the Hegelian programme of universal history, he emphatically stated his approval of the *comparative* approach for the determination of essence, and praised Schleiermacher's *Ethics* for its breadth of view over the spiritual life [*GS* II, 396–7]. Although this form of essence definition is a 'purely historical matter', the formulation of the necessary abstractions is a task beyond what he termed 'inductive-empirical history', and lies at the point of transition to the philosophy of history. The former, of course, uses general terms, but never concerns itself very self-consciously with abstraction. This was Troeltsch's complaint against Harnack, who had not, in his view, sufficiently pondered the difficulties of the transition. It was not enough historically to have analysed the teaching of Jesus, and to have presented it as the simple essence of the total and complex phenomenon of Christianity. Nor, on the other hand, would it do, with Loisy, simply to presuppose the view that the catholic church superseded the concept of essence; that would be to lapse into the old unhistorical realm of dogma. The only way of avoiding these mistakes was to operate the correct method. One ought to proceed not on the basis of dogma, but 'from history in general, and its methods, to Christianity in its overall extent, and to the question of its validity' [GS II, 400].

But even the correct method itself presented new problems. The only easy way of avoiding these was to suppose that a single force of some kind underlay the basic idea, and expressed itself in history as a single law of development (*Entwickelungsgesetz*). This was the solution offered by the Hegelian school, and might be seen especially in Baur and his pupils.[6] The trouble with this theory of a single law is that it explains too much. All the forms of Christianity would have to be shown to be teleologically necessary; and that, declared Troeltsch, would be impossible for a protestant, who considers catholicism to be 'a deviation from the essence of Christianity' [GS II, 404].

At this point the differences between the two editions of the text become important. In the original edition of 1903 Troeltsch, after offering his objection that the theory of a single law of development was biased in favour of catholicism [cf. GS II text, 403–5], immediately drew from the opposition between catholicism and protestantism the conclusion that the history of Christianity contains absolute opposites [GS II, 405]. This, he admitted, was a protestant judgment (a sentence omitted in the later edition), but at the same time a result of purely historical considerations. The idea of essence in any case only existed as a construct of the historian. In the later edition, he evidently felt obliged to admit at once that in offering his objection as a protestant he had departed from 'purely historical thinking' [GS II, 403]; and subsequently he added that the justification of his objection was a matter of 'our own conception and interpretation of Christianity' [GS II, 405]. The difference is significant. In the original edition he seemed content to be understood to be saying that the protestant and the purely historical, or impartial view of Christianity simply coincide. It was a view which, as we shall see, Troeltsch did not really abandon. But it seems that in his later edition he

---

[6] In the later version of the essay, Troeltsch added the idea that both Ritschl and Harnack are likewise dominated by a similar idea of 'progressive development' (*Fortentwickelung*) based not on the idea of incarnation, as in Hegel's case, but on the biblical idea of the kingdom of God. In view of the objection Troeltsch was going to offer in what follows, it was a curious addition.

proposed to be more circumspect, and, so to speak, to set his 'protestant' objection within brackets by raising the (wholly theoretical) possibility that even protestantism itself might be viewed as 'a falling away or peripheral variety of the essence' [*GS* II, 405]. The conclusion of the argument is thus made much more general in the later edition. The oppositions apparent in church history (he has now reinforced the original argument by reference to the history of heresy and sectarianism) presuppose the necessity of criticism from a particular standpoint; but that statement is at the same time a historical judgment. 'It cannot be otherwise even for the most impartial approach, if one considers it possible to achieve a concept of the essence at all' [added, *GS* II, 405]. The qualification in the conditional clause is vital. Troeltsch was now arguing that, if one wants to do essence construction at all, one is bound to accept the fact that the concept will be formed by the judgment of the historian. Thus the 'impartiality' claimed for the judgment cannot literally mean non-partisan-ship; it must refer, rather, to the conscientiousness of the historian in his handling of material from his own particular standpoint. The difficulty in which he has landed is seen repeatedly throughout the essay.

Troeltsch, however, was thoroughly aware of the point, and gave it at once an airing. If essence-definition was at the same time criticism, what provided the criterion? To this his immediate answer was: 'It is a criticism of historical formations in terms of the ideal which lies within their main driving force' [*GS* II, 407]. Here he was referring to Heinrich Rickert's programme of the elucidation of 'immanent values', a theory whose importance for his essay he acknowledged in a subse-quently added footnote [*GS* II, 450]. The critical character of essence-definition is still part of the historical task, even if the transition to philosophy of history has taken place. Its criteria are, therefore, supposed to be objective; and this is why Troeltsch, though manifestly now on difficult ground, defended the impartiality of the critical viewpoint he felt compelled to adopt.

When partisan spirit and personal wishes are left in the background, and if one simply gives oneself over to the impression made by the material and attempts to distinguish the specific within the whole and to judge the distortion and the accidental additions in terms of the whole then such a problem is soluble, at least to the extent that unprejudiced persons ready to learn may be brought to a sympathetic understanding or at least inducted into the main direction and evaluation of the essence [*GS* II, 408].

The objectivity of the solution thus depended on its being tackled by men with the necessary intellectual, moral and spiritual gifts; it was a matter both of historical competence and ethical insight [*GS* II, 411].

Troeltsch was 38 years old when he wrote this essay, and we look in vain for any self-effacing disclaimers about his own competence to fulfil the task. Not even when banning 'the amateurs, the doctrinaire, the fanatics, the narrow-minded, subordinates and specialists' from the work does he hint at the enormity of the claim he is making on his own and his like-minded contemporaries' behalf. It is clear too from other work he was doing at the time, especially his long discussion of Rickert in his essay, 'Modern Philosophy of History' (1904), that this new theory was intended to replace the old theological dogma that norms had been given by 'an isolated divine revelation'.[7] But he was clearly torn about the extent to which personal factors influence the historian's judgment. The method for defining the essence of Christianity with the aid of immanent criticism could in principle be used on every other historical phenomenon; but there existed the truth that 'history is ceaselessly striving to realise values which have an objective, inner necessity', and this was no ethically indifferent standpoint. Ultimately Troeltsch's view was circular, as he frankly recognised [*GS* II, 709]. But he defended its circularity on the grounds that it necessarily arose out of the structure of our consciousness. The values which we detect by impartial enquiry into history, we order according to a criterion personally convincing to ourselves which spontaneously arises in the course of a comparative estimate. This criterion emerges in the active correlation of a historical heritage and the living present [*GS* II, 709]. Troeltsch's own deployment of the criterion led him to the view (which he did not attempt to alter in his later edition) that the *critical* definition of the essence was in fact

---

[7] Troeltsch indicates that so thoroughly has this view been discredited by historical writing it is not even mentioned by Rickert, *GS* II, 704.

only possible in protestantism, 'which is based precisely upon the principle that personal insight into what is essential in Christianity is able to evaluate selectively the mass of actual historical manifestations' [*GS* II, 411].

Does Troeltsch really think that insight into the phenomenon of Christianity is restricted to neo-protestant (or neo-protestant-thinking) professors of history? A lecture which he gave to the ninth congress of German historians and which formed the basis of his *Protestantism and Progress* (1906[1], 1911[2], ET 1912), indicates that the answer to this question is in the affirmative. In the Preface to the English translation, Troeltsch stated that his work had two main centres of interest: the first, that of describing with complete impartiality and objectivity the relation of protestantism to modern civilisation; and the second, on the basis of the first, of correlating the valuable elements of both in a constructive synthesis. The second task, he recognised, was based on 'very personal and subjective, although at the same time carefully reasoned, convictions and presuppositions' [*PP*, p. viii]; but his book 'belongs distinctly to the former circle of interests'. Even in the final chapter on 'Protestantism and Modern Religious Feeling', where if anywhere he approached most closely the constructive task, he explicitly asserted that he was confining himself to purely historical thought and the realm of fact rather than of opinion. The question he proposed to tackle was 'whether the religious life which lives in the context of the contemporary world and is inwardly bound up with it, actually bears the features of protestantism'.[8] For all its difficulty, Troeltsch was prepared to respond to this question, given the assumption that without a metaphysic and an ethic a strong self-consistent spirit of civilisation cannot exist. His answer runs as follows:

If we confine our attention to the actual religious life of the modern world and not to those portions of it which are religiously atrophied, it is, after all, unmistakable that, as a simple matter of fact, on the one hand an essentially practical protestantism, conservative in doctrine but not intensely dogmatic, forms the backbone of the great Anglo-Saxon portion of our modern world, and that, on the other hand, along with it, the influences of German idealism, which are closely

---

[8] My translation. *Die Bedeutung des Protestantismus für die Entstehung der modernen Welt* (2nd ed., 1911), p. 89. Cf. *PP*, p. 178.

connected with protestantism, are the directive forces. All other kinds
of religious aspiration and imagination are rather a flight from the
modern world than an inner religious conquest of it, a flight, in
general, from the practical and real. Thus, on grounds of pure fact,
we are warranted in saying that the religion of the modern world is
essentially determined by protestantism, and that this constitutes the
greatest historical significance of protestantism [*PP*, p. 185].

Even supposing that the presumptuous identification of 'the
modern world' with civilisation developed in Europe and
America does no more than 'extend rather unduly [*sic*] the
sphere of our own existence' [*PP*, p. 9], this passage is
remarkable for its tacit assumptions. By confining its attention
to the Anglo-Saxon and German world it establishes the
proposition that protestantism is most prevalent. This factual
statement is then combined with the moral judgment that
non-protestant religious thought has an atrophied or escapist
character, to yield the assertion 'on grounds of pure fact', that
the religion of the modern world is essentially determined by
protestantism. As usual one immediately finds Troeltsch
taking into consideration the obvious objection that, on this
occasion, he had passed well beyond a factual statement into a
value judgment [*PP*, pp. 203–4]. His answer is not reassuring:
'It may well be so; but if so, it no longer has a place within the
limits of this enquiry.' The enquiry, he asserted, was only
concerned with the causal connection between protestantism
and the modern world. Contradicting his subsequent statement in the English preface, he claimed that he was not even
concerned with providing a basis for any judgment of value.
'What we have had to do with is simply the actual significance
of protestantism for the arising of modern civilisation, including its religious elements, not the provision of a norm for its
present-day existence, maintenance, or development. Nor do I
wish to bring on such a judgment even here at the close' [*PP*, p.
204]. But to reaffirm the *intentions* of his enquiry is by no means
to answer the objection that he had gone well beyond his own
limits by speaking of religious atrophy or escapism. To admit
that the charge, if true, would contradict his intentions, leaves
the substantive question quite untouched; and it is here that
Troeltsch's position has one of its most obvious weaknesses.

As hitherto described, Troeltsch's method for defining the

essence of Christianity, which has striking points of resemblance to Schleiermacher's, is as much art as science, and depends heavily on such qualities as sympathy, maturity of judgment and insight. Troeltsch recognised, however, that the peculiar problem of Christianity lay in the importance for its whole development of its origins in the person of Jesus. Not just artificial dogmatism, but the historically developed tradition of christian teaching as a whole, recognised in Jesus the founder of the religion in an exceptionally strong sense. Troeltsch preferred the term, 'classical time', to designate the importance of the New Testament period for subsequent developments, and within this classical time further pinpointed the historically reconstructed preaching and personality of Jesus as the 'finally decisive point' [*GS* ii, 414]. Here it is again instructive to observe the development of Troeltsch's thought from the writing of the original article to the edition published in the collected works, as mirrored in the changes to the text. They begin at once in the answer to the question, at what point is the preeminently important revelation of the essence to be found. 'To begin with', affirmed the Troeltsch of the first edition, 'the answer is very simple'; by the second edition it only 'seems' simple. Accordingly, the difficulties which Troeltsch proposed to introduce in the second edition are of a more radical kind. In the first edition Troeltsch touched on the following three complications; first that there can be no artificial isolation of the canon; secondly that within the New Testament it is the words and personality of Jesus, as elucidated by the historian, that are preeminently important; and thirdly that these are only mediated to us by the faith of the community, influenced (and rightly so) especially by Paul to emphasise the spirit of Christ, always active in its midst. From this last the conclusion is drawn that the essence of Christianity is not exhausted by an examination of the teaching of Jesus.

Retaining all that, Troeltsch by 1912 wanted to complicate and radicalise the problem considerably. Much earlier in the discussion he signalled the fact that Jesus' preaching of the kingdom was not for him the essence of Christianity; also the novelty of the influence of Paul on early Christianity was greatly emphasised, and his christocentrism was bluntly stated to be a 'new picture of Christ'. Whereas earlier Troeltsch had

himself affirmed that the spirit and meaning of Jesus' preaching was contained in Paul, he now presented this position as an
argument likely to be brought forward with which he did not
fully agree. Paul cannot be understood as preaching, like the
fourth evangelist, a spiritual Christ, leading the Church into all
truth. 'Paul's preaching has a quite different relationship to the
present and to the possession of salvation'; it contains 'a
substantively new religious element of the highest significance'
[GS II, 415–16]. Thus Christianity contains from the start
different basic trends; it has 'two distinct accents, if not indeed
two altogether distinct elements' [GS II, 416]. This conclusion is
used to justify the introduction of a stronger reference to 'the
truths of Platonism and Stoicism', without which Christianity is
actually said to be culturally inconceivable [GS II, 416] or even,
in the case of Platonism, untenable scientifically and as a
philosophy of religion [GS II, 423]. Where the first edition
spoke of the essence being a complex entity containing in itself
an oscillation between several basic ideas, the second edition
radicalised by asserting that it 'must go so far as to bear
opposites and tensions within itself' [GS II, 420–1].

Even without the addition of this new perspective, the
problem of recognising the essence had become, at Troeltsch's
hand, incredibly complex – too complex for any single
Hegelian 'law of development'. Nonetheless Troeltsch per-
sisted in maintaining that the careful historian may acquire a
sense (Gefühl) for what is christian.

Our sense for this is corrected by history and yet at the same time our
sense for it plays a leading part in our grouping of the historical facts.
According to our own inward reflection on the christian idea and
according to the conscientiousness of our grasp of the historical
material we shall arrive at differing conceptions of the course of
development, and from these positions conceive differently the
seminal potential of the original form [GS II, 419].

To counterbalance the inescapable subjectivity of this position
Troeltsch quickly added his usual reservation about the need
for 'real historical mastery' [GS II, 420] in the execution of the
task.

Thus the continuum so discerned must be capable of
accounting for the tendency of Christianity to reformulate
itself ever anew. Especially it must take into account the

ambiguity of its attitude towards culture, in which it experiences a fundamental polarity. Troeltsch expressed it thus:

Christianity is an ethic of redemption whose world-view combines optimism and pessimism, transcendence and immanence, an abrupt polarisation of the world and God and the inward linking of these two, a dualism, in principle, which is transcended (*aufgehoben*) again and again in faith and action. It is a purely religious ethic which refers man baldly and onesidedly to the values of the inner life, and yet again it is a humane ethic which forms and transfigures nature, overcoming the struggle with her through love [*GS* II, 422].

The original form of Christianity, however, was a 'onesided and abruptly transcendent ethic'; the immanent ethic was a subsequent development as Christianity was forced to abandon its belief in an early end to the world order. The significance of the 'classical time' was and still is, however, that through the gospel of redemption characteristic of this time the christian would be preserved from total immersion in the world and culture. Troeltsch saw the tension resolved not in a synthetic viewpoint balanced between extremes, but in a temporal process of circular movement between the two poles, in which the preaching of Jesus is the stronger. This, at least, is the message of the first edition. But Troeltsch's radicalisation required an emphatic strengthening on the side of the legitimate incorporation into Christianity of genuine novelty. Accordingly he later added two sentences expressing the view that the changes and assimilations which have occurred within the history of Christianity 'themselves belong to the essence, as it has now become and as alone it is capable of carrying a general culture' [*GS* II, 423]. The supporting reference is not to Paul, used earlier as the grounds for introducing novelty, but to platonic philosophy, social ethics and art. Thus the concluding words of the section, which are identical in both editions, are given in the later edition an entirely new meaning. Whereas in the first edition the circular movement occurs between two poles found in Christianity virtually from the start, of which the redemptive pole (emphasised by Jesus and original Christianity) is the stronger, in the later edition the idea is conveyed that Christianity itself is being progressively altered by its encounters with culture, and that its essence for today could not be the same as in earlier centuries. Any contemporary essence of Christianity would therefore be construed out of the interrelationship between a progressively transformed accommodation of original Christianity and general culture on the one hand, and the preaching of Jesus on the other.

Troeltsch does not, however, pursue this thought; indeed it is not entirely clear that he wholly envisaged the extent to which the addition changed the sense of the original discussion. But the radical tenor of the alterations in the section is good evidence for supposing that he was ready to defend the increased possibility it gave for accommodating novelty in the Christian tradition. Indeed his own theological position by 1912 demanded such a defence.[9]

Troeltsch now turned his attention to a theme which had been implicit from the start in his concept of the essence as the 'driving force' in Christianity, namely whether that which had carried forward the historical phenomenon in the past had any power to do so in the future. The plain fact is that a historian would view Christianity very differently according to whether or not he considered it had any future. Thus the attitude adopted to the Christianity of the present would decisively influence one's view of the whole phenomenon [GS II, 424].

Troeltsch, in admitting this, sought to mitigate the further impression of subjectivity it imported by insisting that, in this situation, Christianity was in no different case from any other phenomenon, such as classical culture, the Renaissance, Buddhism, Islam and so forth. 'The purpose of history is indeed never simply to reflect a past world in the memory. Quite apart from the fact that this is impossible it would also be empty and superfluous' [GS II, 425]. Not even the most distant past is without an indirect relevance to the present and future. History is never merely antiquarian curiosity.

The purpose of this rather confused introduction was to attempt to show that the historian's personal attitude towards the future validity of Christianity conditioned his view of its essence. The carefully defended objective status of the definition was not destroyed, however, because, according to Troeltsch, all historical abstractions (in Troeltsch's sense of

---

[9] See below, p. 167, for Troeltsch's subsequently expressed belief that the *essence* differs in different epochs of history.

historical) contained this evaluative element, and, in any case, the conditioning of the historian is only partial.[10] Nonetheless Troeltsch was emphatic that he was pinpointing one of the conditions of the definition of an essence. 'Almost all essence concepts have the tendency to transmute into ideal concepts.' The historian has to attempt to foresee how the basic ideas of the essence will unfold in the future.

No exposition of Troeltsch's view at this point can avoid the question whether he now flatly contradicts all that he said above about the impartiality or objectivity of the historian's approach to the material. The issue turns on whether sense can be made of the notion that the historian is only 'partially conditioned' by his positive or negative decision about Christianity. Once he has asserted, however, that 'none of the possible decisions about the problem can be absolutely presuppositionless and impartial' [*GS* II, 427], it is my view that his protestations about objectivity become redundant, and his further defence of it mere rationalisation. What Troeltsch speaks of in a 1912 addition as 'a thoroughly personal matter conditioned by personal religious feeling (*Empfindung*) and attitude towards the christian idea'[11] is, in fact, in Lonergan's useful notion, the acquisition of a horizon.[12] Such a perspective of history is all-embracing, and, in this specific sense all-conditioning. The case is *not*, of course, that because of his attitude the historian is free, for example, to invent the past. In this sense the actuality or facticity of past events continues to 'condition' one's work; and, indeed, new considerations may in due time trigger a change of horizon. But the sheer impossibility of being neutral in the matter of the decision about Christianity's claims requires the conclusion that what is at stake is our whole way of viewing the world. Troeltsch's personal presupposition that

no physics and no biology, no psychology and no theory of evolution can take from us our belief in the living, creative purpose of God, and that no anti-teleology, no brutality and no fortuitousness of nature, no

[10] 'Mitbedingt' heisst nicht ausschließlich bedingt, und so bleibt der Objektivität der historischen Forschung ihr Recht gewahrt' [*GS* II, 425].

[11] *GS* II, 427. The original phrase was simply 'conditioned by inner experience'.

[12] 'The history one writes depends upon one's horizon', B. Lonergan, *Method in Theology* (1971), p. 247.

contradition between the ideal and the real, can take from us our
belief in redemption as the destination of the whole world [*GS* II, 427].

is an all-embracing affirmation of faith. The historian who
makes it already has a view about the past, present and future
of Christianity, which his work on the historical material will
certainly exemplify. For should the historical work turn out
otherwise, he would, by strict logic, fall into self-contradiction;
and from this position, the only release would be, as Troeltsch
himself admitted, the negative decision on Christianity's
future.

It is thus noteworthy that Troeltsch's defence of the objectivity of the work became, in the pages which followed, an
intra-christian discussion. Having roundly stated that the
combining of objective and subjective considerations is a
creative act, which shapes the essence of Christianity afresh,
having spoken of 'an ever-renewed, purely factual and irrational combination of that which is recognised to be necessary
and true with historical tradition and experience' [*GS* II, 435],[13]
he is forced to consider whether he has not now permitted a
dangerous subjectivism to creep in. But the objection is only
tackled from the standpoint of the needs of the *christian*
community. At this crucial point in the argument, in other
words, he is principally contending with those conservative
theologians worried about the loss of authority and direction,
which Troeltsch's method seems to import into the consideration of the church's future. Thus his replies do not by any
means touch the crucial point, namely the utter gulf he has
introduced between the christian's and non-christian's conclusions about Christianity's future.

This is not to minimise the importance of Troeltsch's
contribution to the discussion. By speaking of the relation of
the historian or theologian to Christianity's past as involving
his own will, and by emphasising the creativity of the statements about Christianity's essence, Troeltsch was bringing into
the open what was implicit in much of the previous history of
essence talk. To define the essence frequently had a reforma-
tory intention, a judgment upon the present by means of a

[13] 'Factual and irrational' are Rickert's terms for an individual event, the
proper subject of history [*GS* II, 690–1].

hoped-for future. Harnack made much the same point when he said:

There is no doubt that, with respect to the past, the historian assumes the royal function of a judge, for in order to decide what of the past shall continue to be of effect and what must be done away with or transformed, the historian must judge like a king. Everything must be designed to furnish a preparation for the future, for only the discipline of learning has the right to exist which lays the foundation for what is to be.[14]

That this was the intention of Harnack's book on the essence of Christianity Troeltsch recognised in a passage inserted in 1912 [*GS* II, 430–1].

Similarly important are the terms of the discussion of the limits to subjectivism. Troeltsch quite rightly says that 'the less effort one spends in self-deceit, trying to find a theoretical escape from subjectivism, the more one's hands are freed to limit it in practice and to render it harmless' [*GS* II, 436]. The open acceptance of the possibility of novelty, confidence in scholarly conscientiousness, awareness that the laity are often more flexible than official church circles, and the sense of continuity achieved in 'the abiding relationship to the christian community'[15] – all these considerations comprise a genuinely important contribution to understanding the theological task implicit in the quest for Christianity's essence.

But they are considerations persuasive only to those already concerned about the integrity of the future of Christianity. At this point in the discussion Troeltsch does not introduce any objection stemming from a historian convinced that Christianity has no future, or discuss the 'objectivity' of the very radically different picture which such a view-point would provide. Nonetheless he does consider the work of Eduard von Hartmann, who had attacked the whole tradition of neo-protestantism, and Harnack especially, as an abandonment of Christianity, in the interest not of orthodoxy but of a philosophical transmutation of orthodoxy. The discussion of

[14] A. Harnack, 'Über die Sicherheit und Grenzen geschichtlicher Erkenntnis', *Reden und Aufsätze*, IV, 7, cited in J. C. Livingstone, *Modern Christian Thought* (1971), p. 258.
[15] A phrase significantly qualified in 1912 by the addition of the words 'closer or remoter' [*GS* II, 440].

von Hartmann is especially interesting, because here Troeltsch
entirely rewrote the meagre paragraph assigned to the question in 1903, expanding it to cover seven pages of his collected
works. In the original version Troeltsch contented himself
with a brief description of von Hartmann's 'pantheistic'
transmutation of the idea of incarnation into the essential
unity of divine and human spirit. Von Hartmann, too, clearly
saw as the essence of Christianity those features of it which had
in his eyes future value. He was accordingly, said Troeltsch,
operating the same method. The difference lay both in
historical interpretation and in personal conviction. In both
respects Troeltsch believed his to be a sounder view, but would
not have expected a neutral tribunal to be able to arbitrate
between them. There is a reciprocal effect of ideas; 'the
historical conception works on the conviction and the conviction on the historical conception'. Hence it is not a matter of
proof, but of conscientious historical study and personal
religious judgment.[16]

By 1913 Troeltsch was evidently convinced that von
Hartmann's thesis needed to be met head-on, if the claims for
an objective basis for essence definition were to carry much
weight. The blandness of the 1903 article was replaced by a
slashing attack on von Hartmann's interpretation of Christianity, said to constitute 'an extremely violent construction
falsifying all real history' [GS II, 443]. In support of this
assertion Troeltsch argued that the philosophical interpretation of the incarnation was quite new and alien to the orthodox
tradition, that pantheism was ruled out by the essentially
christian doctrine of the living God and that the suffering of
the Incarnate had nothing to do with any 'pessimistic' view of a
suffering God. The true historical connections of such ideas
'are with Brahmanism and Buddhism, and not with Christianity' [GS II, 444].

Historical argument is also adduced to dispense with the
objection which von Hartmann raised against the non-
christian, innovatory character of neo-protestantism. It is said
to be certain 'on the grounds of objective history' that what for
von Hartmann is mere limitation and husk (namely the
personalist doctrine of God and belief in salvation) is actually

[16] *Die Christliche Welt* 29 (1903), 682–3.

the essential. Of course, it is true that in neo-protestantism the old christology of protestantism falls away with the advent of a new understanding of the relationship of God and history; similarly a new understanding of culture has emerged to meet present needs. But the genuine link with the actual history of Christianity is perfectly clear [*GS* II, 445].

Now whether Troeltsch had actually contributed more to the argument than increased vigour of assertion may be doubted. His own doubts are possibly evident in the defensiveness of the following paragraphs of the discussion. Here he admitted, yet again, that continuity cannot actually be *proved* in an exact historical sense, but claimed that religious subjectivity can find its inner rapport confirmed by conscientious historical research.[17] He also appealed for confirmation to the future, which he feels will support the basic correctness of the movement of neo-protestantism, and refute von Hartmann's pessimistic monism. Ultimately, however, the appeal was to the truth; compared with this, the argument about whether what we believe is 'no longer Christianity' or 'still Christianity' is unimportant.

But none of these appeals extract Troeltsch from his difficulty. They may successfully defend his own construction as a *possible* view of the essence of Christianity, against von Hartmann's charge that it was a fundamentally new religion. But that is to offer an *argumentum ad hominem*. The supposed refutation of von Hartmann is otherwise sheer rhetoric. Not more than Troeltsch, was von Hartmann obliged to prove that his 'development' of Christianity was identical with historical Christianity; and the appeals to the future and to truth could equally have been made by him. The weakest facet of the whole discussion remains, however, its essentially intra-christian character. Von Hartmann, because he was operating within the Hegelian notion of development was only apparently a non-christian opponent. Troeltsch had still to discuss a case where a serious and qualified historian conscientiously studying the history of Christianity had reached the conclusion that its course has run into the sand. Only in the context of such a discussion would the true nature of his assumed 'horizon' have

[17] We may note that the appeal is now to the *integrity* of the historian, rather than to his *impartiality*.

become apparent to him, and his protestations about objectivity seem less like special pleading.

It remains to enquire why the impression conveyed by the essay is so muddled. To make sense of his work on this topic one must suppose, I believe, that while had he proved by his own discussion that the definition of the essence of Christianity necessarily involved the historian's whole approach to history, for various reasons he was unwilling to accept the theological consequences of this view. What could these reasons be? One is certainly obvious, namely that he was rightly convinced that personal conviction was no substitute for expertise. Here however he failed to distinguish between the capacity of the expert historian to point out the mistakes of improper historical reconstructions, that is, the technique of falsification, and the requirements for the task of construction. The objectivity which properly belongs to the former task, he imported into the latter. The verification, however, of a *total* way of viewing history, such as is implied in the christian's decision to accept a christian account of this matter, is a vastly more complicated business. Troeltsch attempted to unravel the complications, by speaking of an initial *foundation* of objective history, and a subsequent personal act. 'The concept of the essence seeks and has, at any rate in the first instance, an objective, historical foundation' [*GS* II, 428]. But the metaphor of 'foundations' is notoriously ambiguous in intellectual matters, and the temporal precedence accorded to history at the very least problematic. Then the problem was further complicated by his talk of the essence 'changing automatically' or 'tending to turn' into an ideal concept [*GS* II, 426]. Since Troeltsch was not in the least unaware of the unity of all human thought, and affirmed that any divisions and distinctions he had made were 'admittedly only provisional and hypothetical' [*GS* II, 451], one is puzzled to know why he was so intent on making them in the first place.

The reason has evidently to do with his sense of the gains made in the understanding of the past by contemporary historians. These gains Troeltsch attributed to the operation of a method, specifiable under the three headings of probability judgment, analogy and correlation [*GS* II, 731–3]. The method had resulted in objective gains in human knowledge.

Moreover, if you admitted its usefulness in even one instance you were obliged to accept the revolution which the whole method implied; and this revolution consisted in that new view of the relation of God and history, the very hall-mark of the modern world, with which it was Christianity's duty to come to terms. Troeltsch was especially scornful of those who tried to mediate between the methods imposed by the modern world, and the old dogmatic supernaturalism. Even the 'evolutionary apologetic', which appeared thoroughly to immerse Christianity in the stream of history, was presented by him as 'the philosophical substitute for the dogmatic supernaturalism of the church' [*AC*, p. 55]. Troeltsch believed himself, therefore, to be committed to following the new method wherever it led; to do otherwise would be implicitly to put himself in the position of those theologians he most scorned. Yet, on the other hand, he was convinced that it was necessary to stop short of scepticism. Contemporary critics, both theologians and sceptics, were glad to impale him firmly on the horns of this dilemma. His route of escape they were quick to identify as the covert smuggling in of a religious presupposition, biased towards Christianity for no better than cultural reasons.[18] Indeed, in due course, Troeltsch frankly admitted that no better ground existed for maintaining the truth of Christianity as against that of the 'great world religions' than that it was the religion of western culture [*CT*, pp. 54f.]; and as for the escape route being a religious presupposition, Troeltsch was fully prepared to acknowledge that the real existence of an absolute value as the *a priori* of all knowledge was 'a belief and to this extent a religious thought' [*GS* II, 758]. The question then is whether his analysis of what the membership of 'the modern world' implies simply stopped short at an arbitrarily chosen point – a point which, for example, Bertrand Russell or A. J. P. Taylor would certainly not accept? This point is arbitrary, not in the sense of haphazard, but in respect of its character as a chosen point, beyond which the implications of relativism are termed 'spiritual suicide', and before which the imported belief-presuppositions are termed 'dogmatic super-

[18] Cf. Troeltsch's reply in *Theologische Literaturzeitung* 20/20 (1916), 449, in a review of W. Günther, *Die Grundlagen der Religionsgeschichte Ernst Troeltsch* (1914), where this charge is made.

naturalism'. The intellectual mapwork implied in the emotive
labels is correlative to the chosen sticking-point. We can
therefore remain wholly unconvinced by the implicit threat
that in not accepting Troeltsch's depiction of the modern
world we are ruling ourselves out of serious consideration as
'modern' theologians. Von Hügel's gentle, but perceptive
observation of Troeltsch's proneness to vehement judgments
of an apparently quite subjective kind, was wholly
appropriate.[19]

But within the terms laid down by his chosen method
Troeltsch had given himself a narrow ridge on which to
balance. He must polemicise against dogmatic orthodoxy and
maintain the sharpest gulf between it and modernity; yet he
must stop short of naturalism, empiricism or scepticism. He
must depict the orthodox as hopelessly compromised by their
dogmatic commitment; yet he must preserve the right of a
christian to decide for a redemptive view of the world. He must
insist on the necessity of a modern christian belonging to and
participating in the aristocracy of scholarship so influential in
the German state; yet he must allow for the simplest of naïve
commitments to a christian life-style. Throughout the essay we
feel the tensions in this proposed course threatening to pull the
structure of it apart; and despite the fact that Troeltsch
returned to the discussion a number of times, most importantly in the essay of 1913, 'The Dogmatics of the
"Religionsgeschichtliche Schule"', the problem of connecting
the gains of a genuinely historical treatment of Christianity
with the positive task of christian dogmatics manifestly persists
in its old form.

One potential source of liberation from the impasse was to
be found in the work of Max Weber, whom Troeltsch
personally encountered at this time. We find that in Troeltsch's
essay on 'Modern Philosophy of History' [1903; *GS* II,
673–728], devoted to a discussion of Rickert, an explicit parallel
is drawn between the formation of the concept 'essence of

[19] In Friedrich von Hügel, 'On the specific Genius and Capacities of
Christianity', *Essays and Addresses on the Philosophy of Religion* (1921), p. 172.
Although this essay, written in 1914, is a fairly general introduction to
Troeltsch's thought, it contains some penetrating and far-reaching criti-
cisms from a liberal catholic standpoint.

Christianity' and Weber's idea of an 'ideal type'. Almost at once, however, Weber developed an important distinction, which he expounded in an essay 'Die "Objektivität" sozialwissenschaftlicher und sozialpolitischer Erkenntnis' (1904). As against Rickert, on whom Troeltsch had largely relied, Weber distinguished between value-related judgments, necessarily made by any historian in his selection of material for study, and value-judgments, made as a response to moral dilemmas. The historian's selectivity is not to be turned into a bridge on which to pass from observation to value-judgment.

Weber's discussion of ideal types and theory construction makes clear that the ideal type is constructed as a logical possibility, whose usefulness turns on its adequacy. It is a heuristic tool designed to help elucidate the actual character of specific events. He will have nothing to do with the notion of the type as a *force* working itself out in history. Thus it is we who create the artificial construct, 'Christianity', in order to explain to ourselves the 'chaos of infinitely differentiated and highly contradictory complexes of ideas and feelings' which make up, for example, the 'Christianity' of the middle ages. The relation of an ideal type to the history of a phenomenon is as many-sided as Christianity needs careful specification. Turning specifically to the recent 'essence of Christianity' discussions, Weber observed that essence definition is exceedingly problematic if it is supposed to be taken as the historical portrayal of empirically existing facts. On the other hand it is useful as a conceptual instrument for comparing and measuring reality. There is then to be no confusion between the heuristic and the evaluative use of such a definition; an ideal type has nothing to do with a profession of faith.

The *elementary duty of scientific self-control* and the only way to avoid serious and foolish blunders requires a sharp, precise distinction between the logical comparative analysis of reality by ideal-*types* in the logical sense and the *value-judgements* of reality *on the basis of ideals*. An 'ideal type' in our sense, to repeat once more, has no connection at all with 'value-judgements', and it has nothing to do with any type of perfection other than a purely *logical* one.[20]

[20] *Max Weber on the Methodology of the Social Sciences*, tr. and ed. E. A. Shils and H. A. Finch (Glencoe, Ill., 1948) in P. M. Brodbeck (ed.), *Readings in the Philosophy of the Social Sciences* (1968), pp. 496–507; esp. pp. 503–4.

Troeltsch clearly attempted to go a certain way to meet this position, especially in the methodology of the *Social Teachings of the Christian Church*. This is not, of course, a direct study of the essence of Christianity, and the 'ideal types' employed are types observed within the total phenomena of Christianity. But what he had learnt by the study was applicable to his discussion of the essence. For example, at the close of the work he asks himself the question whether anything of lasting significance could be learnt from this study about the future form or content of the christian social ethos. His reply is characteristic:

It certainly is in the position of being able to teach us something of this kind. But perceptions of eternal ethical values are not scientific perceptions and cannot be proved along scientific lines. These perceptions [i.e. the 'permanent ethical values' he is about to expound] have been selected from life in history, which the living conviction and the active will fully apprehend in the certainty that here we perceive absolute Reason in the revelation which is addressed to us and formed in the present connection [*STCC*, p. 1004].

He then offers a list of four social and ethical 'ideas and energies' springing out of the christian religion. What these are is less important than the fact that he sees them as having been 'selected', but that the 'living conviction and the active will' have provided 'certainty' about their status as revelation. The separation of the tasks of history and evaluation, so strongly insisted on by Weber, is only thinly disguised; but it is achieved at the cost of making the subjective 'certainty' of the perception of 'eternal ethical values' hardly distinguishable from the privileged supernaturalism he so scornfully dismissed.

Similarly in the conclusion to the discussion of the essence of Christianity, which he added as a wholly new section in the collected works, he explicitly recognised that in the present situation it was 'perhaps good to separate more sharply the properly historical and the philosophically normative in history' [*GS* II, 449]. This, he remarked in a footnote, was his procedure in the *Social Teachings*, which he claimed had 'consciously...no direct connection to doctrine or ethics and may seem to many to be over-realistic or sceptical' [*GS* II, 449]. The normative and systematic task, on the other hand, by which the essence is defined anew with reference to future development, is quite distinct; but the distinction is a gain both for the impartial understanding of history, and for the free creative nature of the act of normative essence-definition [*GS* II, 451].

That should in effect have been the conclusion of the whole essay. Indeed it thoroughly accords with what Troeltsch was to say in his article of 1913, 'The Dogmatics of the "Religions-geschichtliche Schule"', in which the definition of the essence is presented as a matter of personal intuition, and nothing to do with a single force working itself out in history.[21] The 'essence of Christianity differs in different epochs; to formu-late it means to draw on the historical tradition and to reinterpret and shape it according to the needs of the present'.[22] This conclusion had, indeed, been hinted at already in a 1912 addition to the text (cf. above p. 156 and *GS* II, 423). But the more emphatically he affirmed the separation of history and constructive reinterpretation, the weaker became the whole purpose of his argument to associate the prestige of the historical movement with the necessity for *his* reconstruc-tion. Hence the final paragraph of the whole essay tried to reestablish some semblance of unity to the tasks he now had come to feel must be separated.

Just as history and the philosophy of history can only be separated artificially and methodologically, while in reality the first of these always contains an element of the second, while the second can only be built up on the first, so too the historical essence and the essence of faith will have to seek and find each other again and again. The task of theology consists in their unity, whether the two tasks are carefully shared out and solved as far as possible independently, or whether they are brought together again in a great comprehensive account of Christianity which is at the same time both history and faith [*GS* II, 451].

When compared with the extremely sharp criticism of his contemporaries which Troeltsch was handing out in the name of the *necessity* of a particular view of the contemporary task of theology, this conclusion is exceedingly generalised and tame. So conflicting, however, were the basic tenets of his argument

---

[21] *American Journal of Theology* XVII (1913), 1–21, esp. pp. 11f. and 16. The German version published in the *Gesammelte Schriften* II contains certain additions.   [22] *American Journal of Theology*, XVII (1913), 12–13.

that the only conclusion possible was this weakly-defined programme for future realisation. In order to learn from Troeltsch's work we have to retrace our steps, and work through the whole course of the argument.

We may very well begin with the fact of change within the christian tradition. One of the most solid advantages of Troeltsch's work was its basis in the activities of the *religions-geschichtliche Schule*. The scholarship sponsored by this group has contributed greatly to the improved grasp of the christian churches' place in the history of man's religious, social and economic activity. It has become less and less possible to pursue Old and New Testament studies or the study of church history and the history of dogma in isolation from their setting in the total context of human life; comparative study has continually proved illuminating in respect of material grown stale and unsurprising through the artificial limitations imposed by ecclesiastical interests.

Historiography has, of course, undergone its own changes of fashion and emphasis since Troeltsch's day. The kind of works to which he referred, dealing with the 'essence' of classical culture or of the Renaissance, have disappeared, and the place of the history of ideas in relation to other branches of historical study is greatly disputed. Nonetheless it remains true, as Troeltsch indicated, that if one is going to write the history of cultural, religious or ideological movements at all, the conceptual work of indicating what is meant by terms like 'classical', 'romantic', 'idealist', and 'democratic', and thus also of terms like 'jewish', 'christian', 'buddhist' and so forth is absolutely unavoidable. The suggestion that such concepts are 'essentially contested' may help to illuminate their status.[23] For here, again, as Troeltsch asserted (in the original text of his discussion of von Hartmann's objection to neo-protestantism), a genuine dispute not *resolvable* by argument is 'nonetheless sustained by perfectly respectable arguments and evidence'.[24] We have, however, to be much more alert than was Troeltsch to the possibility of fundamental disagreement about the *extent and nature of the relevant considerations* in the formation of a concept like 'the christian tradition'. Precisely because that

[23] W. B. Gallie, *Philosophy and the Historical Understanding* (London, 1964), ch. 8.   [24] *Ibid.* p. 158.

tradition addresses itself polemically towards the total human situation, the whole question of who man is is impossible to exclude. Certain views of man, such as that of the marxist, illustrate this fact with some clarity; the readily recognisable marxist reading of church history affirms the fact that the human divisions of social class is a prime consideration in framing the concept of 'the christian tradition'. What may be less apparent are the theoretical assumptions made by other historians, less self-conscious in their reflection about the human situation. But their assumptions too can be exposed and criticised – indeed it is sometimes the task of a christian historian, who has learnt something of the all-pervasive character of views about man, to do so.

This is the point where it is necessary to part company with Troeltsch. He rightly criticised Harnack for failing to reflect with sufficient clarity about the transition from history to philosophy of hstory. But he was not prepared to recognise that *his* philosophy of history had been decisively impregnated with christian assumptions, and thus had to sink or swim as part of the maelstrom of conflicting views, rather than stand apart as the privileged presupposition of a 'modern world view'. Of course in theory his whole work was devoted to the synthesising of a modern philosophy of history with a spiritual-ised form of the christian tradition; mutual impregnation was thus the intended outcome of the programme. But it was the very presupposition with which he approached the synthesis which vitiated the whole enterprise; that is, that philosophy of history provided a view of the human situation which was not in itself of the same essentially contested nature as any view formed through the promptings of christian faith. What man is is essentially contested. This does not mean that merely by virtue of professing christian faith a theologian or historian is freed from the need for providing justification for his view of man. Troeltsch's unsparing self-involvement in contemporary philosophy of history is matched by regretably few theological figures of the nineteenth or twentieth centuries. But the olympian heights of that heady discipline concealed from him the sands on which it rested, sands whose shifting brought down not merely his, but many another theoretical construc-tion of the early twentieth century.

There is a further extension of this criticism of Troeltsch's stance, which has to be brought into the open. Troeltsch was part of what has with justice been described as the 'mandarin' tradition in the German academic community, which saw the resolution of the problem of values and society as an urgent practical question for the German state.[25] On this view, if German historical scholarship could not offer the right answers about the future there was little hope for the nation. Throughout Troeltsch's works the view is expressed that the determination of the essence of Christianity could not be the work of the vulgar or uneducated; it must rather be that of a few, to whom sufficient gifts, training and the necessary leisure had been given. Only such people would be able to lay aside the wild passions and fanaticism of ecclesiastical controversy, and to find their way through passing fashion and external pressures. Hence it followed that they were the ones most suited to fashion the christian tradition anew, and to point the way forward [GS II, 429–30]. Quite apart from the objections to the actual programme for the definers of Christianity's essence, there is something narrow-mindedly theoretical about the manner of approach:

After long and careful consideration of the past, present and future, after extending one's view over as much detail as possible, after taking into account all available cases which might further understanding by comparison: there then remains one final fact, in which the element of purely past history and the element of future nomativeness are bound together in a present judgment. This act achieves a transcendence of space and time in the judgment, and an immediate reimmersion of the judgment into space and time as a means of the further development of the whole, based on the idea grasped by intuitive insight and freed of space and time [GS II, 430].

Once can scarcely criticise Troeltsch for approaching the task of essence definition with a deep sense of responsibility; but in the very solemnity there is concealed a contradiction with his theoretical realism about the driving forces within a living church. Troeltsch believed that the task laid upon neo-protestantism was the accomplishment of the second act of the Reformation; but unlike the Reformation of the sixteenth

---

[25] F. K. Ringer, *The Decline of the German Mandarins, The German Academic Community 1890–1933* (Cambridge, Mass., 1969).

century the programme of the new reformers consisted in 'a scientifically informed restoration of the naïve outlook now raised to a higher level' [*AC*, p. 136]. This had been the self-imposed task of many solitary intellectuals since the eighteenth century, and could be intelligibly construed as an attempt to baptise the gradual secularisation of European culture; but it could not be regarded as providing the guidelines of a *religious* movement of the future.

The tasks of theology, so Troeltsch had learnt from Schleier-macher, are intimately related to church leadership. But in Schleiermacher's *Brief Outline of the Study of Theology* he would have read of the necessity of an ecclesial interest and a scientific spirit being combined in one person; the church cannot exist without a living interchange between priest and theologian.[26] This relationship Troeltsch construed too onesidedly.[27] There is, in his work, considerable reflection on the lessons which the protestant professorial curia would have to teach the church; there is a certain attention given to the way in which the laity can adjust to the new views; but there is very little indeed on the need for the theologian to listen to the contemporary christian, except in contexts where the lay opinion could be marshalled as support for views at which he had already arrived on other grounds. Troeltsch certainly believed that what theologians taught had to be tested out in the world of everyday faith before it could attain its full verification; had he been less immersed in the élitist mentality of his immediate circle, he might have responded in a more practical manner to the very naïveté of which he theoretically approved.

[26] *Brief Outline of the Study on Theology*, tr. T. N. Tice (1966), pp. 21-2.
[27] Troeltsch recognised the need for a philosophically-formed faith to be set out as a religion for the whole christian community, if it was to be in touch with 'elemental power': 'Religionsphilosophie' in *Die Philosophie im Beginn des zwanzigsten Jahrhunderts*, ed. W. Windelband, I (1904), 161f. But this need was essentially conceived in terms of a one-way relationship dictated from on high and was never developed beyond the status of a programme. Had Troeltsch ever attempted to work the programme out, some of its deficiencies might have become more apparent to him.

6. Ernst Troeltsch and the end of the problem about 'other' religions

MICHAEL PYE

THE PROBLEM ABOUT 'OTHER' RELIGIONS

The problem about 'other' religions, as western theologians frequently refer to them, has been a constant appendage to christian theology at least since the days of Justin. Palliatives and surgery have both been tried, but both without ultimate success. The 'other' religions do not go away. They continue to offer their own radical solutions to the problems of human existence or to maintain sociopolitical equivalents of the former Christendom. Even modern Christianity's attempt not to be a religion at all, though ingenious, did not prove satisfactory. It brought renewed depth to the self-understanding of the christian traditions, but as applied to all the 'other' religions it really seemed rather like saying, 'If we can't win, we won't play.'

One of the frequent characteristics of the various christian attitudes, whether denunciatory or appreciative, has been that the 'other' religions have all been treated in one way or another as falling into a single category. Of course distinctions have been made as well, and christian apologists have often been quite specifically pointed in their comments on 'other' religions. Nevertheless there is usually also a generalising thread, such as that the religions reflect the preparatory workings of the Holy Spirit, or that they reflect varying intimations of God, or there is the less complimentary view that they represent more or less skilful wiles of the devil, or the barriers of human pride which block God's search for man as opposed to man's own futile search for God. Perhaps the most polite generalisation is to claim a christian 'presence' among the 'other' religions, though how many christian ministers would welcome say, a saivite presence in their own area of tradition, is one of those widely unasked questions.

The general pattern is therefore a more or less systematically conceived christian dogmatics (whichever sub-system it
happens to be) which through some more or less accidental
encounter is confronted with a range of 'other' religions all
having in common the one obvious fact that they are 'other'
than Christianity. This pattern is reflected also in theological
or missionary training. For example, theological faculties in
universities, not excluding the Germany which produced
Ernst Troeltsch, tend to have appendix courses on 'the history
of religions' in which one or two persons accessory to the main
'theological' work are supposed to deal with the 'other'
religions.[1] Even if the lecturer works in a manner not subser-
vient to a dogmatics which did not originally take his subject-
matter into account, many of his students will in fact be using
his work as a means to correlate the 'other' religions with the
christian dogmatics which is being formulated in their minds.
They will in effect be engaged in the construction of a
compatibility theory which accounts for obtrusive facts and
somehow beds them down into their overall theological
system. As to missionaries trained outside universities and sent
to more or less distant lands, these are given a thorough
grounding in sound doctrine and left as far as possible in
ignorance of the main traditions of the countries to which they
go.

Curiously enough, almost identical statements can be made
about buddhist attitudes towards 'other' religions. Buddhists
are as tolerant as christians are charitable, one may perhaps
fairly observe. They have always cheerfully engaged in
polemics against other religious traditions such as Brahmanism, Taoism and Christianity. They have also attempted in
various ways to assimilate them while asserting the over-riding
validity of buddhist truth, as with Confucianism, Shinto,
shamanism and many other indigenous systems of Asian

---

[1] A similar point was made by Professor Ninian Smart some years ago in
Soundings (ed. A. R. Vidler, Cambridge, 1962), p. 121. As this chapter was
written just after I left the department of religious studies at Lancaster,
which he founded, this is the time to acknowledge with gratitude many
fruitful conversations with him which have no doubt left an indelible mark
on my vocabulary. I should add that my interest in Troeltsch has been
guided as always by Robert Morgan, and also helped more recently by my
colleague John Clayton.

peoples. There is a concept of 'external ways' (*gedō*, in Japanese) which is analogous to the western 'other religions'. In modern buddhist universities some effort is made to deal with other religions such as Christianity, Islam, and the rest. From 1867 there was in Ryūkoku University in Kyōto, a course devoted to the study of Christianity with a view to refuting it.[2]

Troeltsch pointed out these analogies quite adequately long ago in *The Absoluteness of Christianity and the History of Religions* when he argued that religions generally produce apologetic systems which depend on identical motives and processes.[3]

On every hand natural absoluteness gradually grows beyond its naïve, self-contained outlook into a doctrine of unique and miraculous expressions of the divine. This doctrine is then opposed to other religions as the one and only truth, to individual deviations as orthodoxy, and to the questing intellectual life of reflection – whether exalted or profound – as the codification of divine wisdom. Sacred books, sacred dogmas, sacred laws, and materially demarcated and guaranteed means of grace everywhere circumscribe the heritage of the founding prophets. A developed theology – sometimes mythologising, sometimes speculative – establishes a lasting relationship between this one and only truth and the manifestations of the religious life that encompass and adhere to it. [*AC*, p. 154].

To the modern historical consciousness Christianity is one such religion with its doctrine opposed to other religions, etc. However, if we stand within a tradition while recognising this situation, the recognition of it subverts our position as it had been maintained hitherto. Christianity is then not miraculously unique but is itself located among the so-called 'other' religions. The same principle applies naturally to all religions. It is subversive of the way in which all religions have historically framed themselves, considered, that is, up to the point at which they begin to become conscious of these facts of life. Whether this means the end of all the meaning of all the religious traditions is however quite another question. After all, heliocentricity and evolution seemed heady enough in their time. It is the end of any kind of theology based on a

[2] Norihisa Suzuki, 'Nobuta Kishimoto and the beginnings of the scientific study of religion in modern Japan' in *Contemporary Religions in Japan* XI Nos. 3–4 (Sept.–Dec. 1970), 156.
[3] Cf. also the early essay 'Religion und Kirche' (1895), *GS* II, in which analogies are considered with respect to the relationship between doctrinal development and social organisation.

miraculously isolated platform, as Troeltsch never wearied of pointing out, but it does not in itself imply the end of theology.

Of course in many ways what Troeltsch had to point out polemically has now become commonplace. Christian attitudes towards 'other' religious traditions have become increasingly polite and subtle. Indeed the matter has been taken up into the whole discussion and implementation of theologies of culture. Yet there has also been a new blanket-appraisal of 'other' religions from the standpoint of 'neo-orthodoxy', and in many other ways the old model of a ready made christian dogmatics confronted with an appendix problem about 'other' religions still lives on. It seems to be worth stressing therefore that inescapable characteristics of modern thought which have to do with the real world have demanded or eventually will demand a significant methodological shift at this point, on the part of all religious traditions which claim to stand in a coherent relationship to human thought in general. Of course there will remain the responsibility and the opportunity to wrestle with the challenges and the meanings of the great religious traditions, but what is desirable is the elimination of the problem set up as a naïve correlation between one's own ready made system (however fragmentary) and the 'other' religions. This implies a methodological shift which will certainly discourage some of the more naïve formulations of Christianity. However it is most important to stress that this shift does not in itself imply specific results about the meaning-content of Christianity. The same applies to each tradition. That is to say, the methodological demands being made do not imply, for example, the truth or the untruth of propositions such as that God's Word to us is the primary definition of the content of christian theology, or buddhistically, that dis-criminative thought is inimical to an enlightenment which involves non-attachment to this or that point.

In order to bring the matter to a head it is necessary to elaborate two presuppositions which were clearly stated by Troeltsch. The first of these is that *there is a plurality of autonomous religious and cultural traditions in history.* The second is that *tradition is subject to change within history and therefore a creative act is necessary to grasp the essential meaning of a given tradition for our time.* The implications of these presuppositions were partly obscured by other emphases in Troeltsch's thought, as will be pointed out below, but it seems that if they are fully articulated *and taken together* they provide a methodological opening for the interpretation of religious traditions which is not immediately doomed to an 'us–them' dichotomy. Such a beginning involves the rejection of the notion of 'other' religions, at least as a kind of dogmatic shadow, if not from the exigencies of daily speech.

It should be stressed yet again that this abolition of the notion of 'other' religions does not in itself contain an interpretation of the way in which any one religious tradition, such as Christianity, might be meaningful or valid. This is because the whole purpose of the methodological shift is precisely not to foreclose but to open the way for the emergence of the meaning which any religious tradition may turn out to convey. Such a meaning might be in some sense overwhelming, but it would not advance from the position of naïve absolutism or miraculous isolation. Moreover there will remain, of course, questions about the relation between the meaningful content of religious traditions or whatever it is which they convey, but these will not remain in terms of a problem about 'other' religions, which does not arise out of the realities of world history, and which is now as fundamentally misleading as a wrong use of myth. (The points stressed in this paragraph are attended to again briefly in the final extended footnote to this paper, written after it was discussed, but in a manner which also presumes the following argument.)

THE PRESUPPOSITION OF HISTORICAL PLURALITY

In the early essay entitled 'Ueber historische und dogmatische Methode in der Theologie' [(1898), *GS* II, 729–53], Troeltsch characterised the historical method as it concerned christian theology by stressing not only historical criticism but also the importance of analogy and the mutual interrelation between all historical developments. He saw emerging at every point 'unique and autonomous historical forces' which are yet analogous to each other, and which, since their interacting relationships add up to a whole, cannot be interpreted in isolation from each other. This view by no means implies that individual religious or cultural traditions simply vanish in the sands of relativism. They remain both specific and coherent, and they demand coherent interpretation. But it does mean that there is no splendid isolation of any one which can be justified on miraculous or semi-miraculous grounds. The relativism is really an aspect of a proper respect for the whole historical context in which specific elements have their being.[4]

As far as the plurality of religions in particular is concerned, Troeltsch was more specific in *The Absoluteness of Christianity and the History of Religions (1901)*. The passage quoted earlier already gave evidence of his recognition of the important analogies between various distinct and complex traditions. It is interesting, however, that when he begins to name them by name he embarks upon a curious weeding-out process. The aim of this is to restrict the force of relativism. 'Polytheism and the numerous religions of uncivilised peoples' are immediately dismissed as 'irrelevant to the problem of highest religious values' [*AC*, p. 92].[5] The religions of 'ethical and spiritual greatness' are then reduced to Judaism, Christianity and Islam on the one hand, the Hinduism and Buddhism on the other hand. Rationalised forms of religion which are severed from contact with historical tradition are treated as secondary, and in this way, 'The field narrows down, therefore, to the rivalry between three or four basic orientations in which the power of religion is disclosed, orientations that have their counterpart in, and give support to, entire spheres of culture' [*AC*, p. 93]. The three or four dwindle almost to two when he goes on, 'Indeed, it is not too much to say that essentially we have to do with the rivalry between the prophetic, Christian, Platonic and Stoic world of ideas on the one

---

[4] 'Although numerous theologians seek to persuade us that the proper starting point is the isolated claim and judgement of the Christian community, no just estimate of Christianity can be formed except by reference to the total context – even as the self-judgment of the Greeks or the Romans cannot be allowed to determine our estimate of their permanent contribution to the human spirit.' 'Historical and Dogmatic Method in Theology', Eng. trans. in manuscript by Dr Ephraim Fischoff and Dr Walter Bense, p. 9 (of 'Ueber historische und dogmatische Methode in der Theologie', *GS* II).

[5] It is obvious that such a judgment cannot now be so easily made, if only because complicated systems have been built upon the interpretation of archaic symbols and mythology.

hand, and the Buddhist and Eastern world of ideas on the other' [*AC*, p. 93].

Unfortunately the history of religions itself scarcely supports such a drastic simplification. To speak of the east alone, even granted some coexistence between Hinduism and Buddhism, the basic buddhist teaching of *anattā* (*anātman*) must be seen as importantly divergent from Upanishadic Hinduism with its *Ātman-Brahman* teaching. It would be an elementary mistake too, to assimilate Mahayana Buddhism to Hinduism, even though the former could bend a pervasive tantric style to its purposes as convenient. Nor is Buddhism to be packed in together with the confucian tradition of East Asia, nor even with Taoism, although of course all three of these drew from and contributed to the wider Chinese and east Asian culture.

Why did Troeltsch simplify so much? The reason is that by setting up the pluralism of religions in such a diminished form he was able to argue that we have a basic choice between personal and impersonal religion, a choice which then only remains to be made – in favour of the former! Thus he wrote:

It is necessary to make a choice between redemption through meditation on Transcendent Being or non-Being and redemption through faithful, trusting participation in the person-like character of God, the ground of all life and of all genuine value. This is a choice that depends on religious conviction, not scientific demonstration. The higher goal and the greater profundity of life are found on the side of personalistic religion.[6]

Troeltsch's recognition of the pluralism of religious traditions is therefore severely modified in this writing, and indeed the religions are really pressed into service to show that 'Christianity is the pinnacle of religious development thus far' and even 'the basis and presupposition for every distinct and meaningful development in man's religious life in the future' [*AC*, p. 131]. Although Troeltsch certainly arrived at these ideas along a coherent train of thought, they do not provide a basis for the resolution of the problem about 'other' religions, and moreover even if this represents a very special kind of

[6] *AC*, p. 112. Cf. also p. 117: 'The personalistic redemption-religion of Christianity is the highest and most significantly developed world of religious life that we know.'

'absoluteness' the positive evaluation of 'rival' traditions remains so slight as effectively to subvert the original pluralist presupposition.

Troeltsch's basic grasp of the autonomous plurality of the several historical traditions comes out after all most strongly in *Der Historismus und seine Probleme*, which may be taken as his considered statement of the nature of the historical way of thinking supposed to have so many implications for the interpretation of religion. In the section on the 'formal logic of history' he defines the basic category of history to be that of 'the individual complex' (*die individuelle Totalität*), by which is meant a grouping of elementary psychological processes and physical conditions, which however cannot be deduced from psychology but stands before us already in visualisable concreteness as historical fact.[7] Examples of such complexes are individual humans themselves, but more importantly collective individualities: 'peoples, states, classes, cultural periods and trends, religious communities and processes such as wars and revolutions' [*GS* III, 33]. 'In each case', he wrote, 'it is a complex which can be carved out of the river of events precisely because it does have a persisting form and a relative compactness, and which fades away at the edges more or less indistinctly into the total human process [*GS* III, 34]. It is the task of the historian to discern and interpret these complexes, each in its own individuality and in its position relative to the whole. The rest of the formal logic of history develops this theme, stressing the distinctive originality of every such historical complex as well as its continuity with others; and stressing above all the auxiliary character of comparative or typological constructs used in their interpretation as compared with the individual living movements themselves [*GS* III, 66–7].

On such a basis the pluralism of the various religious traditions in their autonomous individuality cannot be gain-

---

[7] *Der Historismus und seine Probleme, GS* II, 32–3. The term *Totalität* (actually *historische Totalitäten*) is given in brackets in Troeltsch's article on 'Historiography' in Hastings' *Encyclopedia of Religion and Ethics* (1913), VII, 720b, for the English 'historical aggregates'. Later the article uses the rather hopeless word 'totality'. Troeltsch's meaning can now be easily conveyed by the term 'complex', as one may satisfactorily speak of a complex of facts or events. His precise meaning must in any case be drawn from his argument at length.

said. Each one demands interpretation in terms of its own coherence which is also conditioned by its position relative to the whole. Such is the fundamental axiom of Troeltsch's historicism, and its implications have to be fully drawn out if a creative and evaluative appraisal of the whole of religious history is to be grounded in the objectively available data. It has been seen above that in his early work Troeltsch plunged headlong into an urgent simplification which would scarcely convince the adherents of the 'other' religious traditions themselves that their autonomous plurality was being taken very seriously. It is regrettable that a better articulation of the autonomous plurality which can be seen in the history of religions continued to be inhibited in his thought in two ways. These inhibitions now need to be explained and set aside so that the full implication of his basic presupposition can be worked out.

TROELTSCH'S EUROPEANISM

Consider first Troeltsch's massive concentration on the European tradition. His appraisal of the total situation of his time led him to the view that European and christian values and meanings were the high point of human development thus far. Although it was by no means inappropriate that he should strive to discern the highest flowering of the human spirit, since he was above all neither a negative nor a petty thinker, the effort which he made in this direction did tend to detract from his methodological contribution to the history of religions. The problem may be summed up in his own striking sentence: 'For us there is only a world history of Europeanism' [GS III, 708]. Universal histories of the world could not in Troeltsch's view, be undertaken, 'for thousands of reasons', some of which are rehearsed in Der Historismus und seine Probleme, Ch. IV, pt 2, which is entitled 'Der Europäismus'. 'Humanity as a whole has no spiritual unity and therefore no unified development', he wrote [GS III, 706]. Or again: 'Our history and that of the people outside...simply cannot be brought on to a common level where it might be forged into a unity' [GS III, 709]. Nor is the non-European world really knowable to the European mind: 'In reality we only know ourselves and our own being' [*GS* III, 709]. Like so many westerners he shook his head (in a footnote) over the disinter-est shown by eastern peoples in 'the individual' and 'time' [*GS* III, 706].

Not that Troeltsch was a cultural imperialist. On the contrary it is precisely because he recognised the particularities of non-European cultures that he pours scorn on those who would drag them in to a western orientated world history. For such, he scoffed, Palestine, Rome, Wittenberg and Geneva are the centres of the world. 'The conqueror, the coloniser and the missionary is to be found in all European thought; and that is a source of practical strength and fruitfulness but also of many theoretical errors and exaggerations.' [*GS* III, 707]. Thus Troeltsch's own restriction of universal history to the Euro-pean development was based not on a blind arrogance but rather on an admittedly curiously stated humility and caution. The world as a whole had too many divergently directed complexes for Troeltsch to feel that a universal history was possible. When he agonised over how far Muslims, Russians and Americans were to be taken into account [*GS* III, 725–30], this was based above all on his assessment of the coherence of individual developments in themselves, on the autonomous pluralism of cultures. Islam, for example, with all its intimate relations to the sources which also produced Europe, has a universal history of its own. The concentration on European values grows out of his very respect for the autonomy of the specific content of historical formations. Yet one has to work to recognise this. His very appraisal of these European values did tend to smother over his theoretically pluralist outlook.

Thus the first factor inhibiting the full articulation of this presupposition was his own superior knowledge of and predilection for the values and principles of European civilisa-tion, as this had emerged from antiquity and the middle ages. Nevertheless behind this emphasis can still be discerned the principles espoused in his 'formal logic of history' with its basic category of 'the individual complex'.

This is because the plurality of historical trends is also to be found *within* Troeltsch's Europe, though in this case he is able to view them as coherent contributions to the modern spirit. In his treatment of the problem of an objective periodisation of

European history he determines four basic powers (*Grundgewalten*), namely Hebrew prophetism, classical Greece, Roman imperialism and the western middle ages, which together constitute the creative drives of the modern European world, and upon which the building of a new cultural synthesis has to be based. In a different writing, the essay entitled 'The Essence of the Modern Spirit', he adduced a different group, namely antiquity and Christianity to begin with, followed by 'the qualities and forces peculiar to the Germanic nations', and finally the modern spirit as such which found its full stature 'as a result of the Enlightenment and the English, American and French revolutions'.[8] Europe alone is a composite abstraction based on the changing interrelationships between several complexes of individual fact, and grasped by experienced historians in subtly different ways.

It must be said however that the modern world is not Europe. The realities of the modern world are different from those of fifty years ago. Troeltsch's theoretical pluralism of historical forces has to be accepted more radically than he himself applied it. The universal history of Europe is now about as important in the world as a whole as is the history of Holland in Europe. A universal history of the world is still not really in view, perhaps. There are too many open perspectives. Yet in many respects there are new analogies and new interdependencies of culture for our consideration. As far as religious traditions are concerned it is becoming increasingly possible to advance beyond the shadow-boxing apologetics of earlier times to seek analogies and appraisals based on truly penetrating empathies.

HISTORICAL PLURALITY AND THE 'ESSENCE' OF RELIGION

It has been said that Troeltsch's grasp of the autonomous plurality of religious traditions, as of all historical movements, was inhibited in two ways. The second factor which inhibits his basic standpoint as far as the history of religions is concerned is his use of the category 'essence of religion' (*Wesen der Religion*), which now merits brief consideration.

[8] 'The Essence of the Modern Spirit', Eng. trans. in draft by W. F. Bense, pp. 3–4.

Troeltsch was open to criticism from other dogmatic theologians because his historically based work failed to give sufficient certainty to christian belief. He reacted to this in two ways. On the one hand he preferred to bring the clash of presuppositions out into the open, as in the reply to Niebergall,[9] and to relish his own thorough-going historical method. On the other hand he laboured hard to find a new location for the stability of faith, that is, the stability of a faith no longer miraculously guaranteed in a manner which isolated its reference points from other historical facts and events. At the general level there was the problem as to how any historical individualities could be linked with any standards of evaluation and general validity, which he treated in *Der Historismus und seine Probleme*. With respect to religion in particular there were various starting points. Above all he elaborated the idea of a historically informed and creative theological act, which determines the 'essence' of the religious traditon both for the past and for the future, in a manner which is at the same time temporary and normative.[10] But he also attempted to establish the independence of 'religion' as a basic factor in human life, either generally as a psychological reality[11] or more specifically as a neo-Kantian *a priori*.[12] He may have had the same goal in view, though at the general cultural level rather than the psychological, in his essay 'Wesen der Religion und der Religionsgeschichte'. Here he argued that the science of religion should be based on 'idealism', an unfortunately over-used word, by which he meant however 'nothing more than the possibility of seeing religion as a qualitatively characteristic and creative power of spiritual life'.[13]

These various attempts were paralleled also by his view of the 'essence' of religion, which is referred to in various places, but most straightforwardly in the posthumously published *Vorlesungen über Glaubenslehre*. Here he took the view that since

---

[9] In 'Ueber historische und dogmatische Methode in der Theologie', *GS* II, 729ff. Cf. also his criticism of Ihmels and Heinrici in the 'Foreword to the First Edition' of *The Absoluteness of Christianity*.

[10] 'Was heißt "Wesen des Christentums"?', *GS* II.

[11] 'Die Selbständigkeit der Religion', *ZThK*, v–vi (1895–6).

[12] 'Zur Frage des religiösen Apriori', *GS* II.

[13] *GS* II, 460 ('eine qualitativ eigentümliche und schöpferische Kraft des seelischen Lebens').

supernatural authoritarianism was replaced by a philosophic-
historical appraisal of Christianity within the history of religions, the starting-point should be an investigation of the
essence of religion leading into a demonstration of the special
position of Christianity as conveying the highest revelation of
this essence. This is clearly stated in the opening paragraphs of
the *Glaubenslehre*, where a characterisation of this essence is
also given.

It seems that Troeltsch was carried away in this line of
thought beyond the limits of his historical work. For the notion
of an 'essence' of religion as set out here is one apparently
pertinent to all mankind. It is quite different from the notion
of the essence of a particular, more or less coherent tradition,
which in so far as it is coherent at all may be amenable to the
project of defining its essence. This is the sense in which
Troeltsch spoke of the 'essence' of Christianity. The 'essence
of religion' by contrast cannot but refer to the whole of
mankind, and is therefore an even more vastly complex
undertaking, if indeed there is any such coherence available to
be grasped at all. It is strange that Troeltsch argued on the one
hand that a universal history of the world is impossible because
of the radical divergence of different cultural principles, while
on the other he held that just in the case of religion there is a
universal coherence of some sort. The simplest way to convey
his position will be to quote from the opening pages of the
Glaubenslehre.

The task of a dogmatic system used to be seen in brief projects which
began with the presupposition of a universal, rational belief in God, or
with natural theology, and moved immediately to the assertion of the
exclusive supernatural revelation of the bible, which was followed by a
mere systematic arrangement and scholastic formulation of biblical
propositions. Since the reorganisation of modern theology by
Schleiermacher this has been replaced by a much more comprehensive philosophical account of the principles of religion. This takes its
starting point not in natural theology but in an examination of the fact
and of the essence of religion in general. It replaces deduction from
an exclusive, supernatural theology by a philosophical and historical
appraisal of Christianity within the history of religions, and in the
bible it sees only the humanly comprehensible record and literary
deposit of christian history.

In this way an *independent section of dogmatics* has been formed which deals with the essence of religion, the stages of its development and the demonstration of the position of Christianity within the history of religions. Nowadays this first part is usually separated off from dogmatics itself and has become an independent discipline known as fundamental theology, or the doctrine of religious certitude, or bearing the name of *philosophy of religion*. The yield of these investigations is usually as follows. Religion is a specific, essentially independent constituent of the human consciousness, which without religion languishes away or is doomed to deep resignation. In this specific area of life there takes place a real interpenetration of the human and the divine spirit. In the course of human development as a whole this presence of God in the human soul has assumed in relation to conditions in general the most varied forms of expression, in which by and large may be recognised a sequence and a progression in ethical and spiritual terms. In all these formations therefore can be discerned the revelations and self-manifestations of God corresponding to the total situation of the time. In this context Christianity represents the final and inclusive break-through of these tendencies leading to the formation of a religion of salvation which is in principle universal, ethical, purely spiritual, and formative of personality. Since it opens up in Christ a divine community which is the most profound and comprehensive, and at the same time the most inward and personal, the community which has the greatest power to overcome suffering and sin, it is the highest revelation. As such it has taken up within itself the highest developments of antiquity.

In this way the doctrine of the principles of religion demonstrates the independence of religious knowledge and the central position of Christianity. This leads however only as far as the concept of Christianity as such, to the general idea of the christian faith in God, or to the *concept of the christian principle*, which refers only in principle and in a summary way to the various religio-ethical ideas and forces of Christianity, which is a power still capable of the most manifold and individual formation and historical development. This concept takes the place of the old authority of the bible, and it signifies within the bible the coherence of the spiritual or religious power for life which speaks from within its historical records. On that basis arises the further task of setting out this living content, conceived first of all as a coherent unity, as a series of beliefs and prescriptions. The first are the responsibility of dogmatics and the second that of ethics. In this way we arrive finally at the concept of a dogmatic system [*Gl.*, pp. 1–3].

Thus Troeltsch used the concept of the essence of religion, framed in a manner friendly to Christianity, to undergird christian theology as a specific enterprise. These are of course abbreviated statements. Yet the *de facto* result is much too quickly a situation in which all the other religions are judged in terms drawn from and hence favourable to the christian tradition. In the more detailed discussion which follows the above quotation, the Schleiermacherian line of thought continues to be developed with approval, leading to the final choice between personal and impersonal salvation already noted in a different context earlier in this argument. The choice is made in favour of the 'personalistic religion of redemption', to use Troeltsch's own formulation.[14] The crucial point is therefore that Troeltsch needed the concept *Wesen der Religion* for reasons connected with the demands of christian theology and not for reasons connected with the interpretation of the inward essence of particular traditions in their historical autonomy and in their divergent plurality. Had he applied his fundamental historicist axioms more consistently he might have come to very different conclusions about the usefulness of this concept. As it is, the shape of christian theology as he envisaged it is thoroughly historical with respect to its own sources, but not with respect to the drawing in of religion in general as a substitute for natural theology. It is one thing for christian theology to have a basis in history in the sense that its sources are those of a historical religious tradition. It is quite another to give it a basis in universal history by drawing on an 'essence' of religion, the definition of which in some ways runs significantly contrary to other highly developed religions. If the first works, the second does not, and it offends against Troeltsch's own 'logic of history'. Let there be no mistake about the fact that Troeltsch's talk of the 'essence' of religion involves a real definition of religion, for example, unbuddhistically, as 'a real interpenetration of the human and the divine spirit'. Indeed, if it did not, it would not serve the purpose to which he puts it.

It is significant that Troeltsch's line of argument here leads to a structural relationship between Christianity and the 'other' religions quite similar to those characterised at the beginning of this argument. Christianity has a special position and the others are all 'revelations and self-manifestations of God corresponding to the total situation of the time'.

[14] *Gl.*, p. 9. The same phrase was used in *Die Absolutheit des Christentums* (Siebenstern Taschenbuch Verlag, 1969), p. 5.

Although Christianity is not 'miraculously' separated from these, Troeltsch nevertheless contrives to put them all into the same basket.

Although the notion of the 'essence' of religion has been widely popular it is doubtful whether it will ever really be able to maintain itself in the history of religions field. The general term 'religion' is perhaps more like the general term 'politics'; and what would be the sense in trying to define the 'essence' of politics? If, as Troeltsch pointed out, the fundamental complexes of history tend to fade away at the edges, what are we to make of the edges of religions or of religion? Some important religions have more in common with apparently non-religious historical forms than with other religions. Yet what in some ways seem to be the fringe cases of religion seem in other ways to be the most important cases. It could be argued precisely that the rarified spirituality which Troeltsch found so significant in Christianity really makes it a very atypical case; the 'essence' of religion by contrast, one might say, is more to do with hunting and agriculture. Finally it would be possible to produce a statement of the 'essence' of religion which is the mirror of Troeltsch's statement quoted above, but which turns out in favour of Buddhism; it would refer to the gradual elimination of self-interest and indeed of the very notion of a self or a soul, a progression from polytheism through monotheism and others towards a general relegation of the gods to harmless realms, and the growing recognition that man can find his release from ignorance and suffering through his own withdrawal of the desire which forever whips the flames forward.

Rather than this outdated 'essence of religion' approach, Troeltsch's own historical presuppositions would seem to demand rather a 'family resemblance' relationship between the religious traditions. While due recognition should be given to all analogies of content and structure, the autonomous individual coherence of each religious tradition should also count significantly for something.

The presupposition of the historical plurality of religious traditions, each with its own internal claim to meaning, and its own demand for attention in appropriate and not alien terms, is really fundamental for Troeltsch, even though it is somewhat obscured by the other traits in his thought which have just been considered. This presupposition is really necessary for a viable history of religions, and it is grounded in the general theory of history as this is understood by Troeltsch. Modern theology, jewish, christian, islamic theology, and the equivalents of theology in the various religious traditions, cannot any longer back away from this presupposition, whatever its implications may be for the structure of their dogmatic systems, unless indeed they are to relapse into an arbitrary supernaturalism or an obscurantist fideism. As Troeltsch would have said, the meaning of any one such tradition lies within itself but also within the meaning of the whole interconnected web of history. At the same time there is no single 'essence' of religion which would miraculously mark off religion from all other matters; and of course Troeltsch himself saw quite clearly the continuities between religion and other social and psychological factors. Above all there is certainly no simple 'essence' of all the 'other' religions, which could somehow be fulfilled by, or contrasted with, the faith of one's choice. Any thought about religion which is based on the history of religions must respect both the analogies and the divergencies between the various traditions.

THE PRESUPPOSITION OF HISTORICAL CHANGE

The second presupposition of Troeltsch's thought which needs to be systematically carried through is that religious tradition is subject to *change* in history. There are two aspects to this. The first is the inescapable modern recognition that this is so, and the second is the creative response made to the meanings conveyed by the tradition under these circumstances. There is no miracle which can isolate one particular phase of a religious tradition, even its original formative phase, as being outside the conditioning by historical change which affects the whole tradition. On the other hand the problem and the responsibility of reinterpretation remain as a continuous possibility. Even saying and doing the same things as are supposed to have been said and done 'originally', for example, giving a literal performance of Saint Paul, has a different meaning in changed circumstances. The reality of historical change cannot be avoided, and there is no short cut to orthodoxy.

It is easy to admit that the features of a religious tradition change more or less coherently in the course of centuries. Indeed at the 'naïve' level this is recognised in all religious movements which call for reform. The cry goes up for a return to the original purity of doctrine, of practice, of experience, and yet another holy community is set up to take its place in the chain. Such religious criticism can also itself contain the seeds of historical criticism, as for example among the confucianists of eighteenth-century Japan. Conversely, however, this very emphasis on the importance of the origins itself tends to isolate these origins as if they were qualitatively different from the subsequent forms of the tradition, which are by implication more or less degenerate. This manoeuvre is particularly visible in protestantism. The result of this natural tendency is that the origins, however defined, whether by holy book, or by persons and events, represent the final stronghold of unhistorical thought, and not only the final one but a strongly reinforced one. It is therefore a point of principle for the historical method to see these origins too, not as an isolated miracle, but as themselves a part of the historical process just as much as later phases of the tradition. The Japanese historicist Tominaga (1715–46) achieved this when he opened his critique of buddhist tradition with the sly words: 'When we now consider first the context in which Buddhism arose it is evident that it began among other religions.'[15] The term for 'other religions', literally 'outside ways' (*gedō*) is ironically taken from the mouths of buddhists who used the term precisely for 'other' religions of ancient India, etc. It may be said that as far as christian theology is concerned (when it goes beyond the naïve) it is now generally recognised that the events first constitutive of the christian religion are subject to the process of history just as much as is the later experience of the church.

[15] Opening sentence of the *Shutsujōkōgo* by Tominaga (Nakamoto), published with a modern Japanese text in *Gendai Bukkyō Meicho Zenshū* I, *Bukkyō no Shomondai*, ed. Nakamura, Masutani and Kitagawa (Tokyo, 1972). For an introductory discussion of the importance of Tominaga's thought, see the present writer's 'Aufklärung and Religion in Europe and Japan', in *Religious Studies*, vol. 9, pp. 201–17, where Tominaga is compared with Lessing.

Similarly it may be said that, today, on the whole, the historical method is the basis for the thoughtful interpretation of buddhist tradition in the east.

Troeltsch himself worked out the notion of Christianity as subject to historical change quite massively in his work *The Social Teachings of the Christian Churches and Sects*, and there is no difference in principle between the assumptions of this work and Harnack's *History of Dogma*. Theoretical reflection on the matter however, which also involves a partial critique of Harnack's work is found in the earlier essay 'What does "Essence of Christianity" mean?'.[16] It is sufficient to recapitulate here that Troeltsch saw the task of theology as being both historical and creative. It is necessary, without any flight to miracle, to grasp the essence (*Wesen*) of Christianity by an objectively disciplined yet critically discerning appraisal of its phases up to now, and in this act, which is a creative act, to set it forth as a possibility for the present and for the future. This combines the importance of the origins with the demands of successive meaningful phases of the tradition in a work which is at once both historical and theological.

Troeltsch's thought here is in line not only empirically with the way in which religions do in fact change and develop in history, but also theoretically with his own general theory of the role of abstractions in history. Whether or not he was himself able to formulate the essence of Christianity adequately or successfully is entirely beside the point and is no indication whatever of the rightness or wrongness of his presuppositions. Nor does it matter very much whether we like the word 'essence' or not (which has a different sense here from that discussed earlier). Some such seizing and reformulation of what is conveyed in the tradition is what comes again and again into question, and the important recognition is that this activity is at once historical and creative, or able to convey insight.

Troeltsch abstracted his methodological reflections at this

---

[16] The argument of this essay is summarised in greater detail than is required here in *The Cardinal Meaning, Essays in Comparative Hermeneutics: Buddhism and Christianity*, eds. Michael Pye and Robert Morgan (Mouton: The Hague, 1973), pp. 9–17, Cf. also Stephen Sykes' extensive (and more sceptical) discussion in his paper contained in the present volume.

point to such an extent that they could be carried on irrespective of the variations in the specific content accorded to Christianity by its various interpreters. Moreover, as mentioned above, his reflections arose not merely on the basis of the writings of his theological contemporaries but also on the basis of his own developing view of historical method. This degree of abstraction makes it possible to relate his analysis to other traditions too. Admittedly Troeltsch himself referred only briefly to religious traditions other than Christianity in the essay in question, though in an earlier piece he had made extended use of a comparative perspective on the relations between doctrine and organisation in religion as a basis for specific recommendations with respect to Christian theology.[17] Nevertheless the implication of his thought is that the same historical presuppositions apply to all religious traditions and that therefore analogous methodological reflections are relevant to theologising (or its equivalents) in any such tradition. There is, for esample, as has been argued elsewhere,[18] a modern question about the 'essence' of Buddhism (if that is the formulation we want), which has its own roots in oriental tradition as well as a common basis in the very nature of all history. Indeed it is to be expected that any individual tradition will develop questions of this sort as it takes on historical depth in the minds of its adherents. It is also to be expected that there is in important respects a common rationality to these problems, which becomes discernible given enough data, both on account of analogies between the claims and functions of religions and because of the nature of history itself as a unifying category. This means that there is some value in a comparative approach to problems about the interpretation of religious traditions, which may be referred to for short as comparative hermeneutics. It also means, and this is a *further* step, that the interpretation of the various traditions (as opposed to the abstract taking of thought about how they interpret themselves), that is, the direct interpretation of the meaning of specific traditions, must also work along lines similiar to those advanced by Troeltsch for the case of Christianity. All modern interpretation presupposes historical

[17] Cf. note 3 above.
[18] 'Comparative Hermeneutics in Religion', in *The Cardinal Meaning*.

change as part and parcel of the tradition whose meaning is supposed to be elucidated. Although it has been treated more briefly, the addition of this presupposition to the present argument is quite essential. Without it the first presupposition, that of the historical plurality of religious traditions in the sense argued for above, remains quite lifeless.

THE END OF THE PROBLEM ABOUT 'OTHER' RELIGIONS

Perhaps it is fair to say that Troeltsch never brought these two important presuppositions together with respect to our problem in a forceful way.[19] First, his theoretical acceptance of a plurality of meaningful complexes in history was over-shadowed in various ways and distinctly impeded by his use of the concept 'essence of religion'. He set Christianity firmly within the history of religions but did not care to articulate the wide divergencies which exist within the real history of religions. This presupposition therefore needs to be radical-ised. Secondly, his presupposition of historical change as an inescapable mode for the work of all interpreters of religion was mainly restricted in its practical application to Christianity. This is understandable in that the problem he set himself was to show the possibility of a christian theology which would be historically based and at the same time both critical and creative. The modern thinking which he helped to nurture demands that this presupposition now be assumed in the interpretation of any religious tradition, and indeed in the interpretation of anything else which is anything like a religious tradition. The two presuppositions complement each other. If we are to see the history of religions as offering various sequences of meaningful tradition, many of which still demand to be stated or conveyed again by those who stand in continuity with them, then the total picture is of a plurality of traditions which are all subject to change in analogous ways. If a specific line of interpretation, such as christian theology, is to

[19] They are admittedly brought together in theory, as, briefly, in the article 'Historiography' in Hastings' *Encyclopedia of Religion and Ethics* VI (1913), 720b, where they are advanced as two of the three fundamental principles of historical reflexion. We are concerned however with the coordinated radicalisation of these principles with respect to the relations between religions in particular.

be carried on in this context of the history of religions as it really is, it cannot sit on some dogmatic throne whence it surveys in retrospect the vanquished rival contributors to an essence of religion which it alone can fully sustain. There can be no priorities among the questions: What is religion? What is Christianity? How best can the superiority (or 'absoluteness' in Troeltsch's modified sense) of Christianity *vis à vis* the 'other' religions be articulated? The question: 'What does our tradition mean?' is *contemporaneous* for all religious traditions which have any role to play. That is the modern situation presaged yet obscured by the writings of Ernst Troeltsch. Any theology which claims to locate its christian tradition within the history of religions must come to terms with this orientation.

If this extrapolation of Troeltschian presuppositions is correct, the implication is that it is extremely odd in our contemporary situation for anyone to be persistently engaged in the interpretation of one tradition in isolation from all the so-called 'others'. Of course there is the pressure of time. Yet this can be an excuse for attitudes which look remarkably like the old flight to miracle, that is, it is like buying a one-way ticket to one's own prejudicially selected and isolated miracle. It is not at all possible here even to outline what would be the pattern of a dogmatics whether mainly christian, mainly buddhist, etc., which took these presuppositions seriously. The requirement remains however that it proceed in such a way that no problem about 'other' religions be set aside in the prolegomena or remain as an appendix. Somehow a contemporary dogmatics has to take the plurality of religious traditions seriously, with all their historical weight and their openness to the future. The meaning of say, Buddhism, Christianity and Marxism for the twenty-first century is *not yet exactly known*. All traditions are equally open and new formulations and phases are sure to emerge. Troeltsch himself was not anticipating significant *new* developments, but even this should not be turned into a lullaby. There is no magical line of defence between one religion and the 'others', and there is no magical line between religion and non-religion. This does not mean that there are not coherencies, for we are all the time shaping tradition both retrospectively and for the future. There are also crisis points.

Troeltsch did not speak much of 'other' religions, but even he, when restricting himself to Europeanism, referred to 'the people outside' [GS III 709, 'die Leute draußen']. The belated political unification of Europe cannot obscure the latently more important fact that the 'we' which we now enjoy has moved beyond the consciousness of European culture prevalent fifty years ago. In a sense all the traditions are 'ours', and 'we' are all tending to get inside. Nothing is to be lost, because we shall be sifting all the traditions and bringing out their meaning for the future. Does this perspective cut some vital nerve for christian faith, or does it perchance rule out *Diamat* (dialectical materialism) *a priori*, or does it unacceptably reduce Buddhism to a par with its theistic rivals and its polytheistic bed-fellows? If so, then it will be the way of the world in so far as this is illuminated by the history of religions. On the other hand, everything of value in all the traditions is available for modern man.

Not that the history of religions should itself be involved in the creative appraisals and interpretations, and transmissions. It merely clarifies the tracks along which things have run so far. But if creative theology is to be consistent with the reality which is known to the history of religions, then it has to respond to a plurality of religious traditions which are all subject to coherent change and open to the future on an equal basis. The notion of 'other' religions, as a general category to be opposed or related to a christian dogmatics worked out in preconceived isolation, is redundant.[20]

---

[20] It must be admitted that this whole argument brings forward only *one* requirement for future systematic theology, and a negative one at that. In discussion of this paper the writer was asked to advance more positively what a dogmatics which satisfies this requirement might in practice look like (in order, no doubt, that it might be open to criticism). It seemed inappropriate to advance such suggestions, however, because the requirement appears to remain regardless of the variety of possibilities for dogmatics, and indeed regardless of whether or not a christian dogmatics is able to satisfy it in any way. In later discussion it was put by Professor Maurice Wiles that the way in which Christianity may be correlated with a religion different from itself should probably be in principle not dissimilar to the way in which it is correlated with the world-views with which it has come into successive contact during its European history. This deceptively simple point has however not yet been taken seriously to heart by christian theology. It would perhaps mean that rather than compressing all the 'other' religions together under some dubious 'essence', each particular instance of importance

would present a whole mode of being for Christianity. Thus one might speak of Christianity in a platonic mode, Christianity in an aristotelian mode and Christianity in a buddhist mode. This should not be thought of as something which can be left to missionary fraternisers in lands far from the supposed centres of christian theology, and also not as finding ways of dressing up Christianity for different climates. Rather it should be seen as a way of critically evaluating potential truths and values from diverse sources. Moreover the whole argument, especially the main negative argument given above, applies equally to the continuing restatement of for example, the buddhist tradition. That is, buddhists also cannot take a supposed general essence of religion as a mere prolegomenon for buddhist doctrine. What is needed is a good-humoured critical interaction between the various traditions, in the course of which all are sifted in terms of each other. Of course there are those who are already engaged in this sharing and searching of traditions. This approach seems to be more interesting than a mere blending or convergence, which often has idealist overtones. By contrast with such blurrings it is necessary (for the theologian) to be at once conservative, critical, and creative of specific tradition.

Bibliography

COMPILED BY JACOB KLAPWIJK

The following abbreviations are used in the Bibliography:

CW   Die Christliche Welt (Marburg i.H.)
HZ   Historische Zeitschrift (München etc.)
JSSR   Journal for the Scientific Study of Religion (New Haven, U.S.A.)
RGG   Die Religion in Geschichte und Gegenwart (Tübingen)
ThLZ   Theologische Literaturzeitung (Leipzig etc.)
ThR   Theologische Rundschau (Tübingen)
VT   Vox Theologica (Assen)
ZThK   Zeitschrift für Theologie und Kirche (Tübingen)

I. RECENT EDITIONS OF TROELTSCH'S WORKS

This section lists works of Troeltsch that have been republished since 1960. It should be used in combination with Hans Baron's bibliography in Troeltsch's *Gesammelte Schriften* (*GS*) IV. The dates preceded by BB refer to that bibliography, which gives further information about the original editions.

'Ueber historische und dogmatische Methode in der Theologie' (BB 1900), in G. Sauter (ed.), *Theologie als Wissenschaft* (Kaiser Verlag: München, 1971), pp. 105–27.

Die Absolutheit des Christentums und die Religionsgeschichte (BB 1902) *und zwei Schriften zur Theologie*: 'Die Bedeutung der Geschichtlichkeit Jesu für den Glauben' (BB 1911), 'Die Kirche im Leben der Gegenwart' (BB 1911), Siebenstern Taschenbuch Verlag: München/Hamburg, 1970.

Die Bedeutung des Protestantismus für die Entstehung der modernen Welt (BB 1906), Otto Zeller Verlag: Aalen, 1963.
  Excerpt (= *Die Bedeutung* (^{5}1928), pp. 46–85) in F. Fürstenberg (ed.), *Religionssoziologie* (Hermann Luchterhand Verlag: Neuwied, 1964, ^{2}1970), pp. 339–73.

'Rückblick auf ein halbes Jahrhundert der theologischen Wissenschaft' (BB 1909), in G. Sauter (ed.), *Theologie als Wissenschaft* (Kaiser Verlag: München, 1971), pp. 73–104.

'Die Bedeutung der Geschichtlichkeit Jesu für den Glauben' (BB 1911), *see Die Absolutheit* (1902).

'Die Kirche im Leben der Gegenwart' (BB 1911), *see Die Absolutheit* (1902).

Die Soziallehren der christlichen Kirchen und Gruppen (BB 1912), *Gesammelte Schriften* I, Scientia Verlag: Aalen, 1961, 1965.

Excerpt (= *GS* I, 362–75) in F. Fürstenberg (ed.), *Religionssoziologie* (Hermann Luchterhand Verlag: Neuwied 1964, ²1970), pp. 299–309.

Zur religiösen Lage, Religionsphilosophie und Ethik (BB 1913), *Gesammelte Schriften* II, Scientia Verlag: Aalen, 1962.

Augustin, die christliche Antike und das Mittelalter (BB 1915), Scientia Verlag: Aalen, 1963.

Der Historismus und seine Probleme (BB 1922), *Gesammelte Schriften* III, Scientia Verlag: Aalen, 1961.

Der Historismus und seine Ueberwindung (BB 1923), Scientia Verlag: Aalen, 1966.

Spektator-Briefe (BB 1924), Scientia Verlag: Aalen, 1966.

Aufsätze zur Geistesgeschichte und Religionssoziologie (BB 1925), *Gesammelte Schriften* IV, Scientia Verlag: Aalen, 1966.

Deutscher Geist und Westeuropa (BB 1925), Scientia Verlag: Aalen, 1966.

2. ENGLISH TRANSLATIONS OF TROELTSCH'S WORKS

This section contains a list of works of Troeltsch that have appeared in English translation. Corresponding German titles are added only where misunderstanding could arise. The dates preceded by BB refer to Hans Baron's chronologically ordered bibliography in Troeltsch's *Gesammelte Schriften* (*GS*) IV. Further information about the original texts and titles can be found in that bibliography.

'Enlightenment' (BB 1897), in Philip Schaff and Joann Herzog (eds.), *New Schaff-Herzog Encyclopedia of Religion*, Baker Book House: Grand Rapids, 1908–14, containing: 'Deism' (BB 1898), III, 391–7, 'Enlightenment' (BB 1897), IV, 141–7, 'Idealism, German' (BB 1900), V, 438–42, 'Moralists, British' (BB 1903), VII, 496–502.

'Deism' (BB 1898), *see* 'Enlightenment' (1897).

'Idealism, German' (BB 1900), *see* 'Enlightenment' (1897).

The Absoluteness of Christianity and the History of Religions (BB 1902), transl. by David Reid; with an introd. by James L. Adams, John Knox Press: Richmond (Virg.), 1971 and SCM Press: London, 1972.

'The Formal Autonomous Ethic of Conviction and the Objective Teleological Ethic of Value', part of 'Grundprobleme der Ethik' (BB 1902), (*GS* II, 618–35), in Warren F. Groff and Donald E. Miller (eds.), *The Shaping of Modern Christian Thought*, The World Publishing Co.: Cleveland and New York, 1968.

'The Ethic of Jesus', part of 'Grundprobleme der Ethik' (BB 1902),

(*GS* II, 629–39), in *The Unitarian Universalist Christian* 34, 1–2 (1974), 38–45.

'Moralists, British' (BB 1903), *see* 'Enlightenment' (1897).

'What Does "Essence of Christianity" Mean?' (BB 1903), in Robert Morgan & Michael Pye (eds.), *Ernst Troeltsch: Essays on Theology and Religion*, Duckworth: London and Beacon Press: Boston, 1976, containing: 'Half a Century of Theology: A Review' (BB 1909), 'The Essence of Religion and the Science of Religion' (BB 1906), 'What Does "Essence of Christianity" Mean?' (BB 1903), 'The Significance of the Historical Existence of Jesus for Faith' (BB 1911).

Protestantism and Progress: A historical study of the relation of protestantism to the modern world (cf. *Die Bedeutung des Protestantismus für die Entstehung der modernen Welt*, BB 1906) transl. by W. Montgomery; Williams & Norgate: London and G. P. Putnam's Sons: New York, 1912; Beacon Press, Inc.: Boston, 1958, ²1966; Gloucester (Mass.), 1964.

'Half a Century of Theology: A Review' (BB 1909), *see* 'What Does "Essence of Christianity" Mean?' (1903).

'Calvin and Calvinism', in *Hibbert Journal* 8 (1909), 102–21.

'On the Possibility of a Free Christianity' (BB 1910), in *Fifth International Congress of Free Christianity and Religious Progress (Berlin), Proceedings and Papers* (London, 1911), pp. 233–49.

Excerpts in: Charles W. Wendte (ed.), *The Fifth World Congress of Free Christians and Other Religious Liberals, Germany, August 5–11, 1910. A summary and appreciation by Charles W. Wendte*, American Unitarian Association: Boston, 1910.

Also in *The Unitarian Universalist Christian* 29, 1–2 (1974), 27–45.

'Contingency' (cf. 'Die Bedeutung des Begriffs der Kontingenz', BB 1910), in James Hastings (ed.), *Encyclopaedia of Religion and Ethics*, T. & T. Clark: Edinburgh and Charles Scribner's Sons: New York, 1908–26, containing: 'Contingency', IV (1911/12), 87–9, 'Free-Thought', VI (1913/14), 120–3, 'Historiography', VI (1913/14), 716–23, 'Idealism', VII (1914/15), 89–95, 'Kant', VII (1914/15), 653–9.

The Social Teaching of the Christian Churches (BB 1912), transl. by Olive Wyon; George Allen & Unwin Ltd: London and The Macmillan Company: New York, 1931, ²1949; Harper & Brothers: New York, 1960; with an introd. by H. Richard Niebuhr.

Excerpts ('The Three Types of Christian Community' = *The Social Teaching*, (1960), pp. 993–4, 997–1002) in Norman Birnbaum and Gertrud Lenzer (eds.), *Sociology and Religion* (Prentice Hall: Englewood Cliffs (N.J.), 1969), pp. 310–14.

Excerpt ('Medieval Christianity' = *The Social Teaching* (1960), pp. 246–56) in R. Robertson (ed.), *Sociology of Religion: Selected*

Readings (Penguin Books Ltd: Harmondsworth, etc., 1969), pp. 115–26.

'Empiricism and Platonism in the Philosophy of Religion (To the Memory of William James)' (BB 1912), in *Harvard Theological Review* 5 (1912), 401–22.

'Renaissance and Reformation' (BB 1913), transl. by Henry A. Finch, in *History: Selected Readings*, vol. II, The University of Chicago Press: Chicago, 1948.

Also in part transl. by Lewis W. Spitz, in Lewis W. Spitz (ed.), *The Reformation: Basic Interpretations* (Series: Problems in European Civilization) (D. C. Heath & Co.: Lexington, Mass./Toronto/London, 1972²), pp. 25–43.

'The Religious Principle' (BB 1913), in J. Pelikan (ed.), *Twentieth Century Theology in the Making*, Harper: New York and Fontana: London, II (1970), 334–41.

'Religion, Economics, and Society' (BB 1913), transl. by David Little/Walter Bense, in Norman Birnbaum and Gertrud Lenzer (eds.), *Sociology and Religion*, (Prentice Hall: Englewood Cliffs (N.J.), 1969), pp. 197–204.

'The dogmatics of the Religionsgeschichtliche Schule' (BB 1913), in *The American Journal of Theology* 17 (1913).

'Free-Thought' (1913/14), *see* 'Contingency' (1910).

'Historiography' (1913/14), *see* 'Contingency' (1910).

'Motley of German War Ideas' (BB 1915), in *New York Times*, 13 August 1915.

'Idealism' (1914/15), *see* 'Contingency' (1910).

'Kant' (1914/15), *see* 'Contingency' (1910).

'The German Idea of Freedom' (BB 1916), in W. Ebenstein, *Modern Political Thought* (New York, 1954), pp. 315–16.

'The Dogma of Guilt (19 June 1919)' (cf. 'Anhang. Das Schulddogma (19 Juni. 1919)' in *Spektator-Briefe*, pp. 314–21, BB 1919 and BB 1924), transl. by B. K. Bennett in Bernard Wishy (ed.), *The Western World in the Twentieth Century. A Source Book* (Columbia University Press: New York, 1961), pp. 151–6.

'Adolf von Harnack and Ferdinand Christian von Baur 1921' (BB 1921), in Wilhelm Pauck, *Harnack and Troeltsch. Two Historical Theologians* (Oxford University Press: New York, 1968), pp. 97–115.

'The Ideas of Natural Law and Humanity in World Politics' (BB 1922), in Otto Gierke, *Natural Law and the Theory of Society, 1500–1800*, Cambridge University Press: Cambridge, 1934; Beacon Press Inc.: Boston, 1957.

Christian Thought. Its History and Application (BB 1923), University of London Press Ltd: London, 1923; Meridian Books Inc.: New York, 1957.

'Public Opinion in Germany' (BB 1923), in *Contemporary Review* 123 (May 1923), 578–83.

The following articles have been translated and are planned for publication in the near future under the editorship of James Luther Adams and Walter F. Bense.
'Historical and Dogmatic Method in Theology' (BB 1900).
'Modern Philosophy of History' (BB 1903).
'The Dispositional Ethic' (part of *Protestantisches Christentum und Kirche in der Neuzeit*, BB 1906), (^{2}1922, pp. 462–3).
'The Essence of the Modern Spirit' (BB 1907).
'On the Question of the Religious A Priori' (BB 1909).
'Eschatology' – 'Faith' – 'Faith and History' – 'Natural Law, Christian' – 'Principle, Religious' – 'Redemption' (BB 1910 and BB 1913).
'Stoic-Christian Natural Law and the Modern Secular Natural Law' (BB 1911).
'The Church in the Life of the Present' (BB 1911).
'Renaissance and Reformation' (BB 1913).
'Logos and Mythos in Theology and Philosophy of Religion' (BB 1913).
'The Concept and Method of Sociology', Review of Paul Barth, *Geschichtsphilosophie als Soziologie* (BB 1916).
'Rival Methods for the Study of Religion' (part of 'Glaube und Ethos der hebräischen Propheten', BB 1916), (*GS* IV, 34–8).
'Max Weber' (BB 1920).
The Social Philosophy of Christianity (BB 1922).
'My Books' (BB 1922).

3. STUDIES OF TROELTSCH'S WORKS

Adams, J. L. 'A Liberal Education for Liberals', *Christian Register* (May 1948).
'Ernst Troeltsch as Analyst of Religion', *JSSR* 1 (1961), 98–109.
'Troeltsch, Ernst' *Encyclopaedia Britannica*, XXII (William Benton: London/Chicago, etc., 1963^{14}), 489.
'Introduction', in Ernst Troeltsch, *The Absoluteness of Christianity* (SCM Press: London, 1972), pp. 7–20.
Althaus, P. Review of E. Troeltsch, *Glaubenslehre*, in *Theologische Literaturzeitung* 52 (1927), 593–5.
Antoni, C. '"La teologia storica" di Ernst Troeltsch', *Studi Germanici* 2 (Florence, 1937), 255–77.
'Problemi e metodi della moderna storiografia: la sociologia e la filosofia della storia di E. Troeltsch', *Studi Germanici* 2 (Florence, 1937), 385–416.
Dallo Storicismo alla Sociologia. Sansoni: Florence, 1940; German

transl., *Vom Historismus zur Soziologie.* Stuttgart, n.d.; English transl., *From History to Sociology: The Transition in German Historical Thinking* (Merlin: London, 1962), pp. 39–85.

Bainton, R. H. 'Ernst Troeltsch – Thirty Years After', *Theology Today* 8 (Princeton, N.J., 1951), 70–96.

Bauer, K. 'Luther bei Troeltsch und bei Holl', *CW* 37 (1923), cols. 36–9.

Beer, R. *Selbstkritik der Geschichtsphilosophie bei Ernst Troeltsch.* UNI-Druck: München, 1957, diss.

Benckert, H. 'Der Begriff der Entscheidung bei Ernst Troeltsch: Ein Beitrag zum Verständnis seines Denkens', *ZThK* N.F. 12 (1931), 422–42. Also in H. Benckert, *Theologische Bagatellen: Gesammelte Aufsätze* (Evangelische Verlagsanstalt: Berlin, 1970), pp. 11–23.

Ernst Troeltsch und das ethische Problem. Vandenhoeck & Ruprecht: Göttingen, 1932.

'Troeltsch, Ernst', *RGG,* VI (J. C. B. Mohr (Paul Siebeck): Tübingen, 1962³), cols. 1044–7.

'Ernst Troeltsch – aktuell?', *Deutsches Pfarrerblatt* 65 (1965), 167–9. Also in H. Benckert, *Theologische Bagatellen: Gesammelte Aufsätze* (Evangelische Verlagsanstalt: Berlin, 1970), pp. 255–60.

Berkhof, H. 'Troeltsch en verder', *VT* 41 (1971), 329–31.

Beth, K. 'Das Wesen des Christentums und die historische Forschung: Eine Auseinandersetzung mit D. Troeltsch', *Neue Kirchliche Zeitschrift* 15 (Erlangen, 1904), 85–100, 173–88, 253–66, 343–60, 468–85. Also published separately: *Das Wesen des Christentums und die moderne historische Denkweise,* Leipzig, 1904.

Review of E. Troeltsch, *Die Absolutheit des Christentums²,* in *ThR* 15 (1912), 321–8.

Bodenstein, W. *Neige des Historismus: Ernst Troeltschs Entwicklungsgang.* Gerd Mohn: Gütersloh, 1959.

Bornhausen, K. 'Das religiöse Apriori bei Ernst Troeltsch und Rudolf Otto', *Zeitschrift für Philosophie und philosophische Kritik* (Leipzig) 139 (1910), 193–206.

'Troeltsch, Ernst', *RGG,* V (J. C. B. Mohr (Paul Siebeck): Tübingen, 1913¹), cols. 1360–4.

'Ernst Troeltsch und das Problem der wissenschaftlichen Theologie', *ZThK* N.F. 4 (1923), 196–223.

'Troeltsch, Ernst', *RGG,* V (J. C. B. Mohr (Paul Siebeck): Tübingen, 1931²), cols. 1284–7.

Bosse, Hans. *Marx–Weber–Troeltsch: Religionssoziologie und marxistische Ideologiekritik.* Kaiser: München and Grünewald: Mainz, 1970, diss.

Brachmann, W. *Ernst Troeltschs historische Weltanschauung.* Max Niemeyer: Halle (Saale), 1940, diss.

Bras, G. le & Séguy, J. 'Christianismes sociaux et sociologie du Christianisme chez Ernst Troeltsch', *Archives de Sociologie des Religions* (Paris) 11 (1961), 3–14.

Brieger, Th. 'Randbemerkungen zu Troeltsch Vortrag über "Die Bedeutung des Protestantismus für die Entstehung der modernen Welt"', *Zeitschrift für Kirchengeschichte* (Gotha, etc.) 27 (1906), 348–55.

Brüning, W. 'Historicismo, naturalismo, apriorismo: La obra de Ernest Troeltsch', *Notas y Estudios de Filosofia* (Tucumán) 4 (1953), 331–42; German transl., 'Naturalismus-Historismus-Apriorismus: Das Werk Ernst Troeltschs', *Studia Philosophica* (Basel) 15 (1955), 35–52; also published separately, Basel, 1955.

Brunstäd, F. 'Ueber die Absolutheit des Christentums', *Neue Kirchliche Zeitschrift* (Erlangen) 16 (1905), 772–800, 815–40.

Christie, F. A. 'Spiritual Values in the Work of Ernst Troeltsch', *Methods in Social Science*, ed. S. A. Rice ed., (Chicago, 1931), pp. 415–23.

Currie, C. 'Ernst Troeltsch's Philosophy of History', 1946, diss. Harvard University (manuscr.).

Deissmann, A. 'Die Absolutheit des Christentums und die Religionsgeschichte', *CW* 16 (1902), cols. 1181ff.

Dermidoff, F. 'Religione e storia nel pensiero de E. Troeltsch'. Genova, 1966, diss.

Dibelius, M. 'Ernst Troeltsch', *Frankfurter Zeitung und Handelsblatt* (Frankfurt) 7.2.1923.

Diehl, H. 'Hermann und Troeltsch', *ZThK* XVIII (1908), 473–8.

Dietrich, A. *Ernst Troeltsch: Ein Gedächtnisrede.* Berlin, 1923.
'Ernst Troeltsch', *Archiv für Politik und Geschichte* (Berlin) 1 (1923), 97–112.
'Ernst Troeltsch', *Deutsche Allgem. Zeitung* 7.2.1923.
'Ernst Troeltsch', *Soziale Praxis* 32 (1923), 143.
'Troeltsch, Ernst Peter Wilhelm', *Deutsches Biographisches Jahrbuch* (Berlin, etc.) V, *Das Jahr 1923* (1930), 349–68.

Dockhorn, K. *Deutscher Geist und angelsächsische Geistesgeschichte: Ein Versuch der Deutung ihres Verhältnisses* (Musterschmidt: Göttingen, 1954), pp. 11–17.

Drescher, H. G. *Glaube und Vernunft bei Ernst Troeltsch: Eine kritische Deutung seiner religionsphilosophischen Grundlegung.* N.p., 1957, diss. Marburg/L.
'Das Problem der Geschichte bei Ernst Troeltsch', *ZThK* N.F. 57 (1960), 186–230.

Dunkmann, K. *Das religiöse Apriori und die Geschichte: Ein Beitrag zur Grundlegung der Religionsphilosophie,* Beiträge zur Förderung christlicher Theologie 14, 3 (1910) (C. Bertelsmann: Gütersloh, 1910), pp. 46ff.

Dyson, A. O. 'History in the Philosophy and Theology of Ernst Troeltsch'. 1968, diss. Oxford.

Eister, A. W. 'Toward a Radical Critique of Church-Sect Typologizing: Comment on "Some Critical Observation on the Church-Sect Dimension"', *JSSR* 6, 1 (1967), 85–90.

Elseman, O. 'Mogelijkheden of onmogelijkheden van een christelijke sociale ethiek', *VT* 44, 3 (1974), 160–74.

Engelmann, H. *Spontaneität und Geschichte: Zum Historismusproblem bei Ernst Troeltsch*. Dipa-Verlag: Frankfurt a.M., 1972, diss.

Eschbach, V. 'Ernst Troeltsch im französischen Urteil', *CW* 37 (1923), cols. 315–16.

Escribano Alberca, I. *Die Gewinnung theologischer Normen aus der Geschichte der Religion bei E. Troeltsch: Eine methodologische Studie.* Max Hueber: München, 1961.

Eucken, R. Review of E. Troeltsch, *Die Absolutheit des Christentums*, in *Göttingische gelehrte Anzeigen* (Göttingen) 165 (1903), 77–106, 177–86.

Faber, H. *De geschiedenis als theologisch probleem: Een studie naar aanleiding van Ernst Troeltsch 'Der Historismus und seine Probleme'.* Van Loghum Slaterus: Arnhem, 1933, diss.

Fellner, K. *Das überweltliche Gut und die innerweltlichen Güter: Eine Auseinandersetzung mit Ernst Troeltschs Theorie über das Verhältnis von Religion und Kultur.* J. C. Hinrichs: Leipzig, 1927, diss.

Fischer, H. 'Luther und seine Reformation in der Sicht Ernst Troeltschs', *Neue Zeitschrift für systematische Theologie und Religionsphilosophie* (Berlin) 5 (1963), 132–72.

Christlicher Glaube und Geschichte: Voraussetzungen und Folgen der Theologie Friedrich Gogartens (Gerd Mohn: Gütersloh, 1967), pp. 13–64.

Förster, E. 'Die Darstellung des lutherischen Protestantismus in E. Troeltsch's "Soziallehren"', *ZThK* N.F. 1 (1920), 103–16.

Frei, H. W. 'The Relation of Faith and History in the Thought of Ernst Troeltsch', *Faith and Ethics: The Theology of H. Richard Niebuhr*, Paul Ramsey (ed.) (Harper & Brothers: New York, 1957), pp. 53–64.

Freisberg, D. *Das Problem der historischen Objektivität in der Geschichtsphilosophie von Ernst Troeltsch.* Heinr. & J. Lechte: Emsdetten, 1940, diss.

Fülling, E. *Geschichte als Offenbarung: Studien zur Frage Historismus und Glaube von Herder bis Troeltsch* (Verlag Alfred Töpelmann: Berlin, 1956), pp. 61–88.

Fürst, E. 'Christliches und profanes Ethos: Ernst Troeltsch und Rudolf Otto', *Theologische Quartalschift* (Rottenburg a. Neckar) 134 (1954), 333–51.

Gerrish, B. A. 'Jesus, Myth, and History: Troeltsch's Stand in the "Christ-Myth" Debate', *The Journal of Religion* (Chicago) 55, 1 (1975), 13–35.

Getzeny, H. 'Troeltsch als Theologe und Soziologe', *Hochland* (Kempten, etc.) 25, 2 (1927/8), 582–97.

'Forscher und Vorkämpfer der Religion: Zum 20. Todestag von Ernst Troeltsch', *Magazin für religiöse Bildung* (Ehingen a.d. Donau) 106 (1943), 15–16.

Goddijn, H. P. M. 'Ernst Troeltsch (1865–1923): Zijn intellectuele en maatschappelijke contekst', *VT* 41 (1971), 297–308.

Gogarten, F. *Ich glaube an den dreieinigen Gott: Eine Untersuchung über Glauben und Geschichte* (Eugen Diederichs: Jena, 1926), pp. 17–39.

Grautoff, O. 'Ernst Troeltsch', *Literarisches Echo* 25 (1923), 673.

Groenewegen, H. Y. 'Het laatste werk van Troeltsch', *Nieuw Theologisch Tijdschrift* (Haarlem) 13 (1924), 226–37.

Günther, W. *Die Grundlagen der Religionsphilosophie Ernst Troeltsch'*. Quelle & Meyer: Leipzig, 1914, diss.

Gustafson, P. 'UO-US-PS-PO: A Restatement of Troeltsch's Church-Sect Typology', *JSSR* 6 (1967), 64–8.

Haan, J. C. de 'Over Troeltsch' historisme', *Tijdschrift voor Geschiedenis* (Groningen) 39 (1924), 77–89.

Habering, E. 'Die Askese in der kantischen Philosophie: Eine historisch-philosophische Studie im Anschluss an die Arbeiten von M. Weber und E. Troeltsch'. Königsberg, 1925, diss.

Harnack, A. von *Ernst Troeltsch: Rede gehalten bei der Trauerfeier am 3. Februar 1923.*

'Ernst Troeltsch. Rede am Sarge Troeltschs', *Berliner Tageblatt* (Berlin) 6.2.1923; also in *CW* 37 (1923), cols. 101–5; also in A. von Harnack, *Erforschtes und Erlebtes* (Giessen, 1923), 360–7.

Harvey, V. A. *The Historian and the Believer: The Morality of Historical Knowledge and Christian Belief* (Macmillan: New York, 1966), pp. 3–9.

Hashagen, J. 'Ernst Troeltsch und Ranke', *Philosophische Anzeiger* (Bonn) 4 (1929/30), 1–12.

Heinrici, C. F. G. *Dürfen wir noch Christen bleiben?: Kritische Betrachtungen zur Theologie der Gegenwart.* Dürr: Leipzig, 1901.

Heinzelmann, G. *Die erkenntnistheoretische Begründung der Religion: Ein Beitrag zur religions-philosophischen Arbeit der gegenwärtigen Theologie.* Verlag von Helbing und Lichtenhahn: Basel, 1915.

Henderson, K. T. 'Ethics and the Control of History: A Study of Troeltsch', *The Church Quarterly Review* (London) (1924), 116–44.

Herberger, K. 'Historismus und Kairos: Die Überwindung des Historismus bei Ernst Troeltsch und Paul Tillich', *Theologische Blätter* (Leipzig) 14 (1935), cols. 129–41, 161–75; also published separately: H. Bauer: Marburg/L., 1935.

Herring, H. 'Max Weber und Ernst Troeltsch als Geschichtsdenker', *Kant-Studien* (Berlin) 59 (1968), 410–34.

Herrmann, Ch. 'Ernst Troeltsch', *Sozialistische Monatsheft* (1923), p. 184.

Herrmann, W. Review of E. Troeltsch, *Die Absolutheit des Christentums*, in *ThLZ* 27 (1902), 330–4.

Review of E. Troeltsch, *Die Bedeutung der Geschichtlichkeit Jesu für den Glauben*, in *ThLZ* 37 (1912), 245–9; also published as an article, 'Wilhelm Herrmann über Ernst Troeltsch', *ZThK* N.F. 57 (1960), 231–7.

Hertefelt, M. d' 'Existeren in overgave: Theologische thematiek in de "Glaubenslehre" van Ernst Troeltsch en "Der Römische Brunnen" van Gertrud von le Fort', *Bijdragen: Tijdschrift voor Filosofie en Theologie* 19 (1958), 247–59.

Hessen, J. *Die Absolutheit des Christentums*. Köln, 1917.

Religionsphilosophie, 1 (Ernst Reinhardt: München/Basel, 1955²), 164–78.

Hintze, O. 'Troeltsch und die Probleme des Historismus', *HZ* 135 (1927), 188–239; also in O. Hintze, *Gesammelte Abhandlungen*, II (Vandenhoeck & Ruprecht: Göttingen, 1964²), 323–73.

Hoffmann, H. Review of E. Troeltsch, *Die Bedeutung des Protestantismus für die Entstehung der modernen Welt*, in *Deutsche Literaturzeitung* (Leipzig) 34 (1913), cols. 1170–2.

'Ernst Troeltsch zum Gedächtnis', *Theologische Blätter* 2 (Leipzig, 1923), cols. 77–83.

Holk, L. J. van 'Troeltsch, de superieure theoloog van het laatburgerlijke tijdperk', *VT* 41 (1971), 315–18.

Hügel, F. von 'On the Specific Genius and Capacities of Christianity, Studied in Connection with the Works of Ernst Troeltsch', *Constructive Quarterly* (New York) (March/December 1914); also in F. von Hügel, *Essays and Addresses on the Philosophy of Religion*, First Series (J. M. Dent & Sons: London and E. P. Dutton & Co.: New York, 1921), pp. 144–94.

'Ernst Troeltsch: To the Editor of the Times', *The Times Literary Supplement*, 29.3.1923, p. 216; German transl., 'Ein Brief F. v. Hügels über Troeltsch', etc., *CW* 37 (1923), cols. 311–15.

'Einleitung', in: E. Troeltsch, *Der Historismus und seine Überwindung* (Pan Verlag Rolf Heise: Berlin, 1924), pp. V–XII. Reprinted: Scientia: Aalen, 1966.

'Introduction', in E. Troeltsch, *Christian Thought: Its History and Application* (Meridian Books: New York, 1957), pp. 13–32.

Hughes, H. S. *Consciousness and Society: The Reorientation of European Social Thought 1890–1930*. Alfred A. Knopf: New York, 1958, and MacGibbon & Kee: London, 1959.

Iggers, G. G. *The German Conception of History: The National Tradition of Historical Thought from Herder to the Present* (Wesleyan University Press: Middletown, 1968), pp. 174–95.

Ittel, G. W. 'Die Hauptgedanken der "religionsgeschichtlichen Schule"', *Zeitschrift für Religions- und Geistesgeschichte* 10 (1958), 61–78.

Jaeger, P. Review of E. Troeltsch, *Die Absolutheit des Christentums*, in *CW* 16 (1902), cols. 914–21, 930–42.

Jelke,. R. J. *Das religiöse Apriori und die Aufgaben der Religions-philosophie: Ein Beitrag zur Kritik der religionsphilosophischen Position Ernst Troeltschs*. C. Bertelsmann: Gütersloh, 1917, diss.

Johnson, B. 'On Church and Sect', *American Sociological Review* (New York), 28 (1963), 539–49.

Johnson, R. A. 'Troeltsch on Christianity and Relativism', *JSSR* 1 (1962), 220–3.

Johnson, W. A. *On Religion: A Study of Theological Method in Schleier-macher and Nygren*. E. J. Brill: Leiden, 1964.

Joó, T. *A történet-filozófia feladata és Ernst Troeltsch elmélete*, etc. Szeged, 1931. With a German summary.

Kaftan, J. 'Die Selbständigkeit des Christentums', *ZThK* VI (1896), 373–94.
'Erwiederung. 1/Die Methode; 2/Der Supranaturalismus', *ZThK* VIII (1898), 70–96.

Kaftan, Th. *Ernst Tröltsch: Eine kritische Zeitstudie*. Julius Bergas: Schleswig, 1912.

Kamstra, J. H. 'Troeltsch en de godsdienstwetenschap', *VT* 41 (1971), 318–23.

Kasch, W. H. *Die Sozialphilosophie von Ernst Troeltsch*. J. C. B. Mohr (Paul Siebeck): Tübingen, 1963.

Kattenbusch, F. Review of E. Troeltsch, *Protestantisches Christentum und Kirche in der Neuzeit*, in *ThR* 16 (1907), 41–54, 71–6.

Keet, B. B. *De theologie van Ernst Troeltsch*. Swets & Zeitlinger: Amsterdam, 1913, diss.

Kesseler, K. 'Ernst Troeltsch: Zu seinem 50. Geburtstage am 17. Februar', *Zeitschrift für Philosophie und philosophische Kritik* 157 (Leipzig, 1915), 1–4.
'Troeltsch als Theologe', *Zeitschrift für den evangelischen Religions-unterricht* 34 (1923), 13–17.
'Vom Lebenswerk Ernst Troeltschs', *Die Hilfe: Zeitschrift für Politik, Literatur und Kunst* 29 (1923), 58–9.
'Ernst Troeltsch', *Deutsches Philologenblatt* 1923, 18.
'Troeltsch als Geschichtsphilosoph', *Monatsschrift für höhere Schulen* (Berlin), 23 (1924), 87–91.

Klapwijk, J. 'Ernst Troeltsch: Het historisme en zijn problemen', *Correspondentie-bladen van de Vereniging voor Calvinistische Wijsbegeerte* (Kampen) 26 (Dec. 1962), 12–24 and 27 (Apr. 1963), 14–23.
'De absoluutheid van het Christendom en zijn historische en sociologische gebondenheid (Ernst Troeltsch)', *Gereformeerd Theologisch Tijdschrift* (Kampen) 70 (1970), 19–33.
Tussen Historisme en Relativisme: Een studie over de dynamiek van het historisme en de wijsgerige ontwikkelingsgang van Ernst Troeltsch.

Van Gorcum & Comp.: Assen, 1970, diss. With a German summary.

'Christelijk geloof en sociale ethiek naar de opvatting van Ernst Troeltsch', *VT* 41 (1971), 335–43.

Klemm, H. 'Die Identifizierung des christlichen Glaubens in Ernst Troeltschs Vorlesung über Glaubenslehre', *Neue Zeitschrift für systematische Theologie und Religionsphilosophie* (Berlin) 16 (1974), 187–98.

Köhler, R. *Der Begriff a priori in der modernen Religionsphilosophie: Eine Untersuchung zur religionsphilosophischen Methode* (J. C. Hinrichs: Leipzig, 1920), pp. 3–22.

Köhler, W. *Ernst Troeltsch.* J. C. B. Mohr (Paul Siebeck): Tübingen, 1941.

'Ernst Troeltsch', *Zeitschrift für deutsche Kulturphilosophie* (Tübingen) 9 (1943), 1–21.

Kollman, E. C. 'Eine Diagnose der Weimarer Republik: Ernst Troeltschs politische Anschauungen', *HZ* 182 (1956), 291–318.

Kracauer, S. 'Die Wissenschaftskrisis: Zu den grundsätzlichen Schriften Max Webers und Ernst Troeltschs', *Hochschulblatt der FZ* 8.3.1923 (Nr. 179) and 22.3.1923 (Nr. 217).

'Ernst Troeltsch', *Frankfurter Zeitung und Handelsblatt* (Frankfurt) 1923 (Nr. 170).

Kübler, O. *Mission und Theologie: Eine Untersuchung über den Missionsgedanken in der syst. Theologie seit Schleiermacher* (Missionswissenschaftliche Forschungen 7, J. C. Hinrichs: Leipzig, 1929), pp. 186–207.

Laeyendecker, L. *Religie en Conflict: De zogenaamde sekten in sociologisch perspectief* (J. A. Boom en Zoon: Meppel, 1967), pp. 37–54, diss. With an English summary.

Leidreiter, E. *Troeltsch und die Absolutheit des Christentums.* C. L. Rautenberg: Mohrungen (Ostpr.), 1927, diss.

Lempp, O. 'Troeltschs theologischer Entwurf', *CW* 28 (1914), cols. 362–70, 410–14, 434–41.

Lessing, E. *Die Geschichtsphilosophie Ernst Troeltschs.* Herbert Reich Evang. Verlag: Hamburg-Bergstedt, 1965, diss.

Lewkowitz, A. 'Ernst Troeltsch', *Monatsschrift für Geschichte und Wissenschaft des Judenthums* (Breslau) 67 (1923), 20–6.

Liebert, A. 'Troeltschs letztes Werk', *Kant-Studien* (Berlin or Bonn) 29 (1924), 359–64.

Liebrich, H. *Die historische Wahrheit bei Ernst Troeltsch.* R. Glagow: Giessen, 1937, diss.

Lindeboom, J. 'De dogmenhistorische theorieën van Ernst Troeltsch', *Theologisch Tijdschrift* 53 (1919), 181–223.

Little, D. 'Religion and Social Analysis in the Thought of Ernst Troeltsch', *JSSR* 1 (1961), 114–17.

Little, H. G. 'History, Decision and Responsibility: A problem central

to the thought of Ernst Troeltsch and Rudolf Bultmann',
Harvard Theological Review (Cambridge, Mass.), 58 (1965), 456–7.
'History, Decision and Responsibility', 1965, diss. Harvard.
'Ernst Troeltsch and the Scope of Historicism', *Journal of Religion*
(Chicago) 46 (1966), 343–64.
Decision and Responsibility: A Wrinkle in Time. Studies in Religion
Series. N.p., Scholars Press, 1975.

Loofs, F. 'Luthers Stellung zum Mittelalter und zur Neuzeit',
Deutsch-evangelische Blätter (Berlin) 22 (1907).
'Troeltschs "Soziallehren der christlichen Kirchen und Gruppen"',
Deutsche Literaturzeitung 34 (Leipzig, 1913), cols. 2885–93.

Lotz, W. 'Das religionsphilosophische Problem der Wahrheit der
Religion bei Ernst Troeltsch'. Bonn, 1924, diss.

Lyman, E. W. 'Ernst Troeltsch's Philosophy of History', *The
Philosophical Review* (New York) 41 (1932), 443–69.

Macintosh, D. C. 'Troeltsch's Theory of Religious Knowledge',
American Journal of Theology (Chicago) 13 (1919), 274–89.

Mackintosh, H. R. *Types of Modern Theology: Schleiermacher to Barth*
(Nisbet and Co.: London, 1937), pp. 181–217.

Mandelbaum, M. *The Problem of Historical Knowledge: An Answer to
Relativism* (Harper & Row: New York, etc., 1967), pp. 155–65.

Mannheim, K. 'Historismus', *Archiv für Sozialwissenschaft und Sozial-
politik* (Tübingen) 52 (1924), 1–60; English transl.: K. Mannheim,
Essays on the Sociology of Knowledge (Routledge & Kegan Paul:
London, 1964³), pp. 84–133.
'Troeltsch, Ernst', *Encyclopaedia of the Social Sciences*, xv (The
Macmillan Company: New York, 1935), 106–7.

Marcuse, L. 'Ernst Troeltsch', *Berliner Tageblatt* (Berlin) 2.2.1923
(Nr. 55).

Maurenbrecher, M. 'Ernst Troeltsch', *Deutsche Zeitung* 2.2.1923 (Nr.
55).

Mazzantini. 'I Problemi della storia secondo E. Troeltsch', *Rivista
Storica Italiana* (Torino, 1924).

Meinecke, F. 'Ernst Troeltsch und das Problem des Historismus', *Die
Deutsche Nation: Eine Zeitschrift für Politik* (Berlin) 5 (1923),
183–92; also in F. Meinecke, *Staat und Persönlichkeit: Studien*
(Mittler & Sohn: Berlin, 1933), pp. 54–64; also in F. Meinecke,
Schaffender Spiegel (Stuttgart, 1948), pp. 211–28; also in
F. Meinecke, *Werke*, iv (K. F. Koehler, etc.: Stuttgart, etc., 1959)
367–78.
'Nachruf auf Ernst Troeltsch', *HZ* 128 (1923), 185–7; also in
F. Meinecke, *Werke*, iv (K. F. Koehler, etc.: Stuttgart, etc., 1959),
364–6.
'Einleitung', in E. Troeltsch, *Spektator-Briefe* (J. C. B. Mohr (Paul
Siebeck): Tübingen, 1924), pp. III–VIII; also in F. Meinecke,
Werke, iv (K. F. Koehler, etc.: Stuttgart, etc., 1959), 379–83.

Meister-Trescher, H. 'Ernst Troeltsch', *Historische Vierteljahrsschrift* 21 (1923), 251, 383 ff.

Mertineit, J. 'Das Wertproblem in der Philosophie der Gegenwart unter besonderer Berücksichtigung von Ernst Troeltsch'. Berlin, 1934, diss.

Meuleman, G. E. 'Christelijk geloof en geschiedenis', *VT* 41 (1971), 332–5.

Meyer, A. 'Ernst Troeltsch nach persönlicher Erinnerung', *Neue Züricher Zeitung* 15.2.1923.

Mezger, P. *Die Absolutheit des Christentums und die Religionsgeschichte.* J. C. B. Mohr (Paul Siebeck): Tübingen, 1912.

Miller, D. E. 'Troeltsch's Critique of Karl Marx', *JSSR* 1 (1961), 117–21.

'Conscience and History'. 1962, diss. Harvard (manuscr.).

Minges, P. '"Freies Christentum" nach Ernst Troeltsch', *Theologisch-praktische Monatsschrift: Zentral-Organ der katholischen Geistlichkeit Bayerns (Passau)* 29 (1919), 227–41.

Morgan, R. *see* Pye, M. & Morgan, R.

Müller, G. 'Die Selbstauflösung der Dogmatik bei Ernst Troeltsch', *Theologische Zeitschrift* (Basel) 22 (1966), 334–46.

Müller-Lauter, W. 'Konsequenzen des Historismus in der Philosophie der Gegenwart', *ZThK* N.F. 59 (1962), 231–35.

Mundle, W. 'Das religiöse Apriori in der Religionsphilosophie Tröltschs in seinem Verhältnis zu Kant', *Theologische Studien und Kritiken* (Gotha) 89 (1916), 427–70.

Neiiendam, M. 'Albrecht Ritschl og Ernst Troeltsch', *Teologisk Tidsskrift for den Danske Folkekirke* (Kobenhavn) (1924), pp. 4–64.

Neumann, C. 'Zum Tode von Ernst Troeltsch', *Deutsche Vierteljahrsschrift für Literaturwissenschaft und Geistesgeschichte* (Halle/Saale etc.) 1 (1923), 161–71.

Niebergall, F. 'Über die Absolutheit des Christentums', *Theologische Arbeiten aus dem Rhein. Wissenschaftl. Predigerverein* (Elberfeld etc.) N.F. 4 (1900), 46–86.

Niebuhr, H. R. 'Ernst Troeltsch's Philosophy of Religion', 1924, Ph.D. dissertation. Yale University.

The Social Sources of Denominationalism. Henry Holt and Co.: New York, 1929.

'Troeltsch, Ernst', *An Encyclopaedia of Religion* (Philosophical Library: New York, 1945), pp. 795–6.

'Introduction', in E. Troeltsch, *The Social Teaching of the Christian Churches* (2 vols., Harper & Brothers: New York, 1960), pp. 7–12.

Niftrik, G. C. van 'De erfenis van Ernst Troeltsch', *VT* 41 (1971), 323–9.

Nome, J. *Det moderne livsproblem: Hos Troeltsch og vår tid.* Gyldendal Norsk Forlag: Oslo, 1950.

Nygren, A. T. S. 'Religiöst Apriori'. Lund, 1921, diss.

Die Gültigkeit der religiösen Erfahrung. Studien des apologetischen Seminars in Wernigerode 8. C. Bertelsmann: Gütersloh, 1922.

O'Dea, Th. F. 'Troeltsch, Ernst', *International Encyclopedia of the Social Sciences,* XVI (The Macmillan Company and the Free Press: New York, 1968), 151–5.

Ogletree, Th. W. *Christian Faith and History: A Critical Comparison of Ernst Troeltsch and Karl Barth.* Abingdon Press: New York/Nashville, 1965.

Palm, G. 'Troeltschs Vermächtnis', *Zeitwende* 1 (1925) Bd 2, 109.

Pannenberg, W. *Basic questions in theology,* vol. 1 (SCM Press: London, 1970), pp. 15–80.

Wissenschaftstheorie und Theologie (Suhrkamp Verlag: Frankfurt a/M, 1973), pp. 105–17.

Parpert, F. *Die Aufgabe der geschichtlichen Abstraktion: Eine Auseinandersetzung mit Ernst Troeltschs Geschichtsmethodologie.* Hubert & Co.: Göttingen, 1919, diss.

Passerin D'Entrèves, A. 'Il concetto del diritto naturale cristiano e la sua storia secondo E. Troeltsch', *Atti della Reale Accademia di scienze di Torino* 61 (1926), 644–704.

Pauck, W. *Harnack and Troeltsch: Two Historical Theologians.* Oxford University Press: New York, 1968.

Paus, A. *Religiöser Erkenntnisgrund: Herkunft und Wesen der Aprioritheorie Rudolf Ottos* (E. J. Brill: Leiden, 1966), pp. 61–75.

Pipkin, C. W. 'Ernst Troeltsch', *Christian Register* 5.4.1923, pp. 319–20.

Planck, R. 'Deutschtum und Christentum bei Ernst Troeltsch', *CW* 31 (1917), cols. 5–9, 23–6, 45–8.

Poehlmann. 'Meister des Lebens: Ernst Troeltsch', *Monatsblätter für den Evangelischen Religionsunterricht* (Göttingen) 18 (1925), 1–10.

Pretzel, U. 'Ernst Troeltschs Berufung an die Berliner Universität', *Studium Berolinense: Aufsätze und Beiträge zu Problemen der Wissenschaft und zur Geschichte der Friedrich-Wilhelms-Universität zu Berlin* (Gedenkschrift der westdeutschen Rektorenkonferenz und der Freien Universität Berlin zur 150. Wiederkehr des Gründungsjahres der Friedrich-Wilhelms-Universität zu Berlin. (Walter de Gruyter & Co.: Berlin, 1960), pp. 507–14.

Przywara, E. 'Ernst Troeltsch', *Stimmen der Zeit* (Freiburg i.B.) 53 (1923, 2), Nr. 105, 75–9; also in E. Przywara, *Ringen der Gegenwart: Gesammelte Aufsätze 1922–1927,* 1 (Augsburg, 1929), 180–90.

Pye, M. & Morgan, R. (eds.) *The Cardinal Meaning.* Mouton: The Hague, 1973.

Quarberg, D. 'Historical Reason, Faith and the Study of Religion', *JSSR* 1 (1961), 122–4.

Quené, C. 'Ernst Troeltsch: Geschiedenis als opgave', *VT* 41 (1971), 278–97.

Rachfall, F. 'Kalvinismus und Kapitalismus', *Internationale*

Wochenschrift für Wissenschaft, Kunst und Technik (Berlin) 3 (1909), Nr. 39–43.

'Nochmals Kalvinismus und Kapitalismus', *Internationale Wochenschrift für Wissenschaft, Kunst und Technik* 4 (1910), Nr. 22–5.

Rand, C. G. 'Two Meanings of Historicism in the Writings of Dilthey, Troeltsch, and Meinecke', *Journal of the History of Ideas* (New York) 25 (1964), 503–18.

Reischle, M. 'Historische und dogmatische Methode in der Theologie', *ThR* 4 (1901), 261–75, 305–24.

Reist, B. A. *Toward a Theology of Involvement: The Thought of Ernst Troeltsch.* SCM Press: London, 1966.

Reitsema, G. W. *Ernst Troeltsch als godsdienstwijsgeer.* Van Gorcum & Comp.: Assen, 1974, diss.

Reymond, B. 'Le concept de religion comme herméneutique théologique de l'existence', *Revue de Théologie et de Philosophie* (Lausanne) 24 (1974), 170–84.

Rhijn, M. van *Studiën over Luther's rechtvaardigingsleer. Met een nawoord over nieuwere Erasmus-waardering (Troeltsch en Pijper).* J. B. Wolters: Groningen/Den Haag, 1921.

Rintelen, F. J. von 'Der Versuch einer Ueberwindung des Historismus bei E. Troeltsch', *Deutsche Vierteljahrsschrift für Literaturwissenschaft und Geistesgeschichte* 8 (Halle/Saale, etc., 1930), 324–72; also published separately: Max Niemeyer Verlag: Halle (Saale), 1930.

Ritzert, G. *Die Religionsphilosophie Ernst Troeltschs: Eine bewusstseinskritische Beurteilung und religiöse Würdigung seiner religionsphilosophischen Schriften.* Hermann Beyer & Söhne (Beyer & Mann): Langensalza, 1924, diss.

Robertson, R. *The Sociological Interpretation of Religion* (Basil Blackwell: Oxford, 1970), pp. 116–26.

Röhricht, R. 'Zwischen Historismus und Existenzdenken: Die Geschichtsphilosophie Ernst Troeltschs'. 1954, diss. Tübingen (manuscr.).

Rossi, P. *La storicismo tedesco contemporaneo.* Giulio Einaudi: Torino, 1956.

Ruler, A. A. van 'Historische Cultuurvorming', *Geschiedenis: Een bundel studies over den zin der Geschiedenis* (Van Gorcum & Comp.: Assen, 1944), pp. 200–21.

Rumpf, M. 'Ernst Troeltsch: Seine Bedeutung für Rechtsgeschichte und Rechtswissenschaft', *Leipziger Zeitschrift für deutsches Recht* (München) 17 (1923), 378–83.

Salis, G. R. de 'La théorie de l'histoire selon E. Troeltsch', *Revue Synthèse de l'Histoire* 43 (1927), 5–13.

Schaaf, J. J. *Geschichte und Begriff: Eine kritische Studie zur Geschichtsmethodologie von Ernst Troeltsch und Max Weber.* J. C. B. Mohr (Paul Siebeck): Tübingen, 1946.

Schaper, E. 'Troeltsch, Ernst', *The Encyclopedia of Philosophy*, VIII (Macmillan etc.: New York, 1967), 162–3.

'Troeltsch, Ernst', *The New Encyclopaedia Britannica, Macropaedia*, VIII (William Benton: Chicago, etc., 1974[15]), 715–16.

Scheler, M. 'Ernst Troeltsch als Soziologe', *Kölner Vierteljahreshefte für Soziologie* 3 (1923/4), 7–21.

Schenk, W. 'Ernst Troeltsch's Conception of History', *The Dublin Review* (London), 108 (1944).

Schlesinger, R. *Probleme eines religiösen Apriori* (Ernst-Reuter-Gesellschaft: Berlin, 1959, diss.), pp. 31–7, 56–60.

Schlippe, G. von *Die Absolutheit des Christentums bei Ernst Troeltsch auf dem Hintergrund der Denkfelder des 19. Jahrhunderts*. Verlag Degener & Co.: Neustadt an der Aisch, 1966, diss.

Schmidt, G. *Deutscher Historismus und der Uebergang zur parlamentarischen Demokratie: Untersuchungen zu den politischen Gedanken von Meinecke-Troeltsch-Max Weber*. Matthiesen Verlag: Lübeck/Hamburg, 1964.

Schmidt, M. 'Züge eines theologischen Geschichtsbegriffs bei Ernst Troeltsch', *Reformatio und Confessio: Festschrift für D. Wilhelm Maurer* (Lutherisches Verlagshaus: Berlin/Hamburg, 1965), 244–58.

Scholz, H. 'Ernst Troeltsch', *Preussische Kirchenzeitung: Kirchenpolitisches Monatsblatt* 19 (1923), cols. 15–16.

Schrey, H. H. 'Ernst Troeltsch und sein Werk', *ThR* N.F. 12 (1940), 130–62.

'Troeltsch, Ernst', *Evangelisches Soziallexikon* (Stuttgart, 1954), p. 1044.

Schröder, A. 'Troeltsch als Geschichtsphilosoph', *Leipziger Neueste Nachrichten*, 25.2.1923.

Schroeter, M. 'Ernst Troeltsch', *Münchener Neueste Nachrichten* 3.2.1923, Nr. 32.

Schüler, A. 'Christlicher Personalismus: Gedanken zu Ernst Troeltschs Werk', *Festschrift für Th. Steinbüchel*, 1948.

Schumann, F. K. *Der Gottesgedanke und der Zerfall der Moderne* (J. C. B. Mohr (Paul Siebeck): Tübingen, 1929), pp. 106–35.

Schwarz, G. M. 'Deutschland und Westeuropa bei Ernst Troeltsch', *HZ* 191 (1960), 510–47.

Seeberg, E. Review of E. Troeltsch, *Glaubenslehre*, in *Deutsche Literaturzeitung* 47 (Leipzig, 1926), cols. 2127–33; also in E. Seeberg, *Menschwerdung und Geschichte: Aufsätze* (Kohlhammer: Stuttgart, 1938), pp. 149–55.

Séguy, J. *Ernst Troeltsch et sa sociologie du Christianisme*. Cahiers du Cercle Ernest Renan 32, Paris, 4e trimestre 1961.

Séguy, J. *see* Bras, G. le & Séguy, J.

Severijn, J. 'Ernst Troeltsch over de betekenis van het Calvinisme voor de cultuurgeschiedenis', *Antirevolutionaire Staatkunde* (Kampen) (Driemaandelijksch orgaan) 1 (1927), 1–71.

Sleigh, R. S. *The Sufficiency of Christianity: An Enquiry concerning the Nature and the Modern Possibilities of the Christian Religion, with Special Reference to the Religious Philosophy of Dr. Ernst Troeltsch.* James Clark & Co.: London, 1923, diss.

Smith, J. S. Boys. 'The Significance of the Historical Element in the Christian Idea of Incarnation', *The Modern Churchman* 28 (1928/9), 372–90.

Smits, P. 'Troeltsch als godsdienstsocioloog', *VT* 41 (1971), 309–15.

Spaleck, G. *Religionssoziologische Grundbegriffe bei Ernst Troeltsch.* C. Nieft: Bleicherode am Herz, 1937, diss.

Spiess, E. *Die Religionstheorie von Ernst Troeltsch.* F. Schönigh: Paderborn, 1927, diss.

Spiess, P. 'Zur Frage des religiösen Apriori', *Zeitschrift für Religion und Geisteskultur* (Göttingen) 3 (1909), 207–15.

Spranger, E. 'Ernst Troeltsch als Religionsphilosoph', *Philosophische Wochenschrift und Literatur-Zeitung* (Leipzig) 2 (1906), Nr. 2–4.

Spranger, E. 'Das Historismusproblem an der Universität Berlin seit 1900', *Studium Berolinense* (Walter de Gruyter & Co.: Berlin, 1960), pp. 425–43. *See* Pretzel, U.

Stackhouse, M. L. 'Troeltsch's Categories of Historical Analysis', *JSSR* 1 (1961), 223–5.

Stephan, H. *Die heutigen Auffassungen vom Neuprotestantismus.* Töpelmann: Giessen, 1911.

Süskind, H. 'Zur Theologie Troeltschs', *ThR* 17 (1914), 1–13, 53–62.

Thomä, J. *Die Absolutheit des Christentums zur Auseinandersetzung mit Troeltsch untersucht.* A. Deichert: Leipzig, 1907.

Tillich, P. 'Ernst Troeltsch', *Vossische Zeitung* 3.2.1923, Nr. 58.
'Ernst Troeltscht. Versuch einer geistesgeschichtlichen Würdigung', *Kant-Studien* (Berlin or Bonn) 29 (1924), 351–8.
Review of E. Troeltsch, *Der Historismus und seine Probleme*, in *ThLZ* 49 (1924), 25–30; English transl., *JSSR* 1 (1961), 109–14.
Review of E. Troeltsch, *Der Historismus und seine Ueberwindung*, in *ThLZ* 49 (1924), 234–35.

Tödt, H. E. 'Ernst Troeltsch', *Tendenzen der Theologie im 20. Jahrhundert: Eine Geschichte in Porträts* (Kreuz-Verlag, etc.: Stuttgart, etc., 1966), pp. 93–8.
'Ernst Troeltschs Bedeutung für die evangelische Sozialethik', *Zeitschrift für evangelische Ethik* (Gütersloh) 10 (1966), 227–36.

Tönnies, F. Review of E. Troeltsch, *Die Soziallehren der christlichen Kirchen*, in *ThLZ* 39 (1914), 8–12; also in F. Tönnies, *Soziologische Studien und Kritiken*, III (Gustav Fischer: Jena, 1929), 432–8.
'Troeltsch und die Philosophie der Geschichte', *Schmollers Jahrbuch*

für Gesetzgebung, Verwaltung und Volkswirtschaft im Deutschen Reiche (München) 49 (1925), 147–93; also in F. Tönnies, *Soziologische Studien und Kritiken*, II (Gustav Fischer: Jena, 1926), 381–429.

Traub, F. 'Die religionsgeschichtliche Methode und die systematische Theologie: Eine Auseinandersetzung mit Tröltschs theologischem Reformprogramm', *ZThK* XI (1901), 301–40.

'Zur Frage des religiösen Apriori', *ZThK* XXIV (1914), 181–99.

Vermeil, E. 'La Philosophie religieuse d'Ernest Troeltsch', *La Revue d'Histoire et de Philosophie Religieuses* (Strasbourg etc.) 1 (1921), 23–44, 154–75; also published separately: E. Vermeil, *La pensée religieuse de Troeltsch*. Librairie Istra: Strasbourg/Paris, 1922.

Vierkandt, A. 'Ein gläubiger Philosoph', *Kölnische Zeitung* 19.7.1924.

Volkelt, H. *Demobilisierung des Geistes?* 1918.

Waismann, A. 'Ernst Troeltsch o el drama de historicismo', *Revista de la Universidad Nacional de Córdoba*, 1955; also published separately: Córdoba, R.A., 1955.

Weinel, H. 'Die ewigen Fragen: Troeltsch und seine Dogmatik', *Münchener Neueste Nachrichten* 2.4.1926.

Wendland, J. 'Zum Begriff "Entwicklung der Religion"', *ZThK* XX (1910), 226–31.

'Philosophie und Christentum bei Ernst Troeltsch im Zusammenhange mit der Philosophie und Theologie des letzten Jahrhunderts', *ZThK* XXIV (1914), 129–65.

Wernle, P. 'Vorläufige Anmerkungen zu den Soziallehren der christlichen Kirchen und Gruppen von Ernst Troeltsch', *ZThK* XXII (1912), 329–68 and XXIII (1913), 18–80.

Wichelhaus, M. *Kirchengeschichtsschreibung und Soziologie im neunzehnten Jahrhundert und bei Ernst Troeltsch*. Carl Winter Universitätsverlag: Heidelberg, 1965.

Wieneke, F. *Die Entwicklung des philosophischen Gottesbegriffes bei Ernst Troeltsch*. H. Madrasch: Berlin/Soldin, 1929, diss.

Wiesenberg, W. *Das Verhältnis von Formal- und Materialethik erörtert an dem Streit zwischen Wilhelm Herrmann und Ernst Troeltsch*. Kranich: Königsberg, 1934, diss.

Wölber, H. O. *Dogma und Ethos: Christentum und Humanismus von Ritschl bis Troeltsch*. C. Bertelsmann: Gütersloh, 1950, diss.

Wünsch, G. 'Ernst Troeltsch zum Gedächtnis', *CW* 37 (1923), cols. 105–8.

Wust, P. 'Vom Wesen der historischen Entwicklung', *Hochland* 20, 2 (1922/3), 19–39, 179–202; also in P. Wust, *Krieg und Aufbau*; also in P. Wust, *Im Sinnkreis des Ewigen* (Verlag Styria: Graz, etc., 1954), pp. 87–97 (abbreviated).

Yinger, J. M. 'The Sociology of Religion of Ernst Troeltsch', *An Introduction to the History of Sociology* (ed. H. E. Barnes, The University of Chicago Press: Chicago, 1948), pp. 309–15.

Index of names